The Economics of Public-Private Partnerships

Stéphane Saussier • Julie de Brux

Editors

The Economics of Public-Private Partnerships

Theoretical and Empirical Developments

 Springer

Editors
Stéphane Saussier
IAE Sorbonne Business School
Paris, France

Julie de Brux
IAE Sorbonne Business School
Paris, France

CITIZING
Paris, France

ISBN 978-3-319-68049-1   ISBN 978-3-319-68050-7   (eBook)
https://doi.org/10.1007/978-3-319-68050-7

Library of Congress Control Number: 2017959881

Translation from the French language edition: Économie des partenariats public-privé, © De Boeck 2015. All Rights Reserved.

Printed on acid-free paper

This Springer imprint is published by Springer Nature
The registered company is Springer International Publishing AG
The registered company address is: Gewerbestrasse 11, 6330 Cham, Switzerland

Foreword

The history of partnerships between the public and private sectors for providing public services goes as far back as the history of the public sector itself. Broadly speaking, the first experiences of public–private partnerships on record date back to antiquity. Ever since then, and at every stage of a country's, a region's, or a city's history, when the choice of such a partnership has been made, it has been the result of various factors which are now well documented. Such a choice has ensued from expected constraints (most often financing constraints, either private or public. But often they have also been the result of constraints associated with *public access to certain technologies* or skills), *from preferences* (out of political or operational pragmatism, or as a result of ideology), *from the rejection of the most extreme production methods* (either purely private or purely public) blamed for quantity or quality rationing or by higher costs of service, or *from a reaction to governance choices* (in some cases to fight corruption, collusion, or political capture but in others to facilitate such perversions of public choice mechanisms).

However, our conceptual and analytical understanding of how important the origin of this decision-making process really is, and of the sheer diversity of the scope the partnership can take, has a much shorter history. It is arguably not much longer than 30 years. It all started with a generation of outstanding researchers whose names and contributions are crucial to any theoretical or applied research focusing on those public–private partnerships. The generation in question includes Akerlof, Baron, Hart, Klemperer, Laffont, Maskin, McAfee, McMillan, Meyerson, Milgrom, Riley, Sappington, Stiglitz, Tirole, Vogelsang, and Williamson (to name but a few). To this day, their 1980s' research still serves as a framework for our collective understanding of the incentives underlying the various stages of any interaction between the public and private sectors in this type of contractual agreement.

If these stages are better known today, it is to a large extent thanks to this initial body of work, but also to developments in the fields of game theory and contract theory, as well as to a long series of subsequent empirical contributions which have come to refine, expand, clarify, and test the theoretical analyses of the 1980s and early 1990s. This research highlights the efficiency conditions at each recurring stages in the timeline of partnerships, from the moment when the decision to start a collaboration is made by a politician or civil servant to the point when the service, asset, or investment the public administration is seeking to procure is delivered.

Once the decision to collaborate has been made, the first stage of its implementation consists in detailing specifically what will be the subject of a contract between the two parties and estimating how consistent these specifications are with the demand side. This initial estimate aims to provide a first assessment of the consistency between the total costs of the various possible specifications and the expected financing structure, particularly its distribution between the taxpayers and the direct beneficiaries of the public service (the two obvious contributors to public finance). Then comes the time to organize a call for tenders and to draw up the regulations to which all involved parties will be subject, as well as their respective rights and obligations. At this point, decisions must be made about implementing the various commitments and about oversight and penalty imposition in case of noncompliance with regulations, and the efforts necessary to ensure a successful collaboration—particularly its consistency with the initial decision—must be anticipated. This stage also involves carrying out a more precise assessment of the financial and economic consistency between the cost of the rights and obligations specified under the final contract and their financing, including financing costs for both the public and private sectors. The next stage consists in implementing the decision and overseeing the process, generally through regulatory mechanisms that often leave significant room for subjectivity, as not everything can be provided for under the contract, which is necessarily incomplete. It also involves taking into account the possibility of a necessity—or at least a desire—on the part of one of the parties to renegotiate certain provisions of the contract. And this series of predictable stages occurs within an institutional context that can be delineated and set up prior to, during, or after partnership preparation and implementation.

As a whole, the theoretical and empirical literature that has allowed for a deeper understanding of each of these stages constitutes what Professor Saussier has called the economics of public–private partnerships. Although rich and fruitful, this literature suffers from a major problem. It is largely perceived as too difficult to understand by stakeholders outside of academia and/or the field of economics. This perception is not unreasonable given that this is an incredibly extensive, heterogeneous, somewhat fragmented, and often very complex literature. The main consequence of this is that at best, the results of this research filter in via interviews or less technical articles published in the general press, which can sometimes be reductive. But among the operators of public–private collaborations—the group which could benefit most from lessons drawn from this research, the most widespread reaction is simply one of rejection.

The book you are reading makes it unacceptable to reject such knowledge on account of it being too difficult to grasp for anyone with a true interest in PPPs who is eager to make sure that expertise furthers the interests of the community instead of serving mere ideological choices or needs arising from political, financial, or institutional constraints. What this book accomplishes is no small feat, as it manages simultaneously to synthetize an extensive literature in a rigorous manner and to "translate" it into a language made simpler by the absence of a jargon which otherwise so often characterizes it. This book perfectly illustrates how to disseminate technical academic knowledge in such a way that it can be put to direct use (if possible) and submitted to informed criticism (as opposed to blind and dogmatic) when necessary. There is no doubt that it will have a major operational impact, both among experts in charge of preparing the legal material for contracts and among civil servants responsible for making key decisions at each stage of partnership implementation.

This book is also a small gem from an academic point of view (although not actually small per se, as it is rather long), in that it covers every essential aspect of the subject to which economists have contributed. Each chapter provides a thorough literature review, thus allowing academic readers to get quickly up to date in the key dimensions of the subject. It will most likely be adopted by many professors as a reference book for courses in the economics of regulation and competition, public economics, or contract theory.

All in all, very few books manage to target such a large audience in such a technical field. The authors of this book have risen brilliantly to the challenge. Public service users and taxpayers will undoubtedly be its main beneficiaries. Indeed, one cannot read it without considering how much is still left to do in order to adjust our use of an instrument that has the potential to be immensely useful but is also far more sensitive to manipulation, incompetence, and ignorance than politicians and economic operators are willing to admit, in Europe or elsewhere.

ECARES, Université Libre de   Antonio Estache
Bruxelles
Brussels, Belgium

Contents

Introduction: The Economics of Public–Private Partnerships

Julie de Brux and Stéphane Saussier

1 Infrastructure Needs Call for More Public and Private Investments

Investment commitments in H1 2016 for private infrastructure projects in low-to-middle-income countries totaled US$29.5 billion across 103 projects. Latin American Countries (LAC) captured 43% of the global total followed by East Asia and Pacific (EAP), with 34%; South Asia (SAR), 12%; Sub-Saharan Africa (SSA), 4%; and Europe and Central Asia (ECA) and the Middle East and North Africa (MENA), both 3% (see Fig. 1).

Infrastructure investment needs to be substantially increased in many developing and emerging economies in order to support more rapid economic growth. According to the OECD (2015), total global infrastructure investment requirements by 2030 for transport, electricity generation, transmission and distribution, water, and telecommunications are no less than USD 71 trillion. This represents 3.5% of the annual World GDP from 2007 to 2030.

Focusing on transport, SSA is expected to meet the fastest average annual growth rate (over 11%). Asia Pacific is expected to be, by far, the largest transport infrastructure market, with investments increasing from $557 billion per year to nearly $900 billion per year in 2025 (PWC 2015). In this part of the world, China is

J. de Brux (✉)
IAE Paris - Sorbonne Business School, Paris, France

Business Advisory Board at United Nations Economic Commission for Europe, Geneva, Switzerland

CITIZING, Paris, France
e-mail: julie.debrux@citizing-consulting.com

S. Saussier
IAE Paris - Sorbonne Business School, Paris, France
e-mail: saussier@univ-paris1.fr

© Springer International Publishing AG 2018
S. Saussier, J. de Brux (eds.), *The Economics of Public-Private Partnerships*,
https://doi.org/10.1007/978-3-319-68050-7_1

1

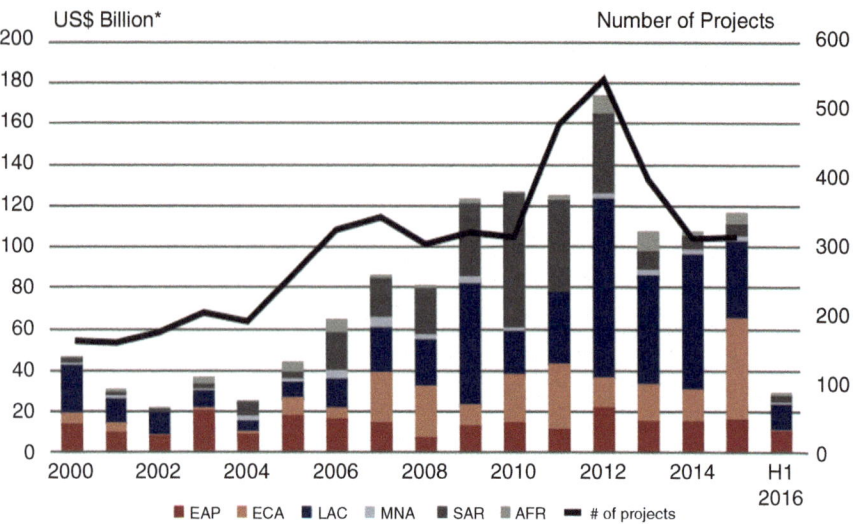

* Adjusted by US CPI

Fig. 1 Total investment in energy, transport, and water by region. Source: World Bank, PPI Project Database

an important player: Recently, China launched more than 1000 PPP projects worth $317.75 billion ("China invites private investors to help build $318 billion of projects," *Reuters,* May 25, 2015—http://www.reuters.com/article/us-china-econ omy-infrastructure-idUSKBN0OA07R20150525). Even if transport investments are projected to increase at an average annual rate of about 5% worldwide over the period of 2014–2025 (see Fig. 2), investments expected in infrastructure are far lower than what is needed.

In addition to those economic infrastructure needs, the needs for social infrastructures are also of primary importance. Social infrastructures typically include assets that accommodate social services such as schools, universities, hospitals, prisons, and community housing. They do not aim at supporting directly economic activity, even if efficient public services may attract foreign investments and increase productivity.

Whatever the kind of infrastructure required, needs are important and public authorities face high financial constraints. That is why, in order to meet these objectives, there is a widespread recognition that greater private involvement in infrastructure is needed, as governments can hardly bridge the growing infrastructure gap through tax revenues and aid alone. Although public–private partnerships (PPPs) should not be viewed as a financing tool, they are often presented as a way of continuing to invest in infrastructure even in financially constrained periods. Private involvement is also frequently presented as a way to optimize productive efficiency while delivering a high level of service. This is typically the kind of issues that will be discussed all along this book, supported by scientific research evidence, without dogma.

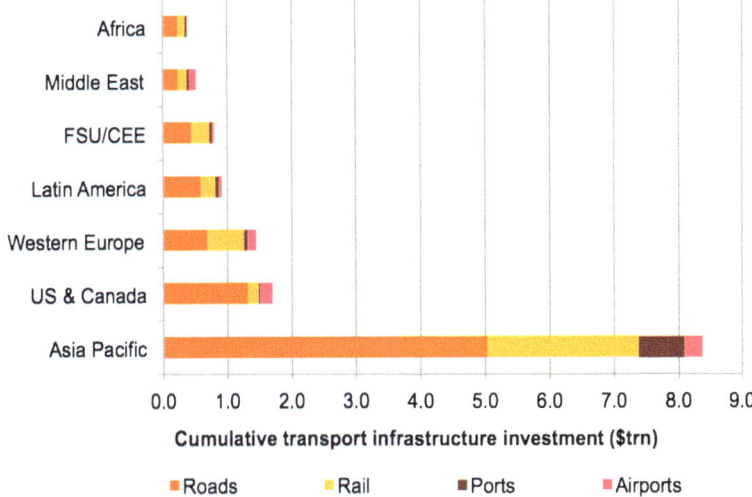

Fig. 2 Expected cumulative transport infrastructure investment to 2025. Source: PWC 2015

2   Which Kind of PPPs to Invest in Public Infrastructures?

There are mainly three tools available for public authorities to invest in public infrastructures: traditional public procurement, concession, and availability-based contracts.

2.1   Public Procurement

Traditional procurement is still all over the world the most widely used delivery option for public projects. Traditional procurement refers to the situation in which a public legal entity entrusts construction or service needs to a public or a private entity in return for an immediate payment. These are generally short-term contracts.

2.2   Concession Contracts

Concession contracts are based on the transfer of a global mission including financing of the investment, eventually the construction of the project, and its operation and maintenance. As part of a concession contract, the public entity assigns the management of the service to a concessionaire that operates it and in fact bears the economic risk associated with it. The concessionaire is in charge of the works to be carried out, it is responsible for financing them, and its remuneration is closely related to service operating results.

As a result, the return on investment of the private operator comes from service operation and more generally from users' payments (tolled highways for example). This is why concession contracts are also sometimes called "user-pay PPPs."

Furthermore, although the public entity delegates the management of the public service, it does not, however, give up its monitoring and control power. The delegated activity must follow the principles governing public services and the delegating authority is in charge of sanctioning any breaches.

Concessions are the oldest historical form of outsourcing of a public service. The private financing of public works or services by a private entity in charge of their operation is a very old process in long-standing use. In the sixteenth century, King of France Henri III decided to build the Pont-Neuf in Paris. It was finished in 1607, in the reign of Henri IV. The construction work was realized under public management. However, on January 2nd, 1602, Henri IV authorized the construction of a large water pump, better known as the Pompe de la Samaritaine. That pump was designed by Flemish engineer Jean Lintlaër, and its purpose was to supply water to the royal palaces of the Louvre and Tuileries. The work was realized under private management and financed by its operator, who was authorized by the King to pump water from the Seine and to charge Parisians for this service as well as a delivery fee. To this occurrence of the concession model in the modern age, we can add other contemporary examples such as contracts for the construction and operation of navigation canals. Along the way, interest in the concession model proved unfailing and, almost three centuries later, Napoleon III turned to private concessionaires for Haussmann's transformation of Paris.

Still today, concession contracts are widely used and mostly employed for mass catering, water and sanitation, district heating, transport, etc.

2.3   Availability-Based PPPs

Many studies limit the definition of PPPs to availability contracts, referring to that of British Private Finance Initiative (PFIs) dating back to 1992, and thereby reducing PPPs to their most recent form.

Availability contracts allow a public entity to entrust a contractor with a comprehensive project as part of a long-term contract, against remuneration paid by the public entity and spread over time. Its objective is thus to maximize the respective performances of the public and private sectors so as to execute projects.

In theory, an availability contract is not an outsourcing of public service duties, the responsibility for which falls on public entities. In reality, through this type of contract, public bodies "purchase" the availability of a service that is necessary to carry out their duties. For instance, it can be the availability of a structure (a hospital, a prison, an office building, a telecommunications network, a railway, etc.) or of a resource (drinking water, meals, heat, etc.).

As part of an availability contract, the private party is in charge of a comprehensive project: its role consists in defining and implementing all means and solutions necessary to achieve the results and meet the objectives requested by the public entity. Generally, the private operator, as project manager, is accountable to the public body for the design, execution, operation, maintenance (including renewals), and financing (debt, equity, and quasi-equity).

The private operator is paid in the form of rent by the public body (and not by users, as it is the case in concession contracts) during the entire duration of the contract, which may be supplemented, if applicable, by additional receipts. Payments of the rent occur provided that the performance criteria specified in the contract are met. Conversely, penalties may be applied.

The structure of penalties varies according to the nature of the tasks entrusted to the private partner. At the realization stage, they are penalties for delay, applicable if the product is not realized within the time stipulated in the contract. At the operation stage, penalties are used in cases where the operator fails to meet its performance objectives. Naturally, these objectives, which give tangible form to the "availability" of a work or service, vary depending on the nature of the project (availability rate of a telecommunications network, observation of the schedule, and deadlines for the realization of preventive and corrective maintenance tasks as part of the provision of a building, etc.). The amount of the penalties applicable by the public body must be adapted to the gravity of the reported breaches and must also be sufficiently dissuasive and capped. Otherwise, the private operator would be exposed to unlimited cost overruns, which it would not be able to assume for very long given the small capitalization of the Special Purpose Vehicles (see Chapter "The Evolution of Financing Conditions for PPP Contracts: Still a Private Financing Model?").

Let us note that although the project is funded by the private contractor, it is repaid by the public authority and *in fine* by taxpayers (and not by users like in concessions). This is what these contracts are sometimes called "public-budget pay PPPs." They are used for major construction projects (educational establishments, train stations, etc.), urban infrastructures (street lighting, roads, etc.) and even sport and cultural facilities (theaters, stadiums, swimming pools, etc.), and prisons.

Those three procurement "tools" (traditional public procurement, concession, and availability contracts) should not be considered as discrete forms: often, public–private contracts entail some mixed characteristics. For example, some availability contracts might condition part of the payment to the number of users. Alternatively, concession contract may specify a minimum guaranteed revenue to the private operator. What is common to all those kinds of public private contracts is that, as soon as investments are needed, long-term contracts are needed opening the rooms to contractual issues that will be studied in this book.

Whatever the kind of infrastructure, a government may delegate them, which gives rise to contractual agreements, at least for the construction period. As such, it is a "partnership" between the public authority and the private entity, leading to transaction cost issues that will be also analyzed in this book.

For the purpose of this book, we will select the broadest definition of PPPs. Not because we consider it to be the most relevant one but rather because the originality and efficiency of one type of PPP can only be assessed by means of a comparative analysis. Incidentally, as we will see in the next contribution (Chapter "An Economic Analysis of Public–Private Partnerships"), it also happens to be the definition selected by contract theory, which takes into account the whole spectrum of possible public–private contractual relationships in order to analyze the efficiency of PPPs in the broad sense of the term.

3   The Award of Public Private Contracts

3.1   The Award of Traditional Public Procurement Contracts

In developed countries, the procedure for the award of public contracts is governed by the fundamental principle of competitive tendering. Whereas economists generally use four criteria to determine the competitive nature of a market (access to information, no dominant position or oligopoly, no barriers to entry, and relative homogeneity of goods and services), legal documents generally refer more specifically to freedom of access, even though the three other features cannot be overlooked. The contracting authority is thus under an obligation to organize competition.

The award procedure is preferably preceded by a needs assessment conducted by the contracting authority. From this needs assessment stems a whole range of services defined through technical specifications listed in the consultation documents addressed to the candidates. The contracting authority then selects which procedure it wishes to apply. Different types of formalized procedures, namely, calls for tenders (open or restricted), negotiated procedures, competitive dialogue, or design contests, are possible.

The call for tenders is the most common type of procedure. The contracting authority selects the successful tenderer without negotiation, on the basis of criteria that are deemed objective and must be communicated to the candidates beforehand. A call for tenders is said to be open when any private economic operator may submit a tender. Conversely, it is said to be restricted when only a limited number of economic operators may participate.

The negotiated procedure differs from calls for tenders in that it involves direct contact with the candidates. This has led the orthodoxy to write that it is therefore less objective and could undermine the principle of equal treatment of candidates.

The competitive dialogue procedure shows some similarities with the negotiated procedure in that, as suggested by its name, it organizes a dialogue between the contracting authority and candidates. This procedure is generally used when the contract is considered to be "complex" (either because the contracting authority is

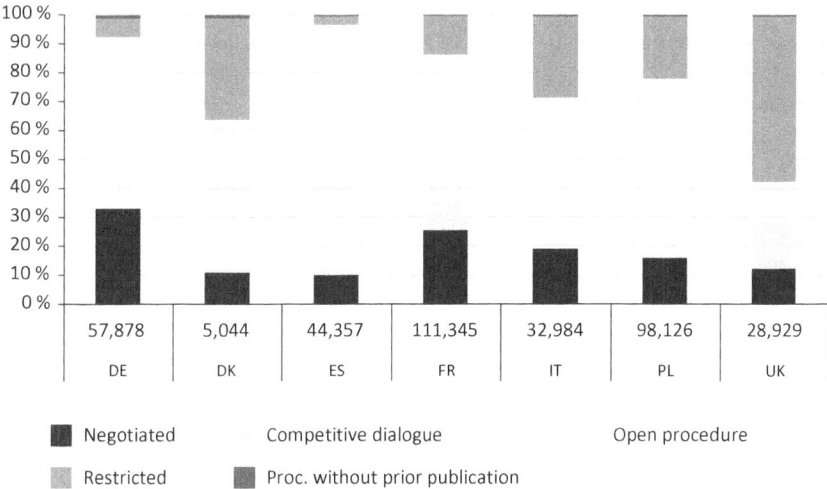

Fig. 3 Use of the various contract award procedures in various European countries (% in value). Source: Saussier and Tirole (2015), based on TED, 2008–2012. Calculations made by the author based on the European database regarding traditional public procurement contracts whose value exceeds the European thresholds. TED distinguishes between several types of restricted and negotiated procedures which are grouped together in this graph. http://ted.europa.eu. The x-axis shows the relevant country and the number of observations over the period

not able to define unaided the technical means to meet its needs or because it is not objectively in a position to specify the legal and financial arrangements for the project).

Finally, the design contest is a specific award procedure whereby the contracting authority chooses a plan or project selected by a jury after its opening up to competition. This last procedure is especially used in the areas of town and country planning.

Few data are available on the use of these different types of contract award procedures for traditional public procurement contracts. The only available database is the TED base (*Tenders Electronic Daily*), which is the online version of the "Supplement to the Official Journal of the EU," dedicated to European traditional public procurement. Based on these data, we can observe that the negotiated procedure is the exception rather than the rule (this is bound to change with the new European directives on public procurement, but there is not enough timescale to assess their impact) and that there are genuine differences between European countries as far as their respective frequency of use of the various procedures is concerned (see Fig. 3).

3.2 The Award of Concession Contracts

The rules applicable to the conclusion of concession contracts are generally made of two subsets, but this may defer depending on the legal frameworks.

The first one is the publication requirement. The delegating public authority must publish a notice so as to allow for the submission of applications. Generally, this publication occurs at least 1 month before the date of effective application submission.

The candidates presenting sufficient guarantees are then selected and receive a document indicating the characteristics of the expected services (functional requirements specifications). Based on this document, the selected economic operators can then submit their tenders, which are then generally negotiated freely, in compliance with legal and statutory requirements.

3.3   The Award of Availability-Based Contracts

In most countries, the use of availability contracts must be justified by a prior value for money analysis. We discuss this issue all along the book as well as the conditions of success. Surprisingly, value for money analysis is less often required when traditional public procurement and concession contracts are envisaged.

Concerning the award of availability contracts, as for concession contracts, a formalized procedure of advertising and opening up to competition under are compulsory in most countries. Three types of award procedures are generally proposed: competitive dialogue (which is recommended when the project is complex, because it makes it possible to determine, together with the candidates, which technical means and financial and legal arrangements are best suited to meet the needs of the public entity), the call for tenders, and the negotiated procedure, below certain thresholds.

4   The Weight of Public–Private Contracts

4.1   The Weight of Traditional Public Procurement

In France, the economic census of public procurement stipulates that a statistical card containing the census data should be drawn up and sent to the French Observatory on Traditional Public Procurement (OEAP) for every contract or framework agreement exceeding 90,000€ in value excluding tax. Thus, in 2013, the annual value of public contracts in France represented over 71.5 billion euros excluding tax for a total of 96,500 contracts (see Fig. 4).

However, we must keep in mind that many low-value public contracts are not taken into account in the OEAP census.[1] Moreover, the expenditure undertaken by

---

[1]Saussier and Tirole (2015) note that, although it is compulsory to send information to the OEAP regarding traditional public procurement contracts whose value exceeds 90 k€, this does not guarantee the exhaustive transmission of data, due to the absence of monitoring and sanctions.

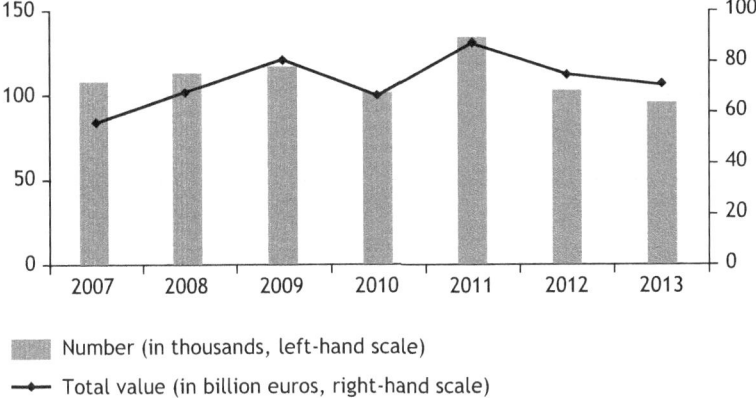

Fig. 4 The total value of public contracts. Source: OEAP (France)

public operators and state-owned companies are not accounted for by the OEAP. The total value of public procurement in France is thus regularly estimated to be around 200 billion euros per year, without being subjected to accurate accounting practices.

In the end, traditional public procurement contracts constitute the preferred tool of public procurement and their total value represents a significant share of the GDP (over 3% according to figures published by the OEAP).

In this respect, France does not appear to be an exception. In the OECD area, general government purchase (a broader concept than purely traditional public procurement, which is what the European Union most often communicates about) represents 13% of the GDP on average, against 19% in the EU (see Fig. 5).

4.2   The Weight of Concession Contracts

Concessions are used in the fields of institutional catering, waste collection, transport infrastructure, etc.

However, at the European level, a lack of available figures can be noted as far as concessions are concerned. The protracted debate that led to the new European directive on concessions being passed in early 2014 highlighted this lack of data, as the Commission was unable to assess the weight of concessions in the economy of European countries to explain the need for a new directive on concessions.

Although France has a long tradition of concessions, there is no monitoring agency for concessions to draw up an annual census of all calls for tenders and signed contracts and thus assess their weight in the French economy. The few existing figures have to do with the turnover generated by these contracts. They indicate that, for the sole operators, the value of concession contracts represents a

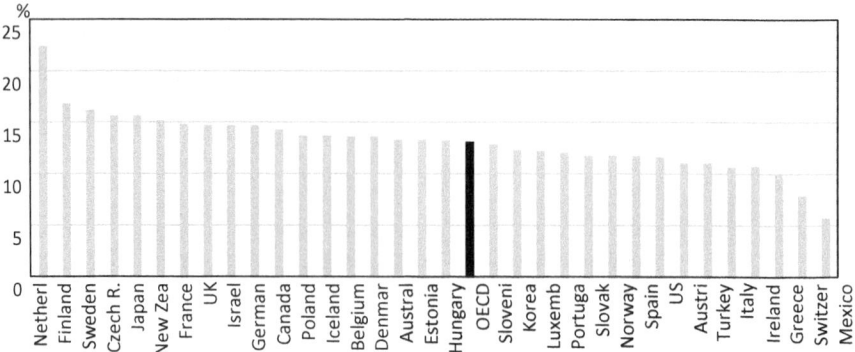

Fig. 5 General government procurement in % of the GDP (2011). Source: OECD (2013)—Government at a Glance. Note: General government procurement is defined as the sum of intermediate consumption (goods and services purchased by governments for their own use, such as information technology or accounting services), gross fixed capital formation (acquisition of capital excluding the sale of fixed assets, such as building new roads), and social transfers in kind via market producers (purchases by general government of goods and services produced by market producers and supplied to households)

market of over 100 billion euros per year (of which about half in the transport industry), that is to say around 5% of the value of the French GDP (Le Lannier & Saussier, 2012).

4.3   The Weight of Availability Contracts

Availability contracts have helped finance a substantial part of the needs for new infrastructure in Europe (see Fig. 6).

Data includes transactions in EU-28 countries as well as Turkey and countries of the Western Balkans region (i.e., Albania, Bosnia-Herzegovina, FYROM, Kosovo, Montenegro and Serbia); transactions structured as design-build-finance-operate (DBFO) or design-build-finance-maintain (DBFM) or concession arrangements which feature a construction element, the provision of a public service, and genuine risk sharing between the public and the private sector; transactions financed through "project financing" and that reached financial close in the relevant period; and transactions of a value of at least EUR 10 million.

In France, ever since their introduction in 2004, availability contracts have also become an increasingly important part of the French landscape of procurement. After a rough start, in large part due to the innovative nature of this new contractual arrangement and the legal insecurity that characterized its early stages, the number, and especially the total value of availability-based contracts (public-budget pay PPPs) concluded in France have become significant. During the last 10 years, the number of availability contracts concluded each year had increased, reaching over

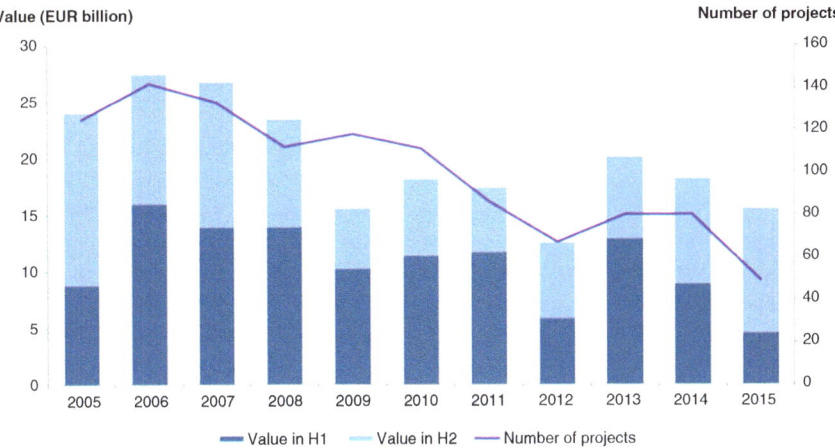

Fig. 6 European PPP market 2005–2015 by value and number of Projects. Source: EPEC (2016)

200 contracts at the end of 2014, for a cumulative amount of over 14 billion euros. By 2011, France was thus the first European country in terms of the value of contracts concluded during the year, well ahead of Great Britain.

Availability contracts are a recent tool of public procurement. Because of the political nature of these contracts (see Chapter "Regulatory Instruments for Public–Private Partnerships"), they have often been in the limelight and not always to their advantage. Despite how difficult it was for them to rise in importance (indeed, even at their highest level, they only represented a small share of public investment, which is estimated at about 70 billion euros per year, depending on the year), their future is currently in the balance. In 2013 and 2014, very few of these contracts were signed. This raises the issue of their efficiency.

There is only little existing feedback to help us assess the efficiency of PPPs. At a quantitative level, a study focuses exclusively on French availability contracts that have reached the operating stage (Saussier & Truong Tran, 2012). The authors thus gathered information about 30 contracts out of the 46 that were in the operating stage on January 1, 2012, when data collection was carried out.

Based on the perception of the performance of such contracts by public entities, and distinguishing six different dimensions of performance, they conclude that a vast majority of these contracts are perceived to be efficient by public authorities and confirm that, in 93% of cases, the infrastructure delivery time was considered to be satisfactory by the public body.

Even though the French experience of availability contracts seems positive in terms of the number and value of signed contracts and of the feedback recorded so far, the fact remains that implementation difficulties continue to arise. These difficulties, coupled with the rather negative image of these contracts among the general public, could challenge the development of such contracts and explain—at least in part—the change in trend observed in 2013 and 2014. Alongside the abovementioned positive feedback, some criticisms have been voiced, based on case studies that brought to light genuine difficulties encountered when setting up an availability contract (see for instance Campagnac & Deffontaines, 2012).

Moreover, the cost of a facility financed through an availability contract is often compared directly with the cost of the same facility when financed through a public procurement contract, even though (i) the cost of the availability contract includes the maintenance of the facility throughout contract duration, which is not the case in a public procurement contract and (ii) the facility is different in nature, since one of the advantages of availability contracts is precisely to offer a custom-made facility that meets the needs of the public authority in complex situations, whereas a public procurement contract generally covers more standardized facilities, thus allowing the builder to benefit from economies of scale insofar as it replicates a facility that it is already in the habit of setting up.

5 Conclusion

Contracting authorities have at their disposal a wide array of tools that vary depending on whether the contract is global (Hart, 2003), whether or not it involves deferred payment, and whether it is remunerated by end-users (concession contracts) or through tax (traditional public procurement contracts and availability contracts). This collection of tools can be summarized according to several criteria (see Table 1) that will feature centrally in the various theoretical analysis grids drawn up by economists.

Table 1 Procurement tools and their characteristics

Tools/Criteria	Traditional public procurement	Concession	Availability contract
Deferred payment	No	Yes (generally by the users)	Yes (by the public authorities)
Transfer of production risk (associated with the service or infrastructure)	Yes	Yes	Yes
Transfer of demand-related risk	No	Yes	No (or very little)
Transfer of risks associated with operating costs	Yes (in public service contracts)	Yes	Yes partially
Global contract	No (with a few exceptions)	Yes	Yes
Project management	Public	Private	Private
Duration of contract	Short-medium term	Medium-long term	Long term

By "transfer of the risk," we mean a transfer toward the contractor, i.e., its accountability in the matter (cost or demand)
Source: Saussier and Tirole (2015)

These tools do not constitute discrete forms; rather, they make up a continuum of contractual solutions for public authorities, one that is bound to evolve, especially under the influence of the new European directives on public procurement and concessions, which have changed the rules in a significant way. Indeed, these directives deeply modify the award and execution of public–private contracts. Firstly, the directives on public procurement give more prominence to the negotiated procedure, which will become the rule rather than the exception; secondly, the extent to which a contract may be renegotiated during its performance stage will increase substantially. Such evolutions are not neutral, and they illustrate the need, in a changing environment, to rely on theoretical frames of reference so as to better predict and understand their future influences. The European Directives include availability-based contracts in the "Public procurement" category. However, we keep traditional public procurement and availability contracts distinct in this book as they have substantially different economic features.

Each contribution of this book can be read independently, depending on the needs of the readers. However, together, they form a coherent unity, providing insights on the most salient issues regarding PPPs.

References

Campagnac, E., & Deffontaines, G. (2012). Une analyse socio-économique critique des PPP. *Revue d'économie industrielle, 140*, 49–79.

EPEC. (2016). Market Update - Review of the European PPP Market in 2016, European Investment Bank document.

Hart, O. (2003). Incomplete contracts and public ownership: Remarks, and an application to public private partnerships. *Economic Journal, 113*(485), c69–c76.

Le Lannier, A., & Saussier, S. (2012). Organisation des partenariats public-privé et gestion des ressources humaines. In Vuibert (Ed.), *Encyclopédie des ressources humaines.*

OECD. (2013). *Government at a glance 2013*. OECD Publishing. en ligne. doi:https://doi.org/10. 1787/gov_glance-2013-en.

OECD. (2015). Fostering Investment in Infrastructure. https://www.oecd.org/daf/inv/invest ment.../Fostering-Investment-in-Infrastructure.pdf.

PWC. (2015). Assessing the global transport infrastructure market: Outlook to 2025, PricewaterhouseCoopers report.

Saussier, S., & Tirole, J. (2015). *Renforcer l'efficacité de la commande publique.* note du Conseil d'analyse économique, avril.

Saussier, S., & Truong Tran, T. (2012). L'efficacité des contrats de partenariat en France: une première évaluation quantitative. *Revue d'Économie Industrielle, 140*, 81–110.

Part I
Definitions, Scope and Economic Analysis of PPPs

An Economic Analysis of Public–Private Partnerships

Jean Beuve, Stéphane Saussier, and Julie de Brux

1 Introduction

The introduction of this book has highlighted the fact that there is no single well-defined "type" of public–private partnership, but rather various types of public–private partnerships (PPPs) that differ depending on whether the contract is global or simple, whether payment is made upon delivery or deferred, and whether the operator is remunerated mostly based on service operating results or, on the contrary, based on its ability to meet the performance objectives described in the contract. The "landscape" of PPPs is thus a complex one, made up of various subcategories, ranging from traditional public procurement contracts, user-pay PPPs (concessions), and public-budget pay PPPs (availability contracts, as most of PFIs). Worse still, there are many possible variants within each group of PPP. For instance, some concession contracts provide for some form of risk sharing between the operator and public authority, the terms of which are defined in contractual clauses. This is typically the case of most Indian concession highways. The National Highways Authority of India in charge of planning investment programs

J. Beuve (✉)
Université de Paris I Panthéon-Sorbonne, Paris, France
e-mail: jean.beuve@univ-paris1.fr

S. Saussier
IAE Paris, Sorbonne Business School, Paris, France
e-mail: saussier@univ-paris1.fr

J. de Brux
IAE Paris - Sorbonne Business School, Paris, France

Business Advisory Board at United Nations Economic Commission for Europe, Geneva, Switzerland

CITIZING, Paris, France
e-mail: julie.debrux@citizing-consulting.com

© Springer International Publishing AG 2018
S. Saussier, J. de Brux (eds.), *The Economics of Public-Private Partnerships*,
https://doi.org/10.1007/978-3-319-68050-7_2

specifies that contract durations can be extended in order to mitigate revenue risk in case traffic is lower than expected. Conversely, if case traffic is 5% higher than traffic forecasts, the concession period is reduced by 3.75%. Other risk sharing mechanisms can take the form of profit sharing above some threshold of revenue or of revenue compensation in case of under underperformance. This type of mechanism is for example in place in the French city of Dijon concerning water management. Such mechanisms enable to mitigate the risks, while still benefiting from the private sector efficiency, but at a lower cost.

Such evolutions of user-pay PPP contracts indicate the parties' acknowledgment of the fact that a significant counter-performance is most often due to exogenous factors, for which the operator cannot reasonably be held responsible alone. This type of contract constitutes a step toward operational risk sharing between the contracting parties. In this respect, it brings user-pay PPP contracts (concession contracts) closer to availability-based contracts (public-budget pay PPPs such as most UK PFIs), thereby creating a real continuum of public–private contracts.

Even though it is difficult to analyze PPPs as discrete and alternative forms of public service organization, they all constitute a more or less partial outsourcing of activities contributing to the realization of a public service. It is therefore from this point of view that the economic analysis proposes to study PPPs, with their potential advantages and drawbacks, by considering them first and foremost as a decision to outsource on the part of public authorities. Moreover, it is essential to emphasize that the economic theory sees PPPs as having advantages and drawbacks that are not only associated with the outsourcing issue but also with the public–private nature of the relationship that makes contracts so particular and more difficult to manage than private–private relationships.

In this chapter, we will first explain the potential advantages of public–private arrangements (first part), before describing their disadvantages (second part). Of course, the economic analysis does not only enumerate these, but it also gives some clues as to how to minimize the disadvantages of PPPs as much as possible while benefiting from the advantages they offer. Depending on the theoretical approaches considered, emphasis will be placed in turn on contractual design, incentives, and the global or incomplete nature of the contract in order to shed light on these issues.

2   Potential Advantages of Public–Private Partnerships

In this section, we will first analyze the economic advantages of outsourcing in general and apply them to the contracting out of public services (Sect. 2.1). In the following section, we will then outline the specific advantages of outsourcing when a public entity is involved in the contractual relationship (Sect. 2.2). Finally, in the last section, we will assume the fact of outsourcing to be given, and we will detail the arguments used in the economic literature in favor of global outsourcing, involving several stages of one project, rather than partial outsourcing focusing on a single stage of a project (Sect. 2.3).

2.1 Advantages of Outsourcing the Provision of Public Services

2.1.1 The Search for Expertise

The first reason identified by the economic literature to justify outsourcing is a lack of in-house expertise. Outsourcing is then an alternative to the integration of a partner or the development of skills, two processes that can take a long time and generate costly irreversibility. Applied to the issue of public service management, this lack of expertise of public entities can lead them to focus on their "core business," namely, the supervision of public service rather than its provision. Indeed, the latter can be realized at a lower cost by private operators, who are experts and benefit from economies of scale, experience, and scope, especially when the technology or knowledge at stake is stabilized. However, this deficit of expertise of the public party compared to private operators depends on the size of the public body, as well as on the complexity of the service in question.

2.1.2 Economies of Scale

The reason most often put forward to justify resorting to an external contractor is the advantage it can represent in terms of economies of scale. Since the average cost incurred to supply a product or service depends on the quantity to be produced, it is generally interesting to outsource the activity in question to a "specialist" who has several customers and can thus make economies of scale (i.e., a reduction in average costs), from which its customers can benefit because of the competitive price it is able to apply. Such economies can generally be explained by the necessity, in order to supply the goods or services, to invest and bear substantial fixed costs that must be amortized on future production.

Of course, this advantage of contracting out disappears when (1) the public entity is in a position of monopoly and (2) when the outsourced activity requires specific assets to be set up, namely, physical or human investments that are specific to the contractual relationship and therefore cannot be redeployed toward other contractors.[1]

If the expertise and investments needed to carry out a given activity are specific, then the advantages of outsourcing the activity in question recede, because the development of new expertise and the benefits related to economies of scale could just as well be realized in-house.

---

[1] Asset specificity is a core concept of the transaction cost approach developed by O.E. Williamson in the early 1970s, and for which he received the Nobel Prize in Economic Sciences in 2009, notably for his work on the optimal boundaries of the firm (i.e., the analysis of which activities should or should not be outsourced by firms). If this concept is essential to understand the advantages of outsourcing, it is even more important to analyze the difficulties associated with externalization, as we will see later.

If we apply this reasoning to public service management, one can easily understand that in-house provision of public services (that is, direct public management)—which is the alternative to externalization, whatever its form—does not enable the same economies of scale as PPPs. Indeed, as demonstrated by many studies in applied economics, operators that are present on several markets can realize economies of scale which is not the case for public authorities, as they only operate in a single market, unless the optimal output level—beyond which average costs increase—is low, or the public body is large enough to be able to realize economies of scale itself. Therefore, these advantages of contracting out are stronger when the value of investments to be set up is substantial (especially in the case of the construction/renovation of infrastructure) and as these investments are not too specific. It should be noted that the existence of such economies of scale can also explain the municipalities'[2] wish to pool their purchase policies and the management of their public services within organizations for intercommunal cooperation. Let us note finally that because private operators usually operate at a very large scale to benefit from those economies of scale, the sectors related to the provision of public services often suffer from high degrees of concentration.[3]

2.1.3 Economies of Experience

Some activities allow companies to benefit from economies resulting from the accumulated experience of their employees and the organizational routines they have set up by coping with and overcoming the problems they have often encountered throughout their history.

This experience effect allows significant improvements to be introduced in the processes on which outsourcing is based, and, moreover, it generally leads to a reduction in operating costs.

2.1.4 Economies of Scope

Although it can be interesting to outsource a service or the production of goods to a specialized firm operating simultaneously in several markets and benefiting from economies of scale, it can also be efficient to conclude a contract with an operator supplying multiple different goods or services, and which therefore benefits from economies of scope. Indeed, some activities can generate synergies when they require similar, complementary expertise and thus enable the operator mastering

---

[2]Metropolis, urban community, conurbation community, community of municipalities, new conurbation syndicate, and intercommunal syndicate.

[3]The existence of substantial economies of scale often leads to a high degree of concentration in the sectors producing public goods. This is why it is necessary that the opening up to competition takes place within an economic space that is large enough (such as the European Union for instance) in order to limit rent appropriation by private operators.

them to reduce its costs. Even more simply, economies of scope may arise from the fact that two different activities use the same imperfectly divisible resources (such as production equipment) and can therefore share the R&D activity, or alternatively share a brand. In such cases, they are very similar to economies of scale.

It is easy to see how economies of scope may be realized when a local authority decides for instance to outsource the production, distribution, and treatment of water to a single operator that can for example establish a common central office to handle customer complaints for all of its activities. As with economies of scale, this argument can also explain why it is sometimes interesting for local authorities to form a group to outsource the management of their public services.

2.1.5 The Search for Incentives

In addition to the technical reasons mentioned so far to understand the advantages of outsourcing, other reasons that are more related to management issues are also alluded to in the economic literature. They justify the use of outsourcing because it is a situation (1) where competition can play its part fully, (2) where management incentive practices are easier to set up, and (3) where risks are more likely to be shared between the public authority and the operator.

Outsourcing and Competition
When a public authority decides to outsource a public service, it has to choose a partner among a certain number of potential suppliers. If one decides to open up a project to competition, for instance by organizing a call for tenders, then outsourcing is considered to guarantee a certain level of cost control that is more difficult to reach with in-house provision, because internal services are not generally put in competition with potential external contractors (or less frequently so). When carried out properly, the opening up to competition realized as part of the outsourcing process thus forces potential partners to disclose information about their costs, by offering a price.

This is an important point, especially as it is raised systematically in the debate on PPP efficiency. With in-house provision, it is not possible to enjoy the benefits of competition since such direct management does not compel the public body to organize competitive calls for tenders, nor to conduct a preliminary assessment to justify this organizational choice. In contrast, when outsourcing is the chosen solution, several operators are likely to compete in a call for tenders for a given contract. Therefore, adopting a direct management method deprives public authorities of the competitive pressures in play in the markets. Incidentally, the French Competition Authority ("Autorité de la Concurrence") recommends conducting an assessment of the costs and advantages related to each mode of provision, that is, both in-house provision and externalization.

Incentives and Management
Whereas internal organization facilitates the control of production activities, outsourcing—although it makes such control more difficult—presents the advantage of increasing the level of incentives to the operator in charge of supplying the

goods or services (see Box 1). As observed by O. E. Williamson, unlike internal organization, the market (i.e., the outsourcing solution), while it does not share out profits, is unforgiving (Williamson, 1985). In other words, as relationships within an organization are based on an employment contract, thus establishing a relation of subordination that leaves little room for incentives (even if incentive wages can be set up), they do not encourage partners to be efficient to the same extent as market relations do. Indeed, in the case of outsourcing, the relationship is based on a contract that can include strong incentives by describing the expected service (that is, a higher degree of precision as to the service to be provided) and by introducing a range of incentive clauses (bonuses and penalties) allowing the operator to keep all the additional revenue it is able to generate by being efficient.

Box 1: Outsourcing and Insourcing in the United Kingdom

While "outsourcing" designates the externalization of public service delivery, the word "insourcing" has little by little become common parlance although its practice has received relatively little attention. A Guardian investigation (from March 2016) of 36 strategic public–private partnerships that local UK authorities signed between 2000 and 2007 has found that 13 of the contracts—that covered IT, back-office functions, property management, and highways—have since gone back in-house, either at the end of the contract or as a result of early terminations.

Examples in the United Kingdom demonstrate that although outsourcing may potentially encourage operators to become more efficient by reducing their costs and by targeting performance indicators, it also puts the public authority at risk of losing control if it is not careful enough.

On one side of the spectrum, one can for example describe the particularly demanding PFI contract (availability-based contract) awarded by the London Borough of Hounslow to maintain roads, pavement, and street lighting across the borough, as well as provide a number of key services including street cleansing, winter maintenance, and enforcement. The contract spans 25 years and describes over 290 performance targets, ranging from network drainage (in case of a storm, the network shall be free from standing water within 2 h of the cessation of storm) to tree management, maximum height of the grass, availability of the road (the service provider shall remove any item or spillage from any affected area of the network within 3 h), etc. The levels of adjustments (sanctions) led to major organizational adjustments and resulted in unrivaled performance in the management of this urban area.

However, other examples illustrate the power of sanction wielded by the market, in that if the operator is not careful to establish and nurture a proper partnership with the public authority, it can be sanctioned without "forgiveness."

A report by the Association for Public Service Excellence on Insourcing (a guide to bringing local authority services back in-house, from 2009) describes several insourcing experiences in the United Kingdom and notably

(continued)

Box 1 (continued)

the return of waste services in-house in Oldham Metropolitan Borough Council in 2000. In the late 1980s, this service was outsourced to SITA, a Suez Environment subsidiary, in a drive to increase competitiveness and commercialism. The experience showed it was difficult for a private operator to deliver this service, as a result of fluctuations in the waste agenda, the sheer scale of the operation, and in some cases the resistance of the Trade Unions to private sector delivery of waste-related services. Additionally, in the late 1990s, the Government had implemented a series of targets with regard to waste collection. These targets were accompanied by financial penalties if not met for the local authority. Increasingly, the council was not meeting the targets, meaning that the service, as it was organized, was not being delivered to standard but also that there were financial implications for the authority.

The return of the delivery of the waste service in Oldham in-house has enabled flexibility in the management and the service. This was particularly remarkable when the indicators relating to reducing the amount of waste sent to landfill and increasing recycling have changed again.

Various reasons are mentioned in the report to explain the insourcing choice in the different case studies. The reasons most frequently put forward are the lack of control over the service delivery, the rigidity of contracts, the trade-off between cost efficiency and service quality, as well as the difficulty to set up real partnerships.

Risk Sharing

Finally, outsourcing can also present advantages as regards risk sharing. Outsourcing the production or the management of a service makes it possible to transfer some risks from the public party to the private one. Depending on the public procurement tool, such a transfer can be focused on production risks, demand-related risks, and risks associated with operating costs (see Table 1). From this point of view, the advantage of outsourcing lies in the greater ability of operators to diversify their risks (because of their level and of the potential diversity of their activities) and their expertise in managing the different types of risks. Consequently, operators bear lower costs when coping with the risks than a public entity.

2.2 Advantages of Outsourcing the Provision of Services to a Private Partner

Aside from the economic advantages, which are common to all transactions, the economic literature also identifies a range of additional reasons that justify the use of outsourcing and which are only relevant when studying the management of

Table 1 Main risks allocation in the various procurement tools

	Public procurement contracts	User pay PPPS (concessions)	Public budget pay PPPs (PFI, availability contracts)
Deferred payment	No	Yes (generally by the user)	Yes (by public authorities)
Transfer of production risk (associated with the service or infrastructure)	Yes	Yes	Yes
Transfer of demand-related risk	No	Yes	No (or very little)
Transfer of risk associated with operating costs	Yes (in service contracts)	Yes	Yes partially
Global contract	Usually No	Yes	Yes
Project management	Public	Private	Private
Duration of contract	Short-medium term	Medium-long term	Long term

Source: Saussier and Tirole (2015)

public services. These reasons mostly have to do with the difficulty of controlling and managing public organizations, as well as with the risk of political interferences that characterizes them. Outsourcing is then seen as a way to reduce or eliminate disadvantages that are specific to in-house provision of public services.

2.2.1 Difficulties in Controlling and Managing Public Organizations

Organizational theory has long since identified a limit that is specific to large-sized companies and collectivities: the delegation of the decision-making power. While delegating becomes indispensable when an organization increases in size and diversifies its activities, it raises the issue of the control of the decision-maker or of its incentives. This is a key point of agency theory, whether in its positive (Jensen & Meckling, 1976) or normative versions (Laffont & Tirole, 1993), and this point has always received special attention in economics. Thus, when talking about company managers to whom owning shareholders delegate their decision-making power, Adam Smith already observed that *"the directors of such companies, however, being the managers rather of other people's money than of their own, it cannot well be expected that they should watch over it with the same anxious vigilance with which the partners in a private copartnery frequently watch over their own"* (Smith, 1776).

Although this problem is not exclusive to public organizations, it is accentuated in their case by the differences between a public and a private organization, the former being more difficult to control when decisions are delegated (especially from citizens to managers). According to Laffont (2000), these particularities have to do with the fact that public entities are generally subjected to several controls, involving various "controllers" with objectives that are potentially antinomic or even variable and with little credibility. Consequently, incentives are limited and it is impossible for public organizations—if it is even desirable—to replicate the incentive rules of the private sector, which is characterized by more efficient corporate governance mechanisms and a single and inviolable objective: profit maximization. Charreaux (1997) also develops an argument along the same line when pondering the reasons why public companies (in France) are "*necessarily*" inefficient. The explanation he suggests has to do with the inability of public organizations to generate the same level of incentive as private companies, precisely because of the characteristics we have just outlined, which are specific to them.[4] Outsourcing is then a way to rationalize the production of a public good or the provision of a public service by restricting the intended objectives to the sole economic performance while implementing more efficient control mechanisms.

2.2.2   Outsourcing as a Way to Reduce Political Interferences

In addition to their low incentives, public organizations are more subject to political interferences, which potentially diverts even further from the pursuit of economic objectives of performance. This point, often put forward in the economic literature (see for example Boycko, Shleifer, & Vishny, 1996), was highlighted by the French Competition Authority ("Conseil de la Concurrence")[5] in its 2003 thematic study on "State monopolies in the competition game" (*Les monopoles publics dans le jeu concurrentiel*), in which it indicated that because of political interferences, public companies may face a multiplicity of sometimes contradictory objectives, which may be detrimental to their efficiency. For instance, supervisory authorities may have a "preference for high levels of production for various reasons, which may have to do in particular with social considerations (sustaining employment)," which may "translate into less attention being paid to losses and the profit criterion, as well as an increased valuation of the scale and range of activities [of the companies they manage]" (thematic study, annual report of the Conseil de la concurrence, year 2003, pages 85–86).

Without trying to be exhaustive, some empirical studies highlight these possible "dysfunctions" and show that the choice to delegate also rests upon noneconomic

---

[4]In his explanation, the author also includes some characteristics that are specific to the French institutional framework of the time (external recruiting, ineffective management boards....) and prevent internal and external corporate governance mechanisms from being efficient.

[5]In January 2009, it was replaced by the Autorité de la concurrence to put an end to the dual system that had been in force since 1986 between the Direction générale de la concurrence, de la consommation et de la répression des fraudes (DGCCRF), in charge of investigations, and the Conseil de la concurrence, in charge of processing cases.

criteria. The political interests associated with the influence of pressure groups are one of these determinants. Their rents may be affected by the organizational form selected by the authorities. Thus, it is generally accepted that public employees and unions are in favor of public supply while industrial users have a preference for private supply (Miralles, 2008). However, a high degree of precariousness (low income per capita or high unemployment rate in the community) may encourage local authorities to retain direct control over the local public service so as to maintain a high level of employment in the public sector. Ideology may also influence the choice of an organizational scheme. For instance, a recent empirical study on water services in Spain has shown that public decision-makers' political affiliation has a significant impact on their outsourcing decisions, thereby illustrating the fact that it is possible for noneconomic considerations to emerge in decisions about public service management (Picazo-Tadeo et al., 2010). Finally, the choice to delegate may also be influenced by tax restrictions that deprive local authorities of funding sources for the local public service. Such difficulties can for example be associated with a tax burden that is deemed too high by taxpayers, or with regulatory constraints regarding local taxation. Generally speaking, tax restrictions increase the budgetary constraints of local authorities and thus bear down on their ability to fund their local public services alone [see for instance Bel and Fageda (2007)'s survey of empirical studies on the reasons motivating the externalization of public services].

2.3   PPPs: Global Contract Versus Simple Contract

We have just highlighted that the issue of optimal public service management can be addressed through the question of outsourcing by showing that direct management (in-house provision) entails sacrificing potential economies of scale, scope, and experience and comes at the cost of low incentives. This makes the efficiency of this governance structure uncertain. However, once the decision has been made to outsource all or part of the stages in the production and supply of a public service, the comparative advantages of the different types of PPPs still need to be discussed, instead of only comparing them with the public solution (direct management), as we have done until now.[6]

---

[6]Let us note that we do not address the question of the total privatization of public services here. In the economic literature, "privatization" often refers to externalization [see for instance Bel and Fageda (2007)]. However, total privatization induces a complete transfer of rights from the public to the private entity, and the latter is the only recipient for the exploitation of the public service. Also in privatizations, assets are and remain private. Privatizations are a lot less common than outsourcing and are often led because governments need the proceeds generated by privatization, and/or for political reasons, and especially in times of economic crises (see for instance the wave of privatization of public companies in ex-USSR economies, in the 1990s).

2.3.1   The Power of Incentives in Global Contracts

To compare the performances of the different kinds of PPPs, it is useful to draw a distinction between global contracts and simple contracts.

The economic literature often defines PPPs as long-term contracts whereby a private operator *finances, builds, and operates* a public service, an infrastructure, or a public facility through a global contract (i.e., involving several stages of service provision, such as the design and construction of an infrastructure and its management). This global nature is often put forward as a major advantage of this type of PPP to justify its efficiency compared to traditional public procurement contracts.

By offering a comprehensive "package deal" to a single operator, the public authority encourages the latter to internalize cost reductions at the level of service operation, which can be realized by an appropriate investment in the design of the support infrastructure (Bennett & Iossa, 2006; Hart, 2003; Martimort & Pouyet, 2008). When a private company is endowed with a global contract, it has strong incentives to massively invest at the construction stage, in order to decrease future maintenance costs. This has important consequences for private operators' incentives but also, ultimately, for the nature of the provided service itself.

Indeed, this type of contract leads the operator to take the complementarities and synergies between the different stages of the project into account. Such a consideration may influence the investments that are set up as well as the operator's incentives to ensure that the different stages combine efficiently so as to reduce the infrastructure lead time (i.e., the "interface risk" associated with coordinating all stages of a project: design, construction, and operation).

Comparing the cost of global contracts with traditional public procurement requires being clear about the scope of what is compared. The cost of a global contract can only be compared with the discounted costs of the sum of the various contracts concluded through traditional procedure.

Some feedbacks that will be discussed later in this book highlight the fact that deadlines are more likely to be met in the case of PPPs than under the traditional public procurement when the project relates to the creation of new infrastructure (NAO, 2009; PriceWaterHouseCoopers, 2011; Saussier & Truong Tran, 2012). This can be explained by the introduction of strong incentives for operators (i.e., the fact that payment generally does not start until the service operation phase is reached, penalties for delay, etc.).

It can also be explained by a deeper involvement of the private partner and by the fact that the latter acts alone. Finally, if the type of contract and the call for tenders allow it, pooling all activities necessary to the execution of a project under a single contract encourages the operator to innovate in order to generate more revenue.

In a nutshell, the conclusion of a global contract modifies the nature and intensity of the private operator's incentives. This brings about changes in investment amounts, the revenue or welfare generated by the service, and the infrastructure lead time (incentive to deliver the infrastructure or facility on time).

2.3.2 Political Interferences in Global Contracts

It is obvious that global contracts can allow to maximize the abovementioned beneficial effects associated with economies of scale and scope, provided that the single operator is the most efficient at the various stages of the project that are included in the single contract. Moreover, several studies have also analyzed the ability of such contracts to reduce political interferences.

As soon as one discards the hypothesis of a voluntary and benevolent public authority, which only seeks to maximize citizens' social welfare, the efficiency of a global contract can be challenged. Maskin and Tirole (2008) consider the case of a public authority that does not seek to maximize the social surplus, but whose actions are driven by ideological considerations, or even by political or social relationships, and which therefore gives priority to projects in accordance with its own ideology, or that favors interest groups which are likely to be useful in the future. The authors then demonstrate that global contracts reduce such a risk compared to the use of separate public contracts, because the total cost of the project is estimated ahead and cannot be hidden. This increased transparency in public expenditure thus strengthens the accountability of public decision-makers. However, still according to Maskin and Tirole (2008), resorting to a global contract opens the way for another risk, namely, the transfer of project costs in time (few payments at the beginning of the project, many later on), by common consent among the parties. Thus, a long-term contract, which transfers decision-making rights to the operator, or which allows numerous opportunities for future renegotiations, can allow transferring the operator's rent in the long term, thus making PPPs more attractive... in the short term.

The economic analysis therefore highlights that outsourcing provides many advantages in terms of productive efficiency and production cost reductions for the provision of a public service. It also suggests that setting up global contracts could heighten these advantages by increasing the operators' incentives to minimize costs on the overall projects. However, this analysis is of course only a partial one. Indeed, the advantages mentioned above can generally only be obtained by signing a contract, often a long-term one, which allows private operators to get a return on investment. This is an important point, as the signature of a contract leads to various implementation and performance difficulties for PPPs: transaction costs, renegotiations, adverse effects on quality, etc. The theoretical advantages associated with public–private contractual arrangements must therefore be weighed against the costs they entail, which will now be outlined.

3 The Costs Associated with PPPs

Public–private partnerships generally lead to long-term contracting. The contract forms the basis for the "partnership" between the public and private parties. If it was possible to draw up complete contracts taking into account all future contingencies, and specifying an efficient means to address them in a way that is understandable both to the contracting party and third parties (e.g., law courts in charge of enforcing them), the contracting process would be quite straightforward. Unfortunately, in the case of long-term contracts, and when the context is uncertain or complex and the economic operators are characterized by different levels of information or expertise, contracting becomes much more challenging. Several theoretical approaches, which draw on different assumptions, focus on the contracting problems encountered in such agreements and the ways to minimize them. Those approaches can be considered as complementary. They highlight the major importance of specific investments needed to provide public services (Sect. 3.1), the importance of information asymmetries and risk sharing (Sect. 3.2), the issue of contractual incompleteness (Sect. 3.3), as well as the influence of the political dimension of PPP contracts (Sect. 3.4). In the end, the relative efficiency of PPPs, compared to direct in-house provision of public services, depends on the parties' ability to limit the risks associated with PPP contracting.

3.1   Specific Assets, Uncertainty, and Renegotiations

Transaction cost theory (TCT), which was developed in the 1970s by Williamson (1971, 1975, 1985), takes a special interest in the analysis of firm boundaries, namely, the decision to "make or buy." It suggests that such a decision results from an arbitration between transaction costs (contracting costs associated with resorting to the market) and organizational costs (internal costs). By analogy, this theoretical framework can also be applied to a situation where the public party has to choose between contracting out the provision of a public service and in-house provision. As a matter of fact, this was the first empirical application of the theory in a case study about cable TV franchising by a private operator in Oakland, under a public–private partnership with the municipality (Williamson, 1976). The main predictions of TCT are that such a choice depends on the level of specific investments required by the transaction and on the degree of uncertainty surrounding it.

3.1.1   Investment Specificity

Investment specificity can be measured by the possibility of redeploying the investments in question in alternative transactions. In other words, the more specific the investments, the less easily they can be redeployed for other purposes or with other potential partners. According to Williamson (1985), a direct consequence of the necessity to develop specific assets for a transaction is the switchover from a competitive situation to a situation of bilateral dependence between the parties. Before setting up specific investments, the contract giver can indeed choose between a number of potential partners. However, once these investments have been set up, the parties are intrinsically bound together and it is no longer possible to organize their relationship through a series of short-term contracts. A long-term contract is required, since the contractor is dependent on the contract giver, for whom it has accepted to set up specific investments, while the contract giver is dependent on the contractor, who is best equipped to meet its particular needs. This lock-in situation is the cause of several difficulties, the most obvious of which being that the parties may behave in an opportunistic manner (Klein, Crawford, and Alchian, 1978; Williamson, 1985), in particular by trying to renegotiate the initial contractual terms, or by failing to fulfill completely their obligations. The empirical literature provides numerous examples of opportunistic motivations that are likely to drive renegotiations, coming from both the private and public parties, or from a third party (see Chapter "Renegotiating PPP Contracts: Opportunities and Pitfalls" in the second part of this book). Consequently, TCT recommends resorting to outsourcing when the level of asset specificity is low, because a simple short-term contract is then possible. However, it advocates the use of integrated or complex governance structures when specific investments are necessary and require a long-term contract that will necessarily generate contractual difficulties. Furthermore, these difficulties will be heightened by the complexity and uncertainty of the transaction.

3.1.2 Uncertainty and Complexity

Every transaction is characterized by a certain degree of uncertainty, that is, by future hazards that cannot be anticipated contractually by the parties. Such uncertainty may arise from the economic context (demand shocks, introduction of product or process innovations, etc.), from the regulatory environment (modification of the existing rules or introduction of new rules), as well as from the complexity of the transaction itself. While a long-term contract is an option that can be considered without too many difficulties in a stable environment, things are different in an environment characterized by high uncertainty. Consequently, contract design is of critical importance in the case of outsourcing (see Box 2).

Box 2: The Example of Motorway Concession Contracts in Mexico

From 1989 to 1994, the Mexican government signed 52 motorway concession contracts. This program required around 13 billion USD and was financed by local banks, private concessionaires, and public guarantees and contributions.

With the 1994 devaluation, the program faced major difficulties. Consequently, the government took over 40% of the concessions and a new public entity was created to take the responsibility for outstanding-related bank credits, which amounted to about 5 billion USD. Shareholders were not compensated.

For the remaining 32 projects, the duration of the concession contracts was extended to allow private partners to recover their original investments (Standard & Poor's, 2006).

(continued)

Box 2 (continued)

The analysis of this case study by OECD/ITF (2008) highlights the fact that although the devaluation was a major catalyst, several failures of the contract design could have been avoided:

- The concession periods were very short (on average 10 years), putting high pressure on concessionaires to recover their costs and pay back their debts, leading to tolls above what users were willing to pay.
- The process for adjusting tool rates was complex and required government approval, which may have led the companies to set up high initial rates for fear of not being able to raise them later.
- Competition was limited to national companies only. As a result, the projects did not benefit from the full degree of experience in managing all aspects of toll motorways that may otherwise have been possible.
- Short time frames for the preparation of the bids and their evaluation meant that the government had little opportunity to assess their financial resilience. Notably, the financial structure of the bids was very vulnerable and subject to major exchange rate risk.

3.1.3 The Importance of Contract Design

Many complex public goods or services are regularly contracted out by public entities, under complex contractual arrangements. Such a situation is not at odds with TCT. It refers to the existence of coordination arrangements located between pure market relations and integrated relationships: "hybrid" organizational forms. These intermediate coordination arrangements are based on long-term agreements and imply that the parties pool their resources. They are made possible by the existence of credible commitments (Saussier & Yvrande-Billon, 2007), that is, of contractual provisions favoring the continuity of the relationship and the management of potential conflicts (safeguard clauses, periodic review clauses, etc.). Thus, TCT highlights the importance of contract design and claims that the success of the relationship depends on its quality. The main challenge here is to generate trust by managing to reach two contradictory objectives: secure the relationship by getting steadfast commitment from the parties, while retaining a certain level of flexibility, which is necessary to allow the contractual adaptations to the economic, financial, and statutory environment during the implementation phase (see Chapter "Renegotiating PPP Contracts: Opportunities and Pitfalls" in the second part of this book).

When this is possible as part of a long-term contract (contracts are generally signed after a competitive call for tenders), then outsourcing is possible. When the level of uncertainty is too high, this solution should not be implemented, as it is too expensive in terms of transaction costs. Regulation then appears as the best possible alternative (see Fig. 1).

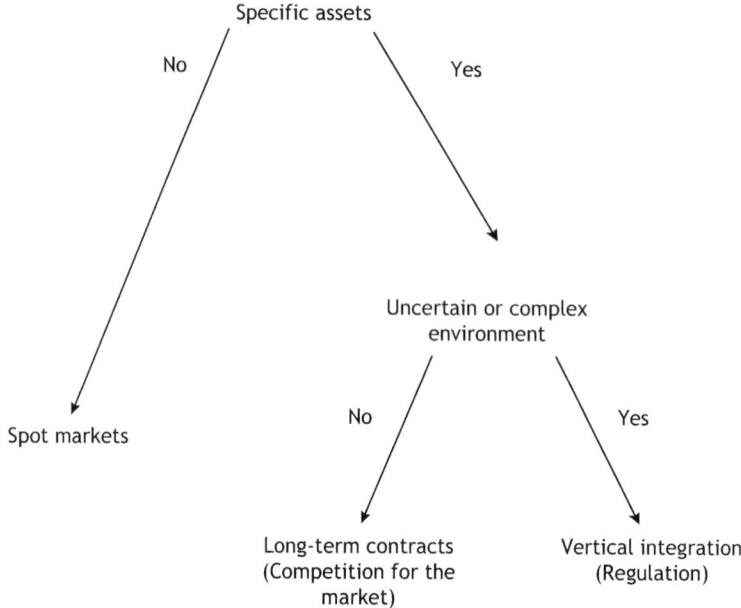

Fig. 1 The choice of public service outsourcing according to transaction cost theory. Source: Crocker and Masten (1996)

3.2 *Information Asymmetries and Incentives*

3.2.1 Information Asymmetries, Adverse Selection, and Moral Hazard

A large part of contractual difficulties encountered in public–private partnerships results from information asymmetries between the contracting parties. Incentive theory focuses on these difficulties. From this theoretical perspective, information asymmetry leads to the existence of an informational rent, which the party with better information may use to maximize its own interest. More precisely, two kinds of opportunistic behaviors resulting from information asymmetry can be identified: adverse selection and moral hazard. Adverse selection occurs prior to contract signing, when an unalterable characteristic of the provided goods or services, or of the supplier, is unobservable. Since they cannot distinguish between good and bad contractors, buyers face the risk of not choosing the "right" partner. As for moral hazard, it occurs after contract signing. Once the contractor has been chosen, it can make use of its informational advantage (often due to a deeper knowledge of the key parameters of the transaction, or to its greater expertise) to reduce its level of effort to the detriment of the contract giver. Thus, unlike TCT, which seeks to find out which organizational arrangement is best suited for the management of different public services, incentive theory mainly focuses on determining which types of mechanisms must be set up to encourage contracting the parties to share their private information and therefore provide the optimal level of effort. The contract therefore aims to establish monitoring and control mechanisms as well as incentive schemes to allow information disclosure and then to ensure that actions align with the revealed information.

3.2.2 Types of Contracts, Risk Sharing, and Incentive Mechanisms

Within the specific framework of public–private partnerships, the contractual clauses that define the remuneration of the operator can be analyzed according to their incentive power and their relevance to the various types of public goods and services. Two contractual arrangements (as well as intermediate schemes in terms of cost sharing) can be used (Laffont & Tirole, 1993).

– Under the first arrangement, the company is repaid the full amount of its costs and additionally receives a predefined payment. This is known as a cost-plus contract for nonmarket services and a cost-of-service regulation indexing user prices on the level of realized costs for market services. This arrangement relieves the company of responsibility but it also limits its potential profits.
– The second arrangement involves a fixed price contract for nonmarket public projects or a price cap regulation—i.e., one where the price is not indexed on effective production costs—for market services. Under this arrangement, the company is granted a fixed amount, regardless of its effective costs and the level of demand. This requires the company to make more efforts to contain its costs, but this offers the possibility to get substantial profits when its costs happen to be especially low (or when demand is particularly high), irrespective of any effort on its part.

Cost-plus contracts have little incentive power and can generate cost overruns, as the operator is not encouraged to be efficient in its management or in suggesting potential innovative solutions. On the contrary, fixed price contracts provide strong incentives and hold the service provider accountable. However, they entail surrendering an informational rent to the operator, which can give rise to cost overruns for the contracting authority that pays a higher price than the effective service production cost.

3.3   Contractual Unverifiability and Adverse Effect on Quality

3.3.1   Unverifiability and Contractual Incompleteness

Like TCT, the incomplete contracts theory (ICT) focuses on the consequences of contractual incompleteness. However, the source of incompleteness does not stem from the parties' inability to anticipate all future contingencies that may arise during contract implementation. Rather, within this theoretical framework, the source of incompleteness comes from third parties' inability to verify certain aspects of the relationship. Indeed, the ICT makes a distinction between actions that are "observable" by the contracting parties and "non-verifiable" actions, which the contracting parties cannot describe perfectly in the contract. Consequently, these non-verifiable actions cannot be made enforceable by a third party, such as a law court. For instance, as part of a PPP, the effort made by an operator to propose innovative solutions is not verifiable, even if it can sometimes be observable by the public authority. Therefore, this kind of effort is not contractible. This is all the more prejudicial as innovations that were not initially planned are likely to happen during the execution phase of a contract.

3.3.2   The Importance of a Good Distribution of Property Rights

Like TCT, contractual incompleteness opens the way for possible opportunistic behaviors. The parties can take advantage of contract adaptation phases to review the contractual terms to their advantage. As a result of parties' anticipations, such a situation then leads to a suboptimal level of initial investment. However, the theory of incomplete contracts shows how this issue can be resolved by an appropriate distribution of property rights *ex ante*. Indeed, the holder of property rights also holds residual control rights over the assets. This means that it falls to this holder to make the final decision regarding the use of these assets in the case where the relationship fails, which gives it a better exit strategy as well as a higher surplus during renegotiations. Its incentives to invest are therefore higher. Consequently, to solve problems of opportunistic renegotiations and underinvestment, property rights should be distributed in favor of the party whose level of specific investment is most important for the success of the relationship.

3.3.3   Cost Reduction and Detrimental Effects on Quality

When applied to the analysis of PPP contracts, models derived from the theory of incomplete contracts state the existence of two kinds of efforts that can be made by the operator. First, there are cost-reduction efforts, which increase the profit of the operator but impede service quality (and therefore at the expense of society as a whole). Secondly, there are efforts that improve quality, which increase the operator's costs but contribute to the provision of a better service. When these efforts are perfectly contractible, it is possible to reach an optimal level of investment. However, if the efforts are non-verifiable, the choice of governance structure will affect the effort levels. Thus, Hart, Shleifer, and Vishny (1997) show that the externalization to a private operator generates stronger incentives to reduce production costs but also stronger incentives to improve service quality.

   Consequently, the theory of incomplete contracts recommends outsourcing public service delivery to solve the issue of public managers' low incentives.

However, it acknowledges the fact that direct public management is preferable in some well-identified cases, namely, when there is little possibility of improving quality and when the detrimental effects of cost reduction on quality are significant. However, although this effect is not directly conceptualized by Hart et al. (1997), public management may be useless even in those specific situations, if there is strong competition among operators (this means that consumers can choose their supplier, which encourages companies to internalize the consequences of their efforts).

3.3.4 Perspective for Future Profit and Reputational Issues

The contractual difficulties encountered in PPPs are real and should be taken into account when the time comes for a public authority to decide whether to make or buy. Nevertheless, the contracting parties' reputation can help simplify things. The theory of relational contracts is based on the same premises as the theory of incomplete contracts: contracts are necessarily incomplete because some aspects of the relationship are non-verifiable. However, this theory takes on a completely different stance regarding the means that should be implemented to resolve opportunistic behaviors and under-investment issues. Adopting an approach based on repeated games, it highlights the fact that the prospect of future profits has a disciplining effect on the behavior of contracting parties. By encouraging them to take into account their reputation and the losses that could be incurred if it came to be damaged, the long-term perspective of the relationship (or its possible repetition) makes it possible to avoid opportunistic renegotiations resulting from contractual incompleteness. Conversely, it encourages the parties to share their information and look for cooperative solutions when faced with contingencies that were not anticipated in the initial contract. Such a solution (that is, selecting a partner based on its reputation and guaranteeing its renewal if the relationship succeeds) would present the advantage of reducing contracting costs in a potentially substantial way. However, it is not easily applicable due to the fact that it is not always possible to make a commitment in the long term. Moreover, the award procedure for public contracts involves that it is impossible to guarantee the repetition of the relationship in time, for regulatory reasons.

3.4 Contestability and Contract Rigidity

Contracting costs associated with outsourcing can also be larger in the case of public contracts because of the political interferences mentioned in Sect. 2.2.2. The specificities of public–private partnerships make them intrinsically different from private–private contracts (that is, contracts concluded between two private partners). Some recent theories (Moszoro & Spiller, 2012; Moszoro, Spiller, & Stolorz, 2016; Spiller, 2008) thus highlight the importance of third-party opportunism in public contracts. Indeed, opportunism can come not only from the signatory parties (private operator, public authority) but also from third parties such as interest groups (consumer associations, lobbies, political opponents of the decision-maker, rival companies of the operator, or citizens): a PPP contract relates to the provision of a public service and implies the investment of public funds and therefore concerns society as a whole. This interest of third parties to PPP contracts may prove useful, especially when it plays a supervisory role by preventing the public party from straying from the announced political agenda, or private operators from renegotiating the terms of the initial agreement in an opportunistic way (McCubbins & Schwartz, 1984). However, third parties may also hinder the running of PPPs when they seek to pursue their own interests instead of the general interest. For example, it can be in their interest to question the integrity of the public party in relation to a public–private contract when they are competing with it in a "political market" (Spiller, 2008). This kind of opportunistic behavior may have significant consequences on contracting costs. Indeed, to protect themselves from political contestability, both the public body and the private party may be tempted to design more rigid public contracts (that is, contracts that include more clauses than contracts concluded between two private parties, as the latter do not have to protect against third-party opportunism). Thus, the public parties will generally draw more rigid contracts to avoid contract renegotiations that could be costly in terms of image if there is a high level of political competition within the municipality. However, setting up rigid contracts presents two drawbacks that should be underlined. First, such contracts are particularly costly. Indeed, drawing them up generates additional transaction costs, both for the public authority (*ex ante* information retrieval, drawing up of detailed specifications, etc.) and for the private party (longer and more complex procedures to participate in calls for tenders), which may result in cost overruns that would cancel out the potential advantages of a rigid contract (that is, the limitation of third-party opportunism). Second, such rigidity can hinder the ability of contracts to adapt to changes in the environment (statutory, technological, financial, etc.), while these evolutions are unavoidable in the case of long-term contracts.

3.5   Importance of the Institutional Environment

The abovementioned issue of contracting costs is raised all the more sharply when institutions happen to be inefficient. Indeed, weak institutions damage the credibility of public authorities and can thus favor opportunistic renegotiations, which could lead to a misappropriation of resources or to a decrease in the quality of the goods or services supplied by the private party. A weak institutional framework also heightens the risk of opportunistic behavior on the part of the public body. Indeed, in the absence of government control systems, it is easier for the government to modify the "ground rules" unilaterally. Guasch (2004) thus observes that the occurrence of renegotiations can be reduced significantly by the presence of a regulatory authority and that it is conversely increased by the incidence of corrupt behaviors (nepotism, clientelism, bribery, etc.).

4   Conclusion

The development of public–private partnerships reflects (among other reasons) the logic of a public authority that increasingly wants to be a steering and managing force, rather than the supplier of public services needed by the population. While these partnerships are a source of potential gains, we have seen that they neverthe-less remain contractual agreements that are likely to cause problems as soon as they are concluded over long periods of time, in complex environments, and with elements that are unverifiable by third parties. While the arbitrations in play can be understood through the works of contract theory dealing with the decision to outsource, one must also consider the intrinsic specificities of these agreements associated with their political dimension, which make them more difficult to manage than purely private transactions.

References

Bel, G., & Fageda, X. (2007). Why do local governments privatise fe.gpublic services? A survey of empirical studies. *Local Government Studies, 33*(4), 517–534.

Bennett, J., & Iossa, E. (2006). Delegation of contracting in the private provision of public services. *Review of Industrial Organization, 29*(1), 75–92.

Boycko, M., Shleifer, A., & Vishny, R. W. (1996). A theory of privatization. *Economic Journal, 106*(435), 309–319.

Charreaux, G. (1997). L'entreprise publique est-elle nécessairement moins efficace? *Revue Française de Gestion*, no spécial Public-Privé, septembre–octobre 1997, pp. 38–56.

Crocker, K. J., & Masten, S. E. (1996). Regulation and administered contracts revisited: Lessons from transaction-cost economics for public utility regulation. *Journal of Regulatory Economics, 9*(1), 5–39.

Guasch, J.-L. (2004). *Granting and renegotiating infrastructure concession: Doing it right.* Washington, DC: The World Bank.

Hart, O. (2003). Incomplete contracts and public ownership: Remarks, and an application to public private partnerships. *Economic Journal, 113*(485), C69–C76.

Hart, O., Shleifer, A., & Vishny, R. W. (1997). The proper scope of government: Theory and an application to prisons. *Quarterly Journal of Economics, 112*(4), 1127–1161.

Jensen, M. C., & Meckling, W. H. (1976). Theory of the firm: Managerial behavior, agency costs and ownership structure. *Journal of Financial Economics, 3*, 305–360.

Klein, B., Crawford, R. G., & Alchian, A. A. (1978). Vertical integration, appropriable rents, and the competitive contracting process. *Journal of Law and Economics, 21*(2), 297–326.

Laffont, J.-J. (2000). *Étapes vers un État moderne: une analyse économique.* dans État et gestion publique, actes du colloque du 16 décembre 1999, Rapport no 24 du Conseil d'Analyse Economique, La Documentation Française.

Laffont, J.-J., & Tirole, J. (1993). *A theory of incentives in procurement and regulation.* Cambridge, MA: MIT Press.

Martimort, D., & Pouyet, J. (2008). Build it or not: Normative and positive theories of public-private partnerships. *International Journal of Industrial Economics, 26*(2), 393–411.

Maskin, E., & Tirole, J. (2008). Public-private partnerships and government spending limits. *International Journal of Industrial Organization, 26*(2), 412–420.

McCubbins, M., & Schwartz, T. (1984). Congressional oversight overlooked: Police patrols versus fire alarms. *American Journal of Political Science, 28*, 16–79.

Miralles, A. (2008). The link between privatization and price distribution among consumer types: Municipal water services in the Spanish region of Catalonia. *Environment and Planning C: Government and Policy, 26*, 159–172.

Moszoro, M., & Spiller, P. (2012). *Third-party opportunism and the (in)efficiency of public contracts*. SSRN eLibrary.

Moszoro, M., Spiller, P., & Stolorz, S. (2016). Rigidity of public contracts. *Journal of Empirical Legal Studies, 13*(3), 396–427.

NAO. (2009). *Private finance projects*. Online, viewed on November 13, 2010, from http://www.nao.org.uk/publications/0809/private_finance_projects.aspx

OECD/ITF. (2008). *Transport infrastructure investment – Options for efficiency*. Transport Research Centre. ISBN:978-92-821-0155-1.

Picazo-Tadeo, A. J., et al. (2010). Do ideological and political motives really matter in the public choice of local services management? Evidence from urban water services in Spain. *Public Choice, 151*(1–2), 215–228.

PriceWaterHouseCoopers. (2011). *Étude sur la performance des contrats de partenariat*.

Saussier, S., & Tirole, J. (2015, April). *Renforcer l'efficacité de la commande publique*. Rapport du Conseil d'analyse économique, no 22.

Saussier, S., & Truong Tran, T. (2012). L'efficacité des contrats de partenariat en France: Une première évaluation quantitative. *Revue d'Économie Industrielle, 140*, 81–110.

Saussier, S., & Yvrande-Billon, A. (2007). *Économie des coûts de transaction*. Paris: La Découverte.

Smith, A. (1776). *An inquiry into the nature and causes of the Wealth of Nations*. Glasgow, R.H. Campbell, Reed (1976).

Spiller, P. T. (2008). *An institutional theory of public contracts: Regulatory implications*. National Bureau of Economic Research, Inc., online http://ideas.repec.org/p/nbr/nberwo/14152.html

Standard & Poor's. (2006). *Revision Crediticia. Sector de Carreteras de Cuota en Mexico*. London and Mexico City: Standard & Poor's.

Williamson, O. E. (1971). The vertical integration of production: Market failure considerations. *American Economic Review, 61*, 112–123.

Williamson, O. E. (1975). *Markets and hierarchies, analysis and antitrust implications: A study in the economics of internal organization*. New York: The Free Press.

Williamson, O. E. (1976). Franchise bidding for natural monopolies: In general and with respect to CATV. *Bell Journal of Economics, 7*(1), 73–104.

Williamson, O. E. (1985). *The economic institutions of capitalism*. New York: The Free Press.

Regulatory Instruments for Public–Private Partnerships

Lisa Chever and Aude Le Lannier

1 Introduction

In the late 1980s, large-scale reforms were undertaken in many Western countries to "modernize" network industries[1] (Armstrong & Sappington, 2006) and public service management.

One of the distinctive characteristics of network industries lies in the monopolistic nature of some of their activities[2]: no production is possible without the prior realization of specific and non-recoverable investments, which will give rise to significant returns to scale. But these returns to scale only deliver their full benefits if the enterprise is "large," which often implies that it operates alone in the market. Thus, the entry of any rival is automatically discouraged. Any entry would indeed result in mediocre or even negative profits in the industry. The economic theory defines such situations as natural monopolies. This formulation reflects the technical inability of such industries to meet the conditions that would allow them to reach the framework of reference—if not the ideal framework—of perfect competition.

In concrete terms, a monopolistic situation leads to excesses in terms of pricing and management. First, a monopoly has strong market power and is therefore

---

[1] Public services such as water, electricity, urban transport, railways, postal services, etc.

[2] This monopolistic nature does not generally extend to the entire industry. It mostly concerns the transport and distribution activities.

L. Chever
IAE Paris - Sorbonne Business School, Paris, France
e-mail: lisa.chever@gmail.com

A. Le Lannier (✉)
IAE Paris - Sorbonne Business School, Paris, France

ARAFER (Railway and Highway Regulation Authority), Paris, France
e-mail: aude.lelannier@arafer.fr

© Springer International Publishing AG 2018
S. Saussier, J. de Brux (eds.), *The Economics of Public-Private Partnerships*,
https://doi.org/10.1007/978-3-319-68050-7_3

encouraged to behave as price maker, as opposed to a competitive system characterized by the presence of several firms, which limits the influence of a single firm on the final equilibrium. Secondly, a monopoly has no incentive to adopt the least costly production methods and is thus a source of "X-inefficiency" (Leibenstein, 1966). Finally, in practice, natural monopolies are often public service providers that are of vital importance to the community. Public intervention thus appears legitimate in order to define the objectives clearly (e.g., to set minimal quantities to be produced)—and potentially to participate in their financing. In the end, the regulation of monopolistic industries is based on motives of allocative and productive efficiency, as well as on objectives of social justice.[3]

Many of the problems raised by natural monopoly regulation overlap with those raised by the supply of more standard public goods or services, such as the construction of a school or the management of a prison. The exact nature of the goods and services to be publicly supplied varies depending on the country, the time, and political persuasions. It is therefore difficult to characterize them and to find the general argument that will justify what *must* fall under public management. But even if one forgoes such a characterization and avoids the debates on the possible superiority of private management over public management, it can still be maintained that systematically delegating the production of a good or service to an agent (even a public one) *de facto* creates a monopolistic situation. There is no reason why it should not generate, to some extent, the same detrimental effects as a natural monopoly.

Thus, in the case of natural monopolies or in the case of a deliberate choice on the part of public authorities to maintain control over the production of certain goods or services, authorities have gradually endeavored to organize competition *for* the market, because of the lack of competition *in* the market. Indeed, if there are several potential suppliers, organizing an auction will make it possible to select the most efficient one to satisfy the needs defined by public authorities (Demsetz, 1968). This idea seems simple enough. Its implementation nevertheless raises a series of questions.

Indeed, let us assume, first, that the objectives to improve general welfare are perfectly defined, observable, and measurable and that the public party has all the information regarding the supplier's efficiency and "efforts." In that case, it can control, observe, and check the performance of each task with precision (adherence to costs and quality levels). But in reality, there is an information asymmetry between the parties, to the advantage of the supplier. Economic theory and practice provide a lot of regulation solutions aimed at limiting such dysfunctions. The development of competition for the market (for the phase known as "*ex ante*," before the contract is awarded) and the setting up of price regulations (for the phase known as "*ex post*," after the contract is awarded) are regulatory tools that are now commonly used but still often discussed.

---

[3]Indeed, public authority intervention in these sectors also aims at guaranteeing that every citizen has equal access to these services.

Indeed, these solutions, inspired by agency theory,[4] stop being beneficial as soon as some assumptions are discarded. Firstly, the public party organizing the opening up to competition does not always know how to define, anticipate, or assess the objectives to be met. Secondly, it does not necessarily have credible sanctioning tools at its disposal in the event of a breach (if there are few potential alternative suppliers, for instance). Finally, it may occur that the objectives of the public party do not contribute to the improvement of general welfare: the authorities may be corrupt; they may favor certain suppliers for reasons other than efficiency.

In the first section of this chapter, we will introduce the tools for efficient partner selection, which have been put forward in the theoretical literature. As these mechanisms are rarely sufficient to guarantee the efficiency of service management throughout the duration of the contract, a second section will focus on *ex post* regulation mechanisms.

2 How to Award a PPP?

When awarding contracts to private partners, several obstacles may arise that could prevent the selection of the most efficient candidate by the public authority. This section does not focus primarily on the difficulties encountered during the contract awarding phase, even though they will be mentioned briefly. Our objective here is, considering these difficulties, to analyze the tools that can increase the efficiency of such procedures.

Thus, the first section will be dedicated to introducing the concept of competition for the market such as it appears in seminal works. After showing that its efficiency is conditional on an exceedingly simplified vision of the real world, we will analyze the works that have tried to develop this principle on the one hand and those that have suggested more radical solutions, thus largely challenging the benefits of a competition that is too intense, on the other hand.

2.1 Selecting the Lowest Tenderer: Advantages and Drawbacks

Taking over an idea first put forward by Chadwick in 1859, Demsetz is often viewed as the first theoretician to show that natural monopolies are not necessarily in complete contradiction with the notion of competition. In his article of 1968, he demonstrated that a public service meeting the criteria of a natural monopoly can be produced more efficiently if it is awarded through an auction to the firm offering the

---

[4]See Chapter "An Economic Analysis of Public–Private Partnerships" of the first part of this book for details about the agency theory.

lowest price in the market. Indeed, if there are enough potential suppliers in the market, then the difference between the winner's price and the unit cost of production will be nonsignificant. In other words, under certain conditions,[5] bidders will be encouraged by competitive forces to disclose their "real" price, after which the contracting authority will only need to select the one offering the lowest price. This mechanism solves problems of adverse selection.

Demsetz' works developed as part of a prolific literature known as "auction theory." As is often the case in economics, this school of thought knew a two-phase progression. During the first, rather normative phase, a simplified vision of reality was used to formalize the issues at stake in an elegant and simple way. Demsetz' article clearly fits into this trend. Other works also laid the foundations for current theoretical models. In particular, Vickrey's famous "revenue equivalence" theorem shows that, under certain hypotheses, oral, written, first-price, and second-price auctions all ensure the same revenue for the contracting authority. The award rule would therefore be neutral! Unfortunately, the recommendations made by these pioneering models, although reassuring, are based on hypotheses that seem to be quite out of touch with reality. Indeed, why would the public body differ to such an extent from the majority of other economic agents, which, for the most part, are risk averse? And besides, is the environment risky, i.e., probabilizable, or radically uncertain? Does the value attributed to a project by a firm depend solely on its cost structure?

Consequently, a second, more positive phase followed the first one. The strongest hypotheses were questioned and then discarded, and simple results gradually gave way to complex arbitrations. Williamson (1975) and Goldberg (1976) both criticized the "Demsetzian" approach and can therefore be considered as initiators of "phase 2."[6] Their influential work did not limit itself to challenging the propositions of auction theory but contributed, directly or indirectly, to the creation of new schools of thought (grouped together under the name of "contract theory"). These authors emphasize the fact that the solution suggested by Demsetz would not be suitable for complex tasks. Such tasks sit uneasily with an award procedure based on the sole criterion of price: they involve other, more subjective dimensions that matter. Now, an auction typically works thanks to the *ex ante* definition of an objective award rule, which is little compatible with notions of reputation, quality, or trust. The abundance of theoretical models that put great effort into finding award rules for complex contracts (and continue to do so today) attests to the relevance of the criticisms put forward by Williamson and Goldberg.

Incidentally, what do theoreticians mean exactly by this notion of complexity? Where does it come from? An exhaustive answer would probably require an entire chapter: some, for instance, consider that complexity derives from an inability to foresee future events, others from the subjective nature of certain tasks, and others

---

[5]Firms have access to the same inputs, the firms' project estimates depend solely on their cost structure, and the environment is risky.

[6]This does not exclude the fact that they may also be the instigators of new theories that develop independently.

still from the prohibitive costs incurred to draw up the contracts. We will limit ourselves to outlining the theoretical approach that we consider to be, if not the most widespread, at least the most compatible with various definitions of complexity, especially as it defines the notion based on its consequences rather than its sources. Most theoreticians agree on the fact that complexity can be modeled as an inability for the public authority to specify all relevant dimensions of the contract. Thus, complex contracts are incomplete contracts made up of two parts: a written part and an unwritten part.

Complexity does not affect all forms of contractual delivery options evenly. On average, it tends to be more significant in public-budget pay PPP contracts (i.e., availability contracts as most PFIs) or user-pay PPPs (concessions) than in traditional public procurement contracts. The latter are generally shorter-term contracts involving a more limited number of tasks, which reduces two potential sources of complexity. In any case, we can assume that PPPs are characterized by contractual incompleteness, although to varying extents. This incompleteness affects the possibility to define *ex ante* the control and sanctioning procedures implemented *ex post* to give the private partner incentives to meet its commitments (see Box 1). PPPs thus give private partners (and the public buyer) the opportunity to go back on their initial commitments in an opportunistic manner during the implementation phase of the contract.

At this stage in our argument, and largely for didactic reasons, we have taken the liberty of investigating the issue of complexity separately. However, this issue generally entails a corollary problem related to competition: a contract that is more complex (in the sense of "less standard," i.e., with a qualitative differentiation) may reduce the number of potential suppliers. This proposition is merely the transposition of a well-identified finding of industrial economics: vertical product differentiation is a way for companies to avoid exceedingly stiff competition. Thus, if the contracting authority wishes to delegate the realization of a nonstandard task, it

---

Box 1: Requirements Definition, Incompleteness, and Efficiency: The Case of Prisons in the United Kingdom

Public authorities are often concerned that, if they limit themselves to stipulating general recommendations in their calls for tenders, tenderers will lower their level of performance. However, public authorities also struggle to define their need *ex ante* in a clear and precise manner. On this topic, Klein (1998) mentions a particularly striking example that occurred in the United Kingdom. Indeed, upon the opening-up to competition of a prison concession contract, the firm that won the call for tenders had assessed the cost of its project based on the assumption that several inmates would be accommodated in a single cell. However, the public authorities wanted to build individual cells but had simply forgotten to specify it in the documents of the call for tenders, thus giving firms the opportunity to submit tenders that were highly attractive financially, although radically different from their expectations.

must expect the number of potential tenderers to be limited. Besides, a competition issue alone may also alter the efficiency of an auction based on prices.[7] This represents an important concern for public authorities during PPP implementation, as illustrated by the 2010 decision from the French Competition Authority ("Autorité de la concurrence") regarding urban public transport, outlined in Box 2 below.

Box 2: Promoting Competition for the Market: The Creation of a Competition Stimulation Fund in the French Sector of Urban Public Transport

In its decision no. 10-DCC-198 of 30 December 2010, made public on 24 January 2011, the French Autorité de la concurrence described the new system as "unprecedented and innovative." Under certain conditions, this decision authorized the merger between Veolia Transport and Transdev in the French sector of public passenger transport. When performing perfectly, urban public transport contracts, which are awarded through calls for tenders, do not require any control of concentrations by a third-party authority, since the market structure could be reconsidered during contract renewals. However, according to the Autorité de la concurrence, the French sector of urban public transport is characterized by effects that give significant advantage to firms already appointed in the market compared to potential entrants. Indeed, the Autorité claim that the analysis of the way competition works in this market shows that the probability of obtaining a network is correlated:

- On the one hand, with having previously been awarded the public–private contract[8] for this network: the experience acquired by the operator increases the probability that it will be awarded the next contract (experience effect). It also increases the possibility for this operator to "signal itself" to the Transport organization authority (AOT for *Autorité organisatrice des transports*) (signaling effect);
- On the other hand, with having previously been awarded transport contracts distinct from the network in question, which allows the operator to demonstrate its ability to operate such networks (showcase effect) or to benefit from geographical synergies.

(continued)

---

[7]For instance, if the value of the contract up for award is high, its realization will require calling on a firm with commensurate financial and human resources. At best, the contracting authority then runs the risk of facing an oligopolistic supply market with only a few companies eligible to apply. Moreover, if these firms anticipate such a situation, it can be in their interest to communicate to divide up the contracts among themselves...

[8]In this sector, most of them are management contracts, with a share of a demand risk borne by the operator.

Box 2 (continued)

The Autorité de la concurrence also highlights the fact that the French market of urban passenger transport is characterized by barriers to entry that tend to lower the probability of a new operator appearing. Although the Autorité admits that the Veolia-Transdev merger will create an entity enjoying a dominant position in the urban transport market and that this could be detrimental to competition in this sector, it chose to take advantage of this operation to give tendering markets a chance to operate in a more competitive manner. With this aim in mind, it accepted, in addition to targeted asset sales, the innovative remedy suggested by the parties, which consists in setting up and financing a "competition stimulation fund." The 6.45 million euro fund is entrusted to an independent manager under the supervision of a trustee. It aims at enabling transport organization authorities to finance the compensation of candidates not selected during calls for tenders organized for the networks in which either Veolia Transport or Transdev is the incumbent operator. It will be used firstly to cover part or all of the costs incurred when responding to the 44 calls for tenders that are about to expire and must therefore be opened up to competition again between 2012 and 2016. Secondly, it will make it easier for small transport organization authorities to resort to project management assistance services so as to help them improve the efficiency of the competitive procedures they organize (they will be granted a lump sum to meet part or all of the costs of outside consultants).

The parties have also undertaken, for 5 years, not to form a group together with the leading national or international stakeholders present in the market in order to respond to intercity calls for tenders.

This innovative solution is thus intended to favor an increase in the number of participants in calls for tenders and to intensify competition between them.

Finally, the efficiency of an auction based solely on the price criterion is subjected to strong hypotheses regarding the characteristics of the awarded good or the level of competition. Theoreticians have developed models that are likely to respond to such limitations.

2.2 Optimizing Open Auction Mechanisms?

Suppose that, as is often the case, a public authority is forced to use what is known in the economic jargon as an "open auction," that is, a procedure in which any interested economic operator can submit a bid. What leeway does the contracting authority have to select a partner as efficiently as possible?

When price is not the only relevant dimension of the awarded project, one solution consists in organizing a multidimensional auction (Che, 1993; McAfee & McMillan, 1987; Milgrom & Weber, 1982). We then switch over from the rule of the "lowest bid" to that of the "best bid." The latter integrates dimensions such as the technical merit of the project, its aesthetic characteristics, or the proposed after-sales service. This type of procedure presents the advantage of limiting the risk of candidates entering into an agreement; indeed, while it may be feasible to coordinate one's actions based on a single and easily quantifiable criterion such as price, coordinating them based on several criteria is more difficult (Caillaud, 2001).

Nevertheless, the benefits of multidimensional auctions may be canceled out by opportunistic behaviors on the part of the public or private party. If the selected qualitative criteria and their respective weight are not defined precisely ahead, then the public authority may "manipulate" the auction (Naegelen, 1990; Williamson, 1975), and uncertainty is generated for potential candidates of the call for tenders. To protect themselves against such uncertainty, they may be tempted to collude or to capture public authority[9] (Burguet & Che, 2004; Celentani & Ganunza, 2002; Compte, Lambert-Mogiliansky, & Verdier, 2005; Lambert-Mogiliansky, 2010). In particular, Burguet and Che (2004) show that, during a multidimensional auction, if the official in charge of awarding the contract is corrupt, there is a positive probability that the most efficient firm will not win the tender: contract allocation is not optimal. In order to limit the risks of corruption and favoritism, it is possible to establish requirements for the contracting authority to make public the reasons for its final choice, as is the case in the sector of bus transportation in London (Amaral et al., 2009). Similarly, another option is to seek to reduce the contracting authorities' discretionary leeway in choosing the award procedure and selection criteria (Iossa & Martimort, 2011). Typically, Lengwiler and Wolfstetter (2006) emphasize how electronic auction mechanisms were developed to limit the risks of manipulation.

Taking into account the partner's reputation when evaluating its bid can be likened to a special form of multidimensional auction.[10] Several authors have claimed that this form helps ensure that commitments are honored and that the informal components of the contract are implemented (Klein & Leffler, 1981; Shapiro, 1983; Wilson, 1985). These models are based on a "repeated-game" framework: if a firm's reputation determines its access to future contracts, and if such contracts are likely to arise, then it is not in the firm's current interest to behave in an opportunistic way. The firm will then submit a credible bid, including all contractual and non-contractual elements, in order to satisfy the public entity and not jeopardize its future prospects. Thus, unlike more conventional multidimensional auctions (which are based on the idea that qualitative dimensions are non-contractible), multidimensional auctions taking into account reputation

---

[9]A firm "captures" a public authority when it exerts an important influence on the latter; the public authority then abnormally protects the interests of the firm.

[10]In practice, this idea is similar to the concept of *intuitu personae* that is used in the case of PSDs.

mitigate a possible inability of contracting authorities to specify their need fully and intelligibly. Nevertheless, European legislators in charge of defining the statutory framework for the opening up to competition of PPPs are very timorous when it comes to this solution. Indeed, the discretionary power it confers on the public party is very difficult to control, paving the way dangerously for problems of corruption and favoritism.

What should be done, then, when the public party's expertise does not enable it to draw up a complete contract? One solution consists in allotting the contracts. The idea is quite simple: publishing calls for tenders one after the other contributes to the improvement of the contracting authorities' expertise, insofar as the gradual nature of the process facilitates the development of skills relating to the organization of calls for tenders as well as the specification of selection criteria. Authorities can learn to detect bids with low credibility, whether they are aggressive or optimistic (Yvrande-Billon, 2008). In Europe, such contract allotment is allowed by Directive 2004/18/EC. It was implemented as early as 1985 as part of the British "Transport Act" for the award of operating contracts for London bus transportation, in which candidates could submit bids on a certain number of routes to be served (Cantillon & Pesendorfer, 2006), which had positive effects on service operating costs.

Nowadays, this possibility is widely used in traditional public procurement. It is even encouraged, largely because of its ability to stimulate competition. Indeed, insofar as allotment reduces the size of contracts up for auction, it can also help increase the number of candidates that are able to respond to the calls for tenders. Moreover, it reduces uncertainty for candidates (as well as the possible risk premium associated with it), since it allows them to receive feedback too: for instance, were the first contracts to be awarded renegotiated by the public authorities?[11] Thus, Preston et al. (2000) demonstrate that the order in which operating contracts for the British railway network were awarded is an explanatory factor for the value of the subsidies that were asked by tenderers: the first candidates asked for a risk premium that was significantly higher than those that followed.

However, de Brux and Desrieux (2014) have shown public contract allotment does not provide an optimal level of incentives for the realization of efforts that are non-contractible, i.e., efforts that aim to increase quality and reduce costs. Moreover, this solution causes some organizational problems: in public service industries, resorting to allotment implies making resources available to guarantee network consistency (in terms of pricing for instance) and the interconnection between the various units (Caillaud, 2001; Yvrande-Billon, 2008). Finally, it is important to ensure that such a division does not lead to losses in economies of

---

[11]Contract renegotiation initiated by the public authority can result from an opportunistic behavior on its part, which potentially and considerably reduces the operator's profit margins. Such behavior increases uncertainty for operators, who can anticipate that the public authority will probably go back on its initial commitments. See Chapter "Renegotiating PPP Contracts: Opportunities and Pitfalls" in the second part of this book for more details on public opportunism and its consequences on PPP efficiency.

scale, or at least to make sure that they are counterbalanced by benefits in terms of competition and learning.

In the end, two types of solutions can be opposed: those implying that the public party can (or will be able to, eventually) define its needs perfectly ("conventional" multidimensional auctions and allotment) and those that are based on the opposite hypothesis (multidimensional auctions taking into account reputation), which is far less demanding. However, because of the risk of discretionary excesses associated with the latter, regulators are reluctant to authorize the use of this second type of auction on a large scale. They sometimes prefer solutions based on dialogue or on a reduction in competition.

2.3   Alternatives to an Open Auction

Alternatives to open competition procedures are based on the idea that the public party is unable to achieve a perfect specification of its need. In the case of certain recurrent services, allotment does mitigate the temporary shortfalls on the side of the public entity. However, this mechanism cannot claim to be suitable for categories of contracts that are inherently singular. It is typically the case of works contracts, which tend to present geographical, temporal, technical, or aesthetic specificities. Thus, assuming that for certain tasks, public authorities cannot provide an exhaustive definition of their need, it can be interesting to resort to other award mechanisms.

From this perspective, it is customary to contrast open auctions and direct negotiation, where the public party holds a dialogue with one single firm *ex ante* to set the conditions of implementation of the contract. The first mechanism provides companies with strong incentives to maximize the price–quality ratio for the elements in the contract. Nevertheless, it exposes the public entity to costly renegotiations if the non-contractible elements determine the success of the project. Now, such renegotiations occur at a time when the public party is in a situation of dependency toward its private partner, who may be tempted to adopt an opportunistic behavior (Williamson, 1975). Conversely, the second mechanism reduces enterprises' incentives to optimize their bid. Its interest lies in the fact that the rent thus generated allows firms to take non-contractible elements into account. The debate of "auctions *versus* negotiations" thus consists in arbitrating between producing incentives *ex ante* and reducing transaction costs associated with renegotiation *ex post* (Bajari & Tadelis, 2001). Two seminal articles can be mentioned to enrich this debate: Bulow and Klemperer (1996) indicate that an additional bid is preferable to stronger bargaining power; in contrast, Manelli and Vincenti (1995) show that negotiation should be favored when the contracting authority attaches importance to the qualitative elements.

The economic literature has also endeavored to analyze the properties of intermediary award procedures, such as restricted auctions, whereby the buyer invites certain enterprises to submit a tender. Unlike direct negotiation, restricted auctions limit competition but do not eliminate the latter. In a dynamic context, an auction where candidates are invited to participate based on their past performances allows the buyer to take advantage of reputational forces and to establish long-term relations (Doni, 2006; Kim, 1998). To avoid jeopardizing their chances of being invited again in the future, companies will submit competitive and credible tenders taking into account non-contractible elements. This argument is quite similar to the one developed for multidimensional auctions based on reputation. The difference lies in the fact that, in this case, the discretionary dimension is supposed to intervene during the invitation to tender (and not in the phase of tender evaluation). These mechanisms are criticized for favoring cartels by reducing the number of competitors. Nevertheless, Calzolari and Spagnolo (2009) show that, when the informal dimensions are important, a restricted auction remains more efficient than an open one.

Therefore, both direct negotiations and restricted auctions constitute alternatives to open tender procedures. These procedures present the disadvantage of granting discretionary power to the public party, whether in the invitation phase or in the negotiation phase (some procedures can combine these two aspects). Simple practices may lead to a solution favoring the most credible tenders while limiting discretionary excesses (see Box 3).

But the fact remains that this tension between rigid rules (which only rarely allow the buyer to select an efficient supplier) and more flexible rules (which increase the risks of a discretionary drift) constitutes the central paradox of the literature on the topic.

Box 3: Prequalification Phases in Tender Procedures: The Example of Electricity Supply in the London Underground

Littlechild (2002) analyzes the tender procedure set up as part of British Private Finance Initiative (PFIs), effective in August 1998, for the distribution of electricity in the London underground. This 30-year contract was signed between Seeboard Powerlink (SPL) and London Underground Limited (LUL).

While four consortia participated in the prequalification phase, only two were given the opportunity to submit tenders. Four criteria were used to prequalify these two candidates. The engineering criterion took into account the consortia's degree of technical expertise. The safety criterion aimed at evaluating their level of knowledge and experience in terms of railway network safety. Finally, the human resources criterion assessed the arrangements made by candidates as regards the incumbent operator's employees, and the commercial criterion corresponded to their propositions in terms of cost and risk sharing with LUL. The first three criteria had to be met by the candidates. The commercial criterion would then allow LUL to make a choice between the candidates that had met the first three. Consortia were set up, gathering several companies, as no company was in position to meet alone all of LUL's requirements. These restrictive prequalification rules allowed LUL to make sure that the selected candidate was not an opportunistic enterprise. They also had the merit of preventing the winning candidate from invoking

(continued)

Box 3 (continued)

financial difficulties or even a risk of bankruptcy to obtain renegotiations to its own advantage. Indeed, the financial guarantees required by LUL to be able to submit a tender rendered such threats devoid of credibility.

In addition, Littlechild highlights the fact that some uncertainty existed regarding future demand as part of this contract. Now, the candidates' tender during the tender procedure strongly depended on the estimate of future demand in electricity specified by LUL in the contract. In order to limit the risk of winner's curse, LUL committed to compensating SPL for the additional costs it might incur if the estimates turned out to differ significantly from effective demand.

It should be noted that this PFI contract was terminated in 2013, that is, 15 years before its expected expiration date. A contractual clause gave the two partners the possibility to put an end to the contract at the halfway point. The sales director of LUL explained that the contract had unfolded in a satisfactory manner, but that LUL had decided to take over management internally in order to save on financial expenses that would have been higher in a PFI.

2.4 Expertise and Award Process

When public authorities are lacking in expertise, a first solution can be to add a preparatory phase to the drawing up of calls for tenders (Caillaud, 2001). Such a phase consists in letting potential candidates make propositions to the public authority regarding the qualitative criteria they deem most relevant. It is then up to the contracting authority to determine which criteria are selected and what their respective weight is, based on the recommendations of independent experts. Moreover, a comparative selection procedure (or "beauty contest"), as it was organized for instance in France for the allocation of third-generation mobile licenses in 2001, may also help reduce information asymmetry for the contracting authority thus benefiting from the tenderers' expertise. "Beauty contests" are based on the submission of an application focusing on qualitative or technical criteria, followed by an evaluation by the contracting authority of the respective qualities of the projects, and the award of the contract to the most deserving applicant, for a price determined by the contracting authority (Morand, Mougeot, & Naegelen, 2001).

Additionally, Bain (2009) stressed the necessity to develop the expertise of contracting authorities. In his report on feedback from PPP projects conducted throughout the world and financed by the European Investment Bank, he highlights the fact that appropriate legislation (such as contract termination rules) is necessary for PPPs to succeed but is not sufficient. Emphasis is placed on institutional elements such as credible regulations, a robust audit system and the support of skilled advisers. The example of the innovation fund created as part of the Veolia-Transdev merger, previously introduced in Box 2, shows the importance granted to the support of contracting authorities by specialist consulting firms. Indeed, part of this fund aims to make it easier for transport authorities to resort to project management assistance services by granting them a lump sum to meet part or all of the costs of outside consultants [see also the example of the Polish case developed by Moszoro and Krzyzanowska (2011), Box 4]. Nevertheless, "*the principle of expertise, as formulated by Gromb and Martimort (2007), stipulates that, in order to encourage the collection of relevant information, the expert must derive financial or reputational gains reflecting the fact that its recommendations are consistent with the success or failure of the project*" (Hiriart & Martimort, 2012). In other words, relying on experts is only efficient insofar as the said experts themselves have an incentive to behave in a non-opportunistic way (for instance, by declaring, without even having undertaken the necessary inquiries, that the project should not be launched).

Box 4: The Use of External Consultants and the Public Authority's Expertise in the Award of Public–Private Contracts: The Example of the City of Warsaw

In an article from 2011 entitled "Implementing Public-Private Partnerships in Municipalities," Moszoro and Krzyzanowska describe the processes set up by the city of Warsaw to manage public–private partnerships. The authors recount the implementation of 20 projects, all sectors combined, and attempt to draw some recommendations from these observations. One of them relates to the expertise of the contracting authority, which appears vital to the smooth running of a PPP. In order to create this expertise, the city of Warsaw started by granting an explicit mandate to a deputy-mayor in charge of the whole award and monitoring process for the city's public–private contracts, *via* the creation of a new body called the "Investors' Service Office" (ISO). After selecting the projects and carrying out feasibility studies, the ISO decided to organize a tender with the aim of resorting to external advisers on financial, legal, and technical issues. Advisers would apply as a consortium to gather all the requested expertise. The winner of the tender was then to advise the city during the award process of certain projects.

Although resorting to external consultants was not legally compulsory, two reasons led the city of Warsaw to set up such a procedure:

- The lack of expertise of the city in terms of PPPs would be (partly) mitigated by the possibility to benefit from the feedbacks of other countries on PPPs thanks to international consulting firms.
- The use of independent firms would strengthen the "objectivity" of the contract award process, thus limiting complaints and criticisms from subsequent administrations, which would have to monitor the contracts in the future without having handled the award process.

(continued)

Box 4 (continued)

The authors stress the importance of this last point, especially in countries where the rule of law is weak and where there can be strong suspicions of corruption.

The selected consortium was chosen through a two-stage public tender procedure. Four consortia were selected in the first phase based on their experience in the field, their credentials, and the proposed conduct of the mission.[12] In the second phase, the public authority negotiated the contractual terms and conditions directly with the four shortlisted consortia.

Once the contract was awarded to an advisory consortium, the public authority and the advisers prepared the business model for the PPP, selected the performance indicators to evaluate the private partner, and drew up the documentation necessary for the call for tenders. The advisors then supported the city during contract negotiations with the future private partners. It should nevertheless be noted that resorting to such external consultants is obviously costly: for the city, it amounted to 3.2 million dollars, which represents 1.2% of the budget estimate for the realization of these projects.

Relying on independent experts such as consulting firms may also help strengthen the objectivity of the award process for public–private contracts, thus limiting accusations from third parties claiming that the cooperation between the contracting authority and private partner has degenerated into collusion (Moszoro & Spiller, 2012).

Such collusion between private interests (firms, lobbies) and public officials involved in contract award (regulators, politicians, office workers) has given rise to an extensive literature.[13] Without going into detail of the various solutions that can limit the risk of capture, one global principle seems to preside over the numerous results found in the literature, in a direct echo of the ambitions of the European directives: it consists in ensuring a high level of transparency during the award of PPPs. Several studies, ranging from the most aggregated to the most disaggregated institutional levels, have indeed managed to derive conditions of optimality in the award of public contracts by seeking to stimulate such transparency. As stipulated by Hiriart and Martimort (2012), "*it is important to understand that capture is related to the opacity of administrative procedures. Consequently, letting different strong arms collect different types of information increases the global transparency*

---

[12]The selected consortia were led by Deloitte Advisory, Depfa Bank, Ernst & Young, and PricewaterhouseCoopers.

[13]See Chapter "Horizontal and vertical agreements in PPPs" of the second part for an analysis of corruption, collusion, and favoritism issues in PPPs.

Table 1 Policy development in the water sector in OECD countries

	Number of stakeholders involved in the development and implementation of public policies	Existence of an agency specifically in charge of water regulation (yes/no)	Role of the central government (main stakeholder, joint role with local stakeholders, neither of the two)
Australia	4	Yes	Joint
Belgium (Flanders)	7	No	Neither
Belgium (Wallonia)	–	No	Neither
Canada	9	No	Joint
Chile	15	No	Main
Korea	5	No	Main
Spain	5	No	Joint
United States	11	No	Joint
France	5	No	Joint
Greece	13	Yes	Main
Israel	4	–	Main
Italy	6	Yes	Joint
Japan	4	No	Main
Mexico	6	Yes	Main
New Zealand	14	Yes	Joint
Netherlands	2	Yes	Joint
Portugal	3	Yes	Main
United Kingdom	11	Yes	Joint

Source: OECD, Water Governance Survey (2011)

of the system and thereby makes it all the more difficult to capture these different entities." Incidentally, it is probably for this type of reason that several stakeholders are generally involved in the implementation of public policies and the regulation of a sector, as illustrated by Table 1 on the water sector.

Nevertheless, as highlighted by Iossa and Martimort (2011), setting up tools aiming to avoid collusive behaviors during the award procedure is not sufficient to prevent them from arising in the implementation phase. For instance, in a literature review on corruption in public procurement, Piga (2011) stresses the fact that corruption during contract implementation is more significant than corruption during contract award. More generally, encouraging compliance with the rules during contract award is a necessary condition to guarantee the optimal performance of public–private partnerships but not a sufficient one. In order to complete the award phase and ensure that commitments made *ex ante* are honored *ex post*, incentive tools must be set up throughout the duration of the contract.

3 Control Tools and Performance Incentives During PPP Implementation

According to agency theory (see for instance Laffont & Tirole, 1993; Laffont & Martimort, 2002), a contract works as an incentive tool when, in a relationship of agency, there is an information asymmetry between the co-contractors. An agency relationship can be defined as "*a contract under which one or more persons (the principal(s)) engage another person (the agent) to perform some service on their behalf which involves delegating some decision making authority to the agent*" (Jensen & Meckling, 1976). A contract between a public authority (the principal) and a firm (the agent) to provide a public service can therefore be described as an agency relationship. In that setting, the agent to whom the principal delegates a task to be executed is likely to be in possession of private information. In such a case, the decisions made by the agent in order to execute the task in question have no reason to match those desired by the principal. Thus, during PPP implementation, the private partner may act opportunistically by seeking for example to conceal or manipulate information regarding its performance (i.e., the extent to which it meets its contractual commitments). The private partner may also apply prices that are higher than the price initially proposed, or deliberately reduce the quality of the service provided. Finally, the partner may renege on its commitments in terms of lead time or investment renewal time and may seek to renegotiate the initial contract to its own advantage by appropriating part of the quasi-rent (Goldberg, 1976; Klein et al., 1978; Williamson, 1975). Incidentally, as an illustration, Table 2 provides a few statistics coming from academic studies on the frequency of renegotiations. While renegotiations seem to occur at a rather variable frequency, the statistics nevertheless suggest that they are not an exception; in other words, contracting parties often enjoy a certain degree of leeway in going back on the initial agreement.

Agency theory highlights how the presence of information asymmetries makes it necessary to sign a contract that can give the agent incentives to operate in the best

Table 2 A few statistics on the frequency of PPP renegotiations

Geographical area	Sector	% of renegotiated contracts	References
Latin America and the Caribbean	All sectors Electricity Transport Water	68% 41% 78% 92%	Guasch (2004)
United States	Motorways	40%	Engel, Fischer, and Galetovic (2001)
France	Motorways Car Parks	50% 73%	Athias and Saussier (2007) Beuve et al. (2013)
United Kingdom	All sectors	55%	NAO (2001)

Source: Estache and Saussier (2014)

interest of the principal. Agency theory considers a situation where the principal implements an incentive scheme so as to lead the agent either to disclose its private information (adverse selection model) or to adopt a behavior that is in keeping with the principal's interest (moral hazard model). The incentive scheme consists in remuneration based on "signals" coming from the agent's behavior.

Section 3.1 outlines contractual solutions based on the introduction of performance indicators that work as "signals" coming from the private partner's behavior. We will also discuss the difficulties associated with these solutions, especially in terms of the public authority's capacity for control. Section 3.2 introduces possible solutions in terms of the regulation of PPP prices by a contracting authority or an independent regulator, which can lead private operators to provide the information necessary to the evaluation of their performance and thus to meet their initial commitments.

3.1   Performance Clauses and Capacity for Control

A first way to introduce contractual incentives and to reduce the risk of opportunism on the part of the private partner (the agent) is to compel its behavior by determining performance indicators and handling (or at least facilitating) the monitoring of these indicators. The incentive mechanisms of a contract rest on the fact that the agent's financial results depend on the performance it achieves.

However, this performance, which can be observed *ex post* by the partners, does not always depend entirely on the "efforts" realized by the private partner. Indeed, *ex post* performance can be affected by exogenous elements that were not anticipated *ex ante* (at the time the contract was drawn up) and are independent of the means implemented by the private partner. Since the principal does not observe the agent's effort, it must define indicators of effort that are observable and correlated with the effort. To summarize, the agent (the private partner) holds an informational rent: it knows its own effort, information which is not available to the principal (the public partner). With this in mind, a number of clauses establishing performance requirements should be specified *ex ante*, which will serve as performance indicators during contract execution. These contractual clauses must be combined with penalties so as to give the private partner incentives to comply with the commitments formulated *ex ante*. The operator thus makes a commitment based on performance promises, and not on a best efforts requirement.

Although we will not go into the details of the theoretical debate on the observable or verifiable nature of an agent's actions, it should be noted at this stage that the efficiency of such performance clauses rests on the essential hypothesis that the proposed remuneration scheme is based on information that is said to be "verifiable," which means that it is observable by a third party (a law court, for instance). Moreover, there is an implicit, yet relevant and benevolent, institutional framework that helps to ensure that the principal honors its commitments (Maskin & Tirole, 1999; Tirole, 1999). If the public entity is able to perfectly observe the work undertaken by its private partner, then it can sanction it in case of noncompliance with the contract stipulating the partner's commitments and the remunerations associated with these commitments. The question is more complex if the private partner's efforts, although observable by the public entity, are not verifiable by a third party. In that case, although it knows that the private partner is not fulfilling its contractual obligations, the public entity cannot prove it and will therefore have difficulties getting the contract implemented. And conversely, although the public entity knows that the private partner *is* fulfilling its contractual obligations, it might be tempted—knowing that the private partner cannot prove it—not to implement the contract. When some clauses are based on non-verifiable elements, dynamic and reputational factors come into play in the decision to execute the contract (Gibbons, 2005).

Another difficulty concerning the setting up of performance indicators can derive from the potential gap between the selected indicator and the actual objective pursued by the public stakeholder. The indicator can then generate perverse effects and lead to pay the private partner for results that were not really desired by the principal. The economic literature has taken an interest in this issue of incentive distortion when imperfect performance measures are implemented and contracted (Baker, 1992, 2000, 2002; Holmström & Milgrom, 1991; Kerr, 1975). Such an issue is especially likely to arise when it is difficult to specify the need in the PPP contract. Incentive mechanisms can give rise to perverse effects because of the "incompleteness" of contracts, especially long-term ones: it is difficult to include contractual specifications about everything that the principal expects from the agent, in all future states. Studies derived in this framework thus propose to reduce the incentive power of the contract, in order to prevent the agent from undertaking efforts that are non-productive from the point of view of the principal for the sole purpose of appearing "efficient" as per the chosen measure of performance.

Such performance indicators were introduced gradually in PPP contracts, as indicated for instance by Moszoro and Krzyzanowska (2011) and Moszoro and Spiller (2012), to ensure in particular that the quality of the service provided is monitored *ex post*. Moszoro and Spiller (2012) add that these indicators also constitute a "signal" for users and voters, indicating that the service in question, even if it is provided by a private operator, remains under the control and respon-sibility of the public authority. Thus, according to these authors, performance indicators are vital elements: they affect the perception of third parties to the PPP contract. Acknowledging the impact of these performance criteria on "social" perception, Moszoro and Krzyzanowska (2011) add that these criteria should be made public to ensure that the performance level of PPPs is widely publicized. This is known as the "sunshine regulation," which will be discussed in more detail in Sect. 3.3 of this chapter.

The theoretical difficulties associated with the introduction of performance criteria, highlighted above, have also been encountered in practice, as shown in Box 5 regarding performance indicators set up for regional rail transport in Île-de-France (the French region which includes the city of Paris).

Box 5: Difficulties Associated with the Introduction of Performance Criteria: The Case of Regional Rail Transport in Île-de-France

In 2010, the Cour des comptes (France's Supreme Court of Audit) published a thematic report entitled "*Les transports ferroviaires régionaux en Île-de-France*" ("Regional rail transport in Île-de-France"). Among other things, this report aimed to evaluate the efficiency of incentive mechanisms set up in this sector, which includes metro, regional train and tramway networks, as well as the regional express railway (RER). These networks make up a total of almost 1700 km of lines, operating over 2.7 billion journeys per year. The organization of this sector is characterized by the presence of two transport operators: the RATP and the SNCF. The planning and management expertise of public transport in Île-de-France is handled, for the most part, by the Syndicat des transports d'Île-de-France (STIF).

Both the monitoring of the execution of the so-called "reference" service and that of the quality of the service are monitored based on indicators that are measured and relayed by the operators. The STIF determines a theoretical supply in kilometers for each subnetwork. If the supply is not materialized beyond a certain threshold,[14] thus resulting in non-operated services, penalties are deducted from the remuneration paid by the STIF.

Contracts concluded between the STIF and the transport operators also define service quality objectives for each subnetwork. These objectives are subjected to financial incentives for the indicators that are most relevant from the passengers' point of view: regularity, passenger information, proper running of the accessibility system for passengers with reduced mobility, safety, appropriate processing of passenger complaints, disruption management, passenger reception, cleanliness, and proper running of the facilities. If the situation observed is better than the set objectives, the remuneration is credited with a bonus; otherwise, a malus is imposed. It should be noted that other quality indicators are also measured without being subjected to a financial incentive, such as passenger comfort, which is calculated based on the production of transport supply.[15]

(continued)

---

[14]This "tolerance threshold" makes it possible to take into account hazards that are independent of the operators' efforts and that could impact their performance (their final supply). If the gap between effective supply and theoretical supply does not exceed this threshold, no penalty is applied. Otherwise, penalties were to be imposed.

[15]For instance, for the metro, the comfort indicator is measured at rush hour based on the share of passengers transported with an occupancy rate below four passengers per square meter, which is the determined contractual threshold used to define the saturation point of a train. This indicator is directly correlated with the level of actual supply.

Box 5 (continued)

In 2009, 78 service quality indicators were used to determine the amount of the bonus-malus given to operators (against 50 in 2008 and 35 in 2007). In 2009, a refined contractual system and reinforced financial incentives aiming to improve service quality brought the highest bonus amount to 23.9 million euros.

However, according to the Cour des comptes, service quality has deteriorated in the regional railway networks over these past few years, with the exception of the metro network, where it remains fairly satisfactory on the whole.

Indeed, the amount of the highest bonuses-maluses remains low when compared to the operating revenues of transport operators (0.6% for the RATP and 0.9% for the SNCF Transilien in 2009) or to the total remuneration they receive from the STIF (1.2% for the RATP and 1.6% for the SNCF Transilien in 2009). Moreover, since their creation in 2000, maluses have never been higher than annual bonuses for the service quality of one of the two operators. According to the Cour des comptes, the system is therefore little discriminating and can be viewed as supplementary remuneration paid to the operators by the organizing authority, rather than as a real incentive mechanism. Besides, the underweighting of regularity and punctuality criteria within the total remuneration for service quality leads to results that are sometimes paradoxical, especially when the total bonus for an operator increases while traffic regularity on some of its main lines simultaneously deteriorates. Indeed, the share of the budget dedicated to train regularity and punctuality only amounts to 5.4 million euros, which represents 22.6% of the total budget allocated to service quality incentives.

Finally, although data are available, the Cour des comptes regrets the absence of a monthly or quarterly communication of results to the general public. Under these conditions, the service quality incentive scheme remains little known and not very intelligible for public transport users.

Once performance criteria have been defined, an ability to control the private partner's performance is an essential asset for the smooth running of such contracts. In France, in the water sector for instance, various laws were passed to try and limit this problem. Since 1995 (Barnier law of 2 February 1995), it has become compulsory for municipalities to draw up an annual report on the price and quality of water services. In parallel, the Mazeaud law of 8 February 1995 decreed that water operators must produce annual reports including a summary of accounts detailing all transactions pertaining to contract performance as well as a service quality analysis. Thus, Ménard, Saussier, and Staropoli (2003) showed that contractual practices in that sector have evolved toward a stronger demand for information on the part of local authorities, as is also the case in the transport and audiovisual industries in the United Kingdom, where concessionaires must publish annual reports or regular accounts (Baldwin & Cave, 1999). However, as highlighted by

Huet (2006), the French Court of Audit ("Cour des comptes") observed in 2003 that *"the presentation of technical and financial records for the service, and the accounting terminology in particular, change every year, making it difficult to draw any kind of comparison. Thus, the principle of consistency in the presentation of accounts, which is necessary to be able to compare results from one year to the next, is still not being observed and, as a consequence, the economy of the contract cannot be assessed over time."* Therefore, a lack of standardization in the presentation of annual reports provided by private partners can limit the possibilities of efficient control from the contracting authority. The Court of Audit also emphasizes the fact that *"many local authorities do not have any internal control system to avoid certain excesses, especially the unjustified increase of certain costs."* In order to limit these difficulties, it can be necessary to supplement such measures with control methods, by including contractual clauses providing for the regular auditing of the service provider's activities and accounts. But once more, as highlighted for instance by Robinson and Scott (2009) and Blanc-Brude and Jenson (2010) in the case of British PFIs, the collection of information by contracting authorities is not an easy task, and besides, once the information is collected, a certain degree of expertise is necessary on the part of the authority to process the information efficiently—hence the idea of pooling information processing and entrusting it to an independent regulatory authority.

As an example, Box 6 below details the arrangements made by London Underground Limited in order to stimulate and control the performances of Seeboard Powerlink as part of a PPP for the distribution of electricity in the London underground. It should be noted that, as highlighted in Box 2, this PPP includes both pre-contractual (at the time of contract award) and post-contractual incentive tools (during contract implementation).

Box 6: Performance Clauses and Controls by the Contracting Authority: The Case of Electricity Distribution in the London Underground

First of all, the PFI contract concluded between Seeboard Powerlink (SPL) and London Underground Limited (LUL) includes performance clauses based on LUL's quality standards. The existing assets at the time of contract signature are to be handed over to LUL under conditions specified in the contract—which aim to improve their quality—when the contract comes to an end. In addition, financial penalties, or damages to be more specific, are also provided for in the contract and will have to be paid by SPL in the event of train delays or station closures due to an electricity supply failure.

Additionally, one of LUL's objectives during the setting up of this PFI was to favor innovations in the London network. This had an impact on the contract design of the PFI: in order to favor innovation, the contract is based on a requirement to achieve specific results rather than on a best efforts

(continued)

Box 6 (continued)

requirement. SPL must comply with specific performance criteria associated with penalties in case of noncompliance with these standards. As an example, the penalties to be paid by SPL in the event of a power outage range from 50£ to 100,000£ per hour of outage, depending on the importance of the damage suffered by LUL in terms of loss of income.

In addition to the specification of performance criteria and penalties, the contract also provides for processes of control by the public authority, as well as for an obligation for SPL to provide feedback to facilitate the control in question. SPL is thus contractually required to adopt standardized accounting procedures that are described very precisely in the contract, in order to limit the possibilities for the private partner to manipulate financial data. Moreover, a control agency made up of 30 LUL employees was created to monitor the observance of commitments made by SPL. Similarly, LUL is authorized to examine electric installations, to control SPL's accounts, and to make copies of any document that is deemed useful, at any moment and without prior notice. As for SPL, it must hand in numerous activity reports as well as accounting and financial reports every year in order to facilitate the control of its activities.

The high degree of precision of the contract as regards the specification of objectives to be met by the private partner, accounting procedures to be observed, and control methods to be implemented thus reduces the possibility for SPL to behave in an opportunistic manner during contract implementation.

It should nevertheless be noted that substantial risks of opportunism may also arise from LUL or the public authorities controlling it (see part 2 - Chapter "Comparative Performances of Delivery Options: Empirical Lessons" on renegotiations in PPPs). In the contract for the London underground, this issue was taken into account by authorizing SPL to terminate the contract unilaterally, especially in the event that LUL should decide to stop paying its bills or would no longer be able to do so because of changing political circumstances.

Another way to introduce contractual incentives and to reduce risks of opportunism on the part of the private partner consists in binding the operator's prices directly to its performance level. The next subsection analyzes these regulatory tools and stresses their strengths and weaknesses for the implementation of PPPs.

3.2   Price Design of the Contracts and Incentives

It is important to remember that, within the framework of agency theory (or incentive theory), the public partner (or alternatively the regulator, which is usually independent from the public authority) is faced with a double information asymmetry. First, it does not know the "quality" of its private partner and therefore ignores the costs the latter has to bear as part of its activity. Consequently, it is in the operator's interest to overestimate its costs and to pass them on to end-user prices (adverse selection). Secondly, the regulator does not know "the effort" realized by the operator as part of its activity. Given that this effort is costly for the operator, it is in its interest to minimize it.[16] In such a situation of moral hazard, the operator's costs will not be minimized and the "additional costs" will impact the prices applied by the operator.

In this regard, price regulation would make it possible to limit the potentially harmful effects associated with the absence of competition in the market.

Cost-plus regulation used to be the prevailing regulation method before the wave of liberalizations of the 1980s. With this mechanism, the regulator uses auditing to observe the monopoly's costs and to compensate the latter on the basis of this observation. The operator is thus guaranteed *ex ante* that all its costs will be covered, in addition to an authorized profit rate. The regulator also sets the user price. This type of regulation eliminates the problem of adverse selection. Nevertheless, it also presents several theoretical limitations. Firstly, a cost-plus regulated enterprise has no incentive to make efforts, since its income is not indexed on its performance. Secondly, firms are encouraged to overcapitalize so as to increase the assessment basis for their authorized profit rate (Averch & Johnson, 1962). In other words, this kind of price regulation leads to inefficiencies in the operators' technological choices and to unnecessary investments: by overcapitalizing, the operator can increase its prices and thus come closer to the unregulated monopoly price. In practice, cost-plus contracts have also been criticized because of frequent and substantial cost overruns as part of PPPs. For instance, a GAO[17] study (2009) focusing on 96 major American supply projects in the defense sector highlights cost overruns of 25% on average, which represents 296 billion dollars throughout the duration of the projects. For 42% of these projects, the cost overruns amount to at least 25%. The report also indicates that the average delay in service provision is 22 months. Based on estimates, only 28% of the projects respect the deadlines provided for in the initial contract. Thus, as highlighted by Fehr, Hart, and Zehnder (2011), cost-plus contracts allow for greater flexibility and capacity for adaptation to hazards, but they are also subject to more frequent cost overruns and a higher risk of information manipulation by the private partner.[18]

---

[16]An information asymmetry can also be advantageous for the public party in some cases, especially when the contract relates to the concession of networks that are better known by the contracting authority than by potential future concessionaires [see for instance Martimort & Sand-Zantman (2006)].

[17]Government Accountability Office (GAO).

[18]As observed by Moszoro and Spiller (2012), cost-plus contracts are viewed as "blank checks" for the partners and are a source of PPP inefficiency. The authors nevertheless highlight the fact that there is at least one exception. Indeed, the PPP set up through a cost-plus contract for the construction of Terminal 5 at Heathrow airport in London was delivered on time and at the cost initially provided for in the contract.

Faced with these difficulties, most countries have introduced incentive mechanisms in order to prevent the operator from passing its cost increases on to the end-user price. The analysis of incentive regulation was developed in the 1980s, largely following the articles of Baron and Myerson (1982) and Laffont and Tirole (1986, 1993). Fixed price regulation (also known as price cap regulation) was then introduced. With this mechanism, the regulator offers the monopoly a lump-sum compensation that is set prior to production, based on its future cost estimates. The amount of the lump sum is independent of the costs borne by the monopoly. Thus, the regulated operator is given an incentive to reduce its costs so as to maximize its profits. This mechanism allows for the minimization of the firm's costs, thus eliminating the moral hazard problem. Nevertheless, it raises the issue of how to set the lump-sum compensation (often called "transfer" in the economic literature on incentives). The regulator does not know the costs actually borne by the operator,[19] and the level of transfer is determined according to estimates based on indicators that do not include the operator's costs. In the absence of detailed information, this mechanism can lead either to excessive profits or to the collapse of the sector (Auriol, 2000). Therefore, the main impediment to the realization of the social optimum once more is of an informational nature. Furthermore, Dixit (1991), Cowan (1998), and Dobbs (2004) underline the fact that the price cap can have a negative impact on incentives to invest in a context of uncertainty. Whether the price cap is set correctly or not by the regulator, the private operator can anticipate a drop in demand and thus protect itself against this risk by underinvesting.

To deal with this double information deficit to which the public partner is subjected (adverse selection and moral hazard), theoretical models of optimal regulation suggest not one contract but a range of contracts, which give more or less incentives (see for instance Laffont & Martimort, 2002). The public authority lets potential partners make their choice among this selection of contracts. By choosing one of them, the private firm reveals "its quality" or "the effort" it is willing to contribute as part of the activity to be contracted. The two extremes of this contract selection can be summarily identified to the two contracts mentioned above (that is, cost-plus and price cap contracts). The more efficient the firm, the more it is in its interest to choose a fixed price contract allowing to obtain a profit that is all the higher as the company reduces its costs. Conversely, a low-performance company will prefer a cost-plus contract guaranteeing the repayment of its costs and setting its profits in advance, irrespective of its performance. Between these two "extremes," the regulator offers contracts that differ in the share of costs repaid by the regulator and the share of revenue retained by the firm. It should be noted that, in practice, the difference between a cost-plus and a price cap contract is not as clear as in theory and that regulators often draw up contracts

---

[19]The regulator is able to observe the monopoly's cost *ex post*, but it does not know whether this cost is "efficient" or not. Indeed, monopolies often benefit from a technological expertise that gives them an informational advantage compared to the regulator.

located in between these two extremes. For instance, in order not to set the authorized price cap arbitrarily, the regulator must take into account the costs actually borne by the monopoly, which constitutes a lightening of the constraint compared to what theory recommends. Moreover, if the price cap contract only lasts a year, and the authorized price upper limit is regularly reevaluated, then the mechanism is equitable with a cost-plus contract. On the contrary, if the duration of the price cap contract is significant, the operator can make efforts to reduce its costs and reap the result of these efforts, which encourages it to improve its efficiency.

Recent developments in contract theory have highlighted the fact that contract design can influence the efficiency of unanticipated adaptations of the contract and, therefore, the final efficiency of the contract. For instance, Bajari and Tadelis (2001) show that there is an arbitration between the incentive power and the efficiency of *ex post* adaptations. The authors assume that during the renegotiation process, there is always an information asymmetry between the contracting parties. They show that an incentive contract (of the fixed price kind) provides strong incentives to reduce costs but is ill-suited for adaptations. These incentives reduce the potential *ex post* surplus as part of the renegotiation process involving information asymmetries. This can lead to inefficient adaptations from the point of view of the social surplus. Conversely, a low-incentive contract (of the cost-plus kind) does not allow for a reduction in the cost of the project, but leads to easier *ex post* adaptations in the event of a hazard, and preserves the surplus during the renegotiation process.

Thus, the design of the contract (the amount of incentives it gives) depends on the likelihood of renegotiations occurring. More precisely, if there is a high probability of renegotiating, then the parties should choose a low-incentive contract that is not too detailed and is therefore able to adapt more easily to potential hazards.

Many empirical studies have been conducted to analyze the effect of the regulation method on the efficiency of public–private arrangements, mostly in Latin America. These studies will be analyzed in greater detail in Chapter "Comparative Performances of Delivery Options: Empirical Lessons" of the second part of this book. Here, let us just briefly stress the fact that the majority of these studies show that introducing a price cap generates productivity gains and cost reductions (see for instance Benitez, Celani, Estache, & Guasch, 2002; Estache & Trujillo, 2002; Estache, Gonzalez, & Trujillo, 2002a, b; Resende & Facanha, 2002; Rossi, 2001, 2002). Nevertheless, Estache, Guasch, and Trujillo (2003) indicate that in reality, the effect of incentive regulation of the price-cap kind is more complex. Among other things, they highlight the fact that investments realized by concessionaires[20] have only represented one-third of the investments deemed necessary in Latin America, thus echoing the theoretical predictions mentioned above (see for instance Dixit, 1991). Moreover, they indicate that the cost reductions do not directly result in a price reduction for users of the services in

---

[20]This study focuses on the sectors of energy, telecommunications, water, and transport.

question, which points to the unclear nature of the profit-sharing scheme between operators and consumers. Finally, Estache et al. (2003) and Guasch (2004) insist on the fact that public–private contracts regulated through a price cap are more often renegotiated and that, for the most part, these renegotiations are initiated by the private partner. Guasch (2004) points out that these renegotiations lead to price increases, delays in investment realization, or even the renunciation of investments that were previously scheduled.

Are such renegotiations and their consequences in terms of prices or investments harmful in the end, or do they result from necessary adaptations of long-term contracts? This question has sparked an extensive debate in the economic literature. We briefly mention this theoretical debate by referring the reader on to Chapter "Renegotiating PPP Contracts: Opportunities and Pitfalls" of the second part of this book, for an analysis of empirical results on this issue.

The economic literature often considers that PPP renegotiations result from actors' opportunistic behaviors, questioning the credibility of their long-term commitments and thus the efficiency of these contractual arrangements (Athias & Saussier, 2007; Crocker & Masten, 1996; Guasch, 2004; Guasch, Laffont, & Straub, 2007, 2008; Williamson, 1975). Transaction cost theory (see for instance Williamson, 1975) views contractual incompleteness as the source of opportunistic and rent-seeking behaviors on the part of stakeholders. During renegotiations, agents seek to appropriate a larger part of the surplus generated by the contract, rather than seek to increase the social surplus. Most studies emphasize the important part played by private partners in such opportunistic strategies. Indeed, the private operator can benefit from a favorable balance of power allowing it to renegotiate the contractual conditions *ex post* to its own advantage, in particular because of a greater experience of the PPP contract and of its renegotiations (compared to the experience of the public authority). Such an asymmetry then confers greater negotiating power on the operator, insofar as it will not be easy for the public authority to find an alternative solution. According to Iossa et al. (2007), the public party's negotiating power is very limited because of the time and transaction costs associated with selecting a new partner, especially as these costs will be all the higher as there is little competition in the market and the number of eligible operators is low (Kerf, 1998). Thus, the public party will be more willing to accept the private party's contractual renegotiations rather than risk an interruption of service that would be contrary to the principle of public service continuity.

Nevertheless, the fact remains that the public authority can also behave opportunistically. For instance, Guasch et al. (2007) developed an agency model in which a new government may choose to renegotiate a PPP contract to take into account the evolution of the agents' preferences (and thus establish its popularity among voters) while maintaining the same utility level for the private partner. However, the new government may also reevaluate the initial contract and, in extreme cases, expropriate the private firm. This situation questions the credibility of the public partner's long-term commitments. Renegotiations are then perceived as an indicator of the government's (or public partner's) ability to commit in the long run (Estache & Wren-Lewis, 2009; Laffont, 2005). In addition, Engel, Fischer, and Galetovic

(2009) show that PPP contract renegotiation may be used by public authorities to circumvent their budgetary constraints and increase their likelihood of being reelected. In their model, the public authority in place is more likely to be reelected if important infrastructure expenditures were realized during its term of office. From this perspective, it is in its interest to renegotiate the PPP contract to increase the volume and value of works, without actually being forced to "bear" the additional costs associated with these renegotiations. Indeed, an important part of these costs will be entered into the budgets of the administrations elected in the future (see Box 7 below).

Transaction cost theory later acknowledges that contracts are imperfect governance structures, which must be adapted to an environment that is often complex, unpredictable, and sometimes poorly apprehended due to the limited rationality of economic operators (Williamson, 1985). Renegotiations are thus viewed as necessary to alleviate the maladaptation costs inherent to long-term contracts and "realign" the contract with its economic environment. The same argument can be found in the theory of incomplete contracts: all long-term contracts must adapt to any new conditions that may arise and that were not anticipated when the contract was signed. The theory of incomplete contracts thus suggests that renegotiations are not only unavoidable, but also and above all useful, given that the private operator must receive compensations in order to develop investments that were not provided

---

Box 7: Contractual Conflicts and Political Stakes: The Case of Water Management in Atlanta

Spiller (2008) provides an example about water management in Atlanta, which illustrates a contractual conflict with an outcome that can be interpreted as resulting more from political stakes than from a will to maintain the social optimum.

Indeed, in January 2003, the public authorities of Atlanta decided to terminate the water management concession concluded 4 years earlier with a private operator (United Water) for a duration that had originally been set at 22 years. Indeed, the private operator was asking for a renegotiation of the initial agreement, arguing that the data that had been used to define its terms were erroneous. According to United Water, in order to comply with the contractual level of service, the firm had to give up 10 million dollars each year for a contract of 28 million dollars per year.

However, the city of Atlanta preferred to put an end to the agreement and take over the contract rather than agree to the firm's requirements. Indeed, according to Spiller, if the city had accepted to renegotiate the agreement in accordance with the firm's expectations, it would have run the risk of its image being badly damaged in the eyes of public opinion. It would have showcased the city's inability to draw up a contract flexible enough to adapt to environmental uncertainties.

for *ex ante* and become verifiable *ex post* (Grossman & Hart, 1986; Hart, 2003). A few empirical studies, although still rare, endeavor to measure the effects of renegotiations on the social surplus (see Gagnepain, Ivaldi, & Martimort, 2013 for urban transport) or the contracting parties' satisfaction (see Beuve, de Brux, & Saussier, 2013 for car park concessions). They do not currently allow us to settle the question of the net effect of renegotiations on long-term contracts once and for all.

Another incentive regulation option designed by Shleifer (1985) has been developing gradually in practice. If the debate on the validity of renegotiations also concerns this regulation method, this one is nevertheless better able to limit difficulties associated with information asymmetries, at least in theory.

3.3   Benchmarking and Yardstick Competition

Auriol (2000) points out that "*an ingenious way to reduce information asymmetries consists in exploiting the correlation between firms producing the same type of goods or services. In that case, it can be assumed that they are faced with the same costs, or at least comparable costs. Even if the regulator ignores the value of these costs, it can exploit their common structure to overcome its informational disadvantage, and thus come closer to the social optimum. This is known as yardstick competition*" (p. 623). Yardstick competition is more commonly known as benchmarking. The theoretical informational advantages that can be derived from interfirm comparisons have been highlighted by authors such as Shleifer (1985), Sobel (1999), Auriol (2000), Boyer and Laffont (2003), and Choné and Lesur (2001). With this mechanism, a regulator or a public authority derives informational externalities from comparing the performances of various PPP private partners that are deemed similar. An operator's profits will depend on its performances, relative to the performances of other regulated firms in the industry. More precisely, the regulator assesses and remunerates (or penalizes) an agent's performances compared to those of other agents, whose characteristics are close enough to allow for comparisons. For the regulator, it is therefore a question of introducing a "fictional" or "virtual" competition between local monopolies. The mechanism of yardstick competition is thus based on assessing the performances of the various regulated firms of the industry (using benchmarking tools) and the financial consequences they may have.

These relative performance measures are realized with benchmarking tools. These tools aim to establish an "efficiency frontier" set by the operators presenting the best practices in the industry. The other operators will then be evaluated as being more or less inefficient, depending on their distance from this efficiency frontier. One essential question lies in the method used to calculate this efficiency frontier. In view of regulators' practices, three main benchmarking techniques can be listed. The corrected ordinary least squares method (COLS) is well known and relatively simple to implement. It is directly derived from the classical method of ordinary least squares (OLS). The "correction" established through the COLS method involves shifting the frontier obtained with the OLS estimation toward the most efficient firm. It is thus merely a shifted average function and not an actual frontier representing the best practices in the sector. Although there is no consensus regarding which benchmarking method is the "best," we can observe the development of parametric methods such as Stochastic Frontier Analysis (SFA),[21] as well as nonparametric methods like Data Envelopment Analysis (DEA)[22] in the literature and in numerous countries. These two models have both advantages and drawbacks, but the attractive features of the SFA method are increasingly highlighted. Compared to the DEA method, SFA presents the advantage of taking into account the effects of statistical noise when measuring relative efficiencies (mistakes made when specifying the cost or production function, or data omission). Indeed, it can be difficult to detect all factors of heterogeneity across companies. Thus, when an unobserved heterogeneity might remain across regulated firms, it is essential to be able to perceive the extent to which distances from the frontier (i.e., deviations from the best practices) are due to statistical noise or to the operators' inefficiency. Conversely, an important advantage of the DEA method is that it does not require making strong assumptions as to the functional form connecting the various inputs to the outputs. In other words, with a DEA method, unlike the SFA method, it is not necessary to assume that firms run their activity based on a certain production or cost function. Finally, and more practically, setting up an SFA requires a relatively extensive database, which is not always possible depending on the regulated sectors. We should bear in mind that this set of tools is imperfect and that many regulators use several methods at the same time to check the consistency of the results, in the manner of the British water regulator or the German energy regulator, for instance.

Thanks to these benchmarking tools, regulators can limit information asymmetry through various channels. First, interfirm comparisons provide the regulator with a yardstick allowing it to better assess observed performances, compared to a simple "nominal" result. For instance, if one of the private partners of a PPP displays better results than other similar partners, it means that it is relatively more efficient than the others. It is then safe to assume that this operator is probably efficient in absolute terms. Second, the comparison of several firms operating in similar environments in different markets (or different contracts) makes it possible to detect signals that are not compatible and thus to give the operators incentives to disclose their private information. For instance, and in broad outline, a regulator can detect firms that wrongly claim to be "inefficient" in order to receive a higher level of transfer from the regulator, by observing the performances of comparable firms.

---

[21]The SFA method was initially developed by Aigner, Lovell, and Schmidt (1977) and Meeusen and Van Den Broeck (1977). See Kumbhakar and Lovell (2001) for an exhaustive analysis of stochastic frontiers and a description of the various existing SFA methodologies.

[22]See Charnes, Cooper, and Rhodes (1978) for an explanation of the DEA method. A complete description of the use of the DEA method for purposes of regulatory policies is provided by Thanassoulis (2000a, b). See also Charnes, Cooper, Lewin, and Seiford (1994) and Cooper, Seiford, and Zhu (2004) for an inventory of DEA applications.

Finally, yardstick competition theoretically creates an "emulation" between operators, which aims to give them incentives to maximize their actions (their "efforts") so as to rank well in relative performances ratings. The objective is then for relatively low-performance firms to "catch up" with the best ones, so that the efficiency of the whole sector improves as a result.

Yardstick competition has been developing gradually in various sectors and countries, such as for instance the water sector in the United Kingdom (see Le Lannier, 2010) and Portugal, the energy sector in Germany, the United Kingdom and the Netherlands, or the hospital sector in the United States. Box 8 below presents in more detail the organization of yardstick competition in Norway to give incentives to operators in bus services, as well as the "innovation" introduced in the Japanese rail industry in terms of yardstick competition.

Box 8: Yardstick Competition: The Case of Bus Transport Services in Norway

Dalen and Gómez-Lobo (2003) analyze how Norway set up a system of yardstick competition in bus transport services. They show that firms regulated with this method reduce their inefficiency more quickly than those regulated through other types of regulatory contracts. In Norway, the responsibility for local transport is entrusted to regional regulators (the "counties") in charge of defining the road network, schedules, transport ticket fares, as well as the transfers granted to network operators. Each region can choose its own type of regulation contract. Because of this setting, regulatory methods vary between regions. Two major approaches can be distinguished, their main similarity lying in the fact that, in every instance, lump-sum transfers are paid to operators.

In the first case, regulators use an "individual" regulation, so that transfers paid to firm i depend on the costs borne by the same firm i. Dalen and Gómez-Lobo (2003) underline the fact that this solution generates ratchet effects,[23] so that firms are not given any incentive to reduce their costs, since they anticipate a decrease in their transfers. Thus, the authors show that this scheme has a low power of incentive in terms of cost reduction.

On the other hand, since the 1980s, some regions have started using a standard-cost model to determine annual transfers to operators. Regulators and firms agree upon a set of criteria for calculating the costs of operating a

(continued)

---

[23]Operators may anticipate the fact that a reduction in their costs provides information to the regulator, who will thus be given an incentive to subsequently increase the power of incentive of the regulatory contract (incentive clauses will be re-evaluated over time based on collected information). Firms may also seek to limit their efforts in terms of cost reduction so as to retain their informational advantage as long as possible and thus prevent the contract from "hardening." This is referred to as a "ratchet effect."

Box 8 (continued)

bus network. Given the estimations regarding ticket fares, the standard-cost model determines the level of transfers granted by the regulator. The same standard-cost model applies to all operators in the region. Once the criteria are set, it is not the costs realized by one firm, but the relative level of cost that will affect the level of its annual lump-sum transfers, in accordance with the principle of yardstick competition. The authors show that firms regulated this way are given an incentive to reduce their costs.

More recently, a third type of regulatory contract was introduced: the subsidy cap. Firms and regional regulators agree upon a reduction in the level of transfers granted by the regulator, by $x\%$ a year, over a period of 5 years. With this in mind, as in the case of the standard-cost model, interfirm comparisons are used to directly set the level of transfers granted to firms and thus form the basis of cost reimbursement.

The Case of the Rail Industry in Japan

Lévêque (2005) describes the "innovative" mechanism of yardstick competition set up in the rail industry in Japan, which includes three different incentive channels. First, and in a "classical" way, benchmarking is implemented through static incentives, based on the gap between the observed cost and the reference cost. As with most yardstick competition applications, an operator's remuneration is thus based on its performances compared to other operators in the industry at a given moment. Secondly, dynamic incentives are set up based on the variation of the gap between the observed cost and the reference cost. In other words, the regulator also compares the evolution of a single operator's costs over time. These dynamic incentives aim to stimulate operators that are low performers, but whose costs are decreasing, and to give a warning to efficient operators whose costs are increasing. Finally, nonfinancial incentives are also provided through the publication of benchmarking results.

Several difficulties associated with yardstick competition have nevertheless been put forward in the literature. First of all, one obvious difficulty is that to set up a yardstick regulation, the productive characteristics of regulated firms must be homogeneous enough to be comparable (Auriol, 2000; Bivand & Szymanski, 1997). Then, agents with homogeneous characteristics may have incentives to coordinate their actions so as to relieve the burden of constraints weighing down on them. The joint adoption of deviant behavior by all regulated operators then introduces a bias into the benchmark and cannot necessarily be detected by the mechanism. This collusion between firms can be explicit (Chong, 2006; Chong & Huet, 2006; Laffont & Martimort, 2000; Pouyet, 2002; Tangerås, 2002) or tacit (Potters, Rockenbach, Sadrieh, & van Damme, 2004). In addition, Sobel (1999) and Dalen (1997) have highlighted how difficult it can be to give firms incentives to invest with such a regulatory method. Investments realized by firms are encouraged by the prospect of future rents generated by these investments. Sobel (1999) underlines the fact that, in the case of yardstick competition, if the regulator's commitment power is limited, it will be tempted to use the information collected through interfirm comparisons to extract the rents produced by the operators' investments. Anticipating such a "hold-up," firms lose all incentive to invest. Yardstick competition thus appears to strengthen the classical "hold-up" problem by allowing access to the private operators' private information at a reduced cost through interfirm comparisons. Dalen (1997) claims that yardstick competition will only have a negative effect on investments creating externalities in the industry as a whole. The assumption is then that a firm will be discouraged from investing if its investments affect the productivity of the whole industry while it bears their costs alone, because it will deteriorate its relative performance.

Because of the limitations associated with setting up a yardstick competition scheme and the imperfection of benchmarking tools, it is not always possible to establish a direct and automatic connection between interfirm comparisons and the authorized price or revenue caps (see Le Lannier, 2010). In other words, it is not always possible to exploit yardstick competition for price regulation purposes. In this respect, many examples show that a more "flexible" form of yardstick competition can also be implemented, without performance comparisons directly influencing the price scheme. This is known as the "sunshine regulation." The objective of this mechanism is to "embarrass" low-performing companies and to bring the industry's best practices in the spotlight through the publication of relative performance rankings, as previously underlined in the case of the Japanese rail industry. In this context, regulators use yardstick competition largely for informational purposes. No direct link between performance rankings and authorized price or revenue caps is envisaged. The incentive received by firms does not derive from financial "rewards" or "penalties" but from the effect their relative performance will have on their reputation because of the publication of benchmarking results. One representative example of sunshine regulation is provided by the Malaysian experience, described in Box 9 below.

Box 9: Incentives Through Information: The Malaysian *Sunshine Regulation*

The construction of the Petronas group's twin towers in Kuala Lumpur is an emblematic example of the application of a sunshine regulation and demonstrates that this informational mechanism is applicable beyond the field of PPPs.

According to the international ranking established by the CTBUH, these towers were the highest in the world from 1998 to 2004 and remain, to this day, the highest twin towers ever built.

(continued)

Box 9 (continued)

Excavation work began in 1993 and construction was completed in 1998. For the realization of this work, Petronas chose to assign the construction of each tower to two different operators (or more precisely, two different consortia). One of the towers was built by a Japanese consortium led by Hazama Corporation, while the other was built by a South Korean consortium led by Samsung C & T Corporation and Kukdong Engineering & Construction.

Putting these two consortia "in the spotlight" introduced "friendly competition" between the two builders: a Korean flag and a Japanese flag were raised above their respective towers and rose in height as the construction of each tower progressed. The Korean consortium won the competition, although by a narrow margin (1 month ahead of the Japanese competitor). This lead can be explained, among other things, by the fact that the Japanese consortium encountered difficulties when it realized that "its" tower deviated from its vertical position by 25 mm.

In the area of public services, the sunshine regulation model is traditionally associated with Sweden, where it is used in the telecommunication, electricity, and gas industries as well as to regulate postal services and railways. Likewise, the IRAR and the VEWIN, the respective regulators of the water sector in Portugal and the Netherlands, have both set up this type of regulation (De Witte & Dijkgraaf, 2007; De Witte & Marques, 2007, 2009, 2010; De Witte & Saal, 2008).

A first theoretical advantage of the sunshine regulation is the promotion of greater efficiency within the industry. De Witte and Dijkgraaf (2007) highlight the fact that the "internal carrots" come from the emulation generated between managers in order to be named the most efficient in the industry. The authors explain that such motivation may be reinforced by indirect financial rewards (other than a higher authorized price or revenue cap). As a corollary, external penalties result from the bad reputation that the worst companies will have to bear after the benchmarking results are disseminated to a large audience (shareholders, consumer associations, media...). Once again, financial penalties can be used to supplement the publications in order to provide companies with incentives to improve their performance. It is important to specify that adding these penalties does not mean that the regulator is heading toward a "stricter" form of yardstick competition. Indeed, yardstick competition remains "flexible" in the sense that the regulator still does not establish a direct connection between interfirm comparisons and the authorized price or revenue caps.

4 Conclusion

The diversity and complexity of public–private partnerships makes it necessary to set up often complex incentive and control mechanisms throughout the duration of the contract. In view of the economic literature and contractual and institutional evolutions observed throughout the world, including in developing countries, it is obvious that the development of such contracts does not lead to a deregulation of public services, but rather to a re-regulation of these sectors.

This chapter analyzed the tools that may be implemented to promote PPP efficiency, both at the time of their award to a private partner and during their enforcement. It is important to highlight the fact that this chapter essentially focused on the solutions, whether contractual or regulatory, that can help limit opportunistic behaviors on the part of private contracting parties. Nevertheless, as we have made it clear throughout this chapter, opportunism can also come from the contracting authority, which may be susceptible to objectives of a personal or political nature. Thus, overall, the economic literature stresses the importance of the institutional context within which the contract is performed: institutions can just as well limit, eliminate, or strengthen the efficiency of regulatory tools.

References

Aigner, D., Lovell, K., & Schmidt, P. (1977). Formulation and estimation of stochastic frontier production function models. *Journal of Econometrics, 6*(1), 21–37.

Amaral, M., Saussier, S., & Yvrande-Billon, A. (2009). Auction procedures and competition in public services: The case of urban public transport in France and London. *Utilities Policy, 17*(2):166–175.

Armstrong, M., & Sappington, D. E. M. (2006). Regulation, competition and liberalization. *Journal of Economic Literature, 44*(2), 325–366. American Economic Association.

Athias, L., & Saussier, S. (2007). Un partenariat public-privé rigide ou flexible ? Théorie et application aux concessions routières à péage. *Revue économique, 58*, 565–576.

Auriol, E. (2000). Concurrence par comparaison: Un point de vue normatif. *Revue économique, 51*(3), 621–634.

Autorité de la concurrence. (2010). Décision no 10-DCC-198 du 30 décembre 2010 relative à la création d'une entreprise commune par Veolia Environnement et la Caisse des dépôts et consignations.

Averch, H., & Johnson, L. L. (1962). Behaviour of the firm under regulatory constraint. *American Economic Review, 52*(5), 1052–1069.

Bain, R. (2009). *Review of lessons from completed PPP projects financed by the EIB*. Luxembourg: European Investment Bank.

Bajari, P., & Tadelis, S. (2001). Incentives versus transaction costs: A theory of procurement contracts. *RAND Journal of Economics, 32*(3), 387–407.

Baker, G. (1992). Incentive contracts and performance measurement. *Journal of Political Economy, 3*(100), 598–614.

Baker, G. (2000). The use of performance measures in incentive contracting. *American Economic Review, 90*(2), 415–420.

Baker, G. (2002). Distortion and risk in optimal incentive contracts. *Journal of Human Resources, 37*(4), 728–751.

Baldwin, R., & Cave, M. (1999). *Understanding regulation: Theory, strategy and practice.* Oxford: Oxford University Press.

Baron, D. P., & Myerson, R. B. (1982). Regulating a monopolist with unknown costs. *Econometrica, 50*(4), 911–930.

Benitez, D., Celani, M., Estache, A., & Guasch, L. (2002). *Efficiency gains in Argentina's telecoms.* mimeo, The World Bank.

Beuve, J., de Brux, J., & Saussier, S. (2013). Renégocier pour durer: une analyse empirique des contrats de concessions. *Revue d'économie industrielle, 141,* 117–148.

Bivand, R., & Szymanski, S. (1997). Spatial dependence through local yardstick competition: Theory and testing. *Economics Letters, 55,* 257–265.

Blanc-Brude, F., & Jenson, O. (2010). *Why the PFI needs a regulator* (Infrastructure Economics Viewpoint Paper).

Boyer, M., & Laffont, J.-J. (2003). Competition and the reform of incentive schemes in the regulated sector. *Journal of Public Economics, 87*(9–10), 2369–2396.

Bulow, J., & Klemperer, P. (1996). Auctions versus negotiations. *American Economic Review, 86* (1), 180–194.

Burguet, R., & Che, Y.-K. (2004). Competitive procurement with corruption. *RAND Journal of Economics, 35*(1), 50–68.

Caillaud, B. (2001). Ententes et capture dans l'attribution des marchés publics. In Cohen & Mougeot (dir.), *Enchères et gestion publique* (pp. 215–244). Paris: Conseil d'analyse économique, La Documentation française.

Calzolari, G., & Spagnolo, G. (2009). *Relational contracts and competitive screening.* SSRN eLibrary.

Cantillon, E., & Pesendorfer, M. (2006). Auctioning bus routes: The London bus experience. In P. Cramton, Y. Shoham, & R. Steinberg (dir.), *Combinatorial auctions* (pp. 573–593). MIT Press.

Celentani, M., & Ganunza, J. (2002). Competition and corruption in procurement. *European Economic Review, 46*(7), 1273–1303.

Chadwick, E. (1859). Results of different principles of legislation and administration in Europe of competition for the field, as compared with competition within the field of service. *Journal of the Royal Statistical Society, 22*(A), 381–420.

Charnes, A., Cooper, W. W., & Rhodes, E. (1978). Measuring the efficiency of decision making units. *European Journal of Operational Research, 2,* 429–444.

Charnes, A., Cooper, W. W., Lewin, A. Y., & Seiford, L. M. (1994). *Data envelopment analysis: Theory, methodology and application.* Boston: Kluwer Academic Publishers.

Che, Y.-K. (1993). Design competition through multidimensional auctions. *RAND Journal of Economics, 24,* 668–680.

Choné, P., & Lesur, R. (2001). *A note on yardstick competition under adverse selection* (CREST Working Paper).

Chong, E. (2006). *Competitive solutions for managing local public services: An economic analysis of water supply in France.* Ph. D dissertation, Université Paris XI-Sud, Orsay, France.

Chong, E., & Huet, F. (2006). Enchères, concurrence par comparaison et collusion. *Revue é conomique, 57*(3), 583–592.

Compte, O., Lambert-Mogiliansky, A., & Verdier, T. (2005). Corruption and competition in procurement auctions. *RAND Journal of Economics, 36*(1), 1–15.

Cooper, W. W., Seiford, L. M., & Zhu, J. (2004). *Handbook on data envelopment analysis.* Boston: Kluwer Academic Publishers.

Cour des comptes. (2010). *Les transports ferroviaires régionaux en Île-de-France.* La Documentation française.

Cowan, S. (1998). Welfare consequences of tight price-cap regulation. *Bulletin of Economic Research, 50*(2), 105–116.

Crocker, K. J., & Masten, S. E. (1996). Regulation and administered contracts revisited: Lessons from transaction-cost economics for public utility regulation. *Journal of Regulatory Economics, 9*(1), 5–39.

Dalen, D. M. (1997). Regulation of quality and the ratchet effect: Does unverifiability hurt the regulator? *Journal of Regulatory Economics, 11*, 139–155.

Dalen, D. M., & Gómez-Lobo, A. (2003). Yardsticks on the road: Regulatory contracts and cost efficiency in the Norwegian bus industry. *Transportation, 30*, 371–386.

de Brux, J., & Desrieux, C. (2014). To allot or not to allot public services in Europe? An incomplete contract approach. *European Journal of Law and Economics, 37*, 455–476.

De Witte, K., & Dijkgraaf, E. (2007). *Mean and bold? On separating merger economies from structural efficiency gains in the drinking water sector* (Tinbergen Institute Discussion Papers 07-092/3). Tinbergen Institute.

De Witte, K., & Marques, R. C. (2007). *Designing incentives in local public utilities, an international comparison of the drinking water sector* (Center for Economic Studies – Discussion papers ces0732). Katholieke Universiteit Leuven, Centrum voor Economische Studiën.

De Witte, K., & Marques, R. C. (2009). *Gaming in a benchmarking environment. A non-parametric analysis of benchmarking in the water sector* (MPRA Paper 14679). University Library of Munich, Germany.

De Witte, K., & Marques, R. C. (2010). Towards a benchmarking paradigm in the European public water and sewerage services. *Public Money & Management, 30*(1), 42–48.

De Witte, K., & Saal, D. S. (2008). *Is a Little Sunshine all we need? On the impact of Sunshine Regulation on profits, productivity and prices in the Dutch Drinking Water Sector* (Center for Economic Studies – Discussion papers ces0828). Katholieke Universiteit Leuven, Centrum voor Economische Studiën.

Demsetz, H. (1968). Why regulate utilities? *Journal of Law and Economics, 11*, 55–66.

Dixit, A. (1991). Irreversible investment with price ceilings. *Journal of Political Economy, 99*, 541–557.

Dobbs, I. M. (2004). Intertemporal price cap regulation under uncertainty. *The Economic Journal, 114*(495), 421–440.

Doni, N. (2006). The importance of reputation in awarding public contracts. *Annals of Public and Cooperative Economics, 77*(4), 401–429.

Engel, E., Fischer, R., & Galetovic, A. (2001). Least-present-value-of-revenue auctions and highway franchising. *Journal of Political Economy, 109*(5), 993–1020.

Engel, E., Fischer, R., & Galetovic, A. (2009). *Soft budgets and renegotiations in public-private partnerships*. New Haven, CT: Cowles Foundation for Research in Economics, Yale University.

Estache, A., & Saussier, S. (2014). Public-private partnerships and efficiency: A short assessment. *CESifo DICE Report, 12*, 8–13.

Estache, A., & Trujillo, L. (2002). *How much did economic efficiency improve in Argentina since privatization – A brief survey of the empirical evidence on the 'X' factor for Argentina's Regulated Industries*. mimeo, The World Bank.

Estache, A., & Wren-Lewis, L. (2009). Toward a theory of regulation for developing countries: Following Jean-Jacques Laffont's lead. *Journal of Economic Literature, 47*(3), 729–770. American Economic Association.

Estache, A., Gonzalez, M., & Trujillo, L. (2002a, November). What does privatization do for efficiency? Evidence from Argentina's and Brazil's railways. *World Development, 30*(11).

Estache, A., Gonzalez, M., & Trujillo, L. (2002b, April). Efficiency gains from port reform and the potential for yardstick competition: Lessons from Mexico. *World Development, 30*(4), 545–560.

Estache, A., Guasch, J.-L., & Trujillo, L. (2003). *Price caps, efficiency payoffs and infrastructure contract renegotiation in Latin America* (Policy Research Working Paper Series 3129). The World Bank.

Fehr, E., Hart, O., & Zehnder, C. (2011). Contracts as reference points-experimental evidence. *American Economic Review, 101*(2), 493–525.

Gagnepain, P., Ivaldi, M., & Martimort, D. (2013). The cost of contract renegotiation: Evidence from the local public sector. *American Economic Review, 103*, 2352–2383.

Gibbons, R. (2005). Four formal(izable) theories of the firm?. *Journal of Economic Behavior & Organization, 58*(2):200–245.

Goldberg, V. P. (1976). Regulation and administered contracts. *The Bell Journal of Economics, 7*(2), 426–448.

Government Accountability Office. (2009). *Defense acquisitions. Assessments of selected weapon programs.* Report to Congressional Committees, GAO-09-326SP.

Gromb, D., & Martimort, D. (2007). Collusion and the organization of delegated expertise. *Journal of Economic Theory, 137*(1), 271–299.

Grossman, S., & Hart, O. (1986). The costs and benefits of ownership: A theory of vertical and lateral integration. *Journal of Political Economy, 94*(4), 691–719. University of Chicago Press.

Guasch, J.-L. (2004). *Granting and renegotiating infrastructure concessions: Doing it right.* Washington, DC: World Bank Institute Development Studies (Processed).

Guasch, J.-L., Laffont, J.-J., & Straub, S. (2007). Concessions of infrastructure in Latin America: Government-led renegotiation. *Journal of Applied Econometrics, 22*(7), 1267–1294.

Guasch, J.-L., Laffont, J.-J., & Straub, S. (2008). Renegotiation of concession contracts in Latin America, evidence from the water and transport sectors. *International Journal of Industrial Organization, 26*(2), 421–442.

Hart, O. (2003). Incomplete contracts and public ownership: Remarks, and an application to public private partnerships. *Economic Journal, 113*(485), C69–C76.

Hiriart, Y., & Martimort, D. (2012). Le citoyen, L'expert et le politique: Une rationalité complexe pour une régulation excessive du risque. In *Annales d'économie et de statistique,* hors-série 1, *Économie, environnement et destin des générations futures* (pp. 153–182).

Holmström, B., & Milgrom, P. (1991). Multitask principal-agency analysis: Incentive contracts, asset ownership and job design. *Journal of Law, Economics and Organization, 7*, 24–51.

Huet, F. (2006). *Partenariats public-privé et performances. Théories et applications au secteur de l'approvisionnement d'eau potable en France.* Ph.D. dissertation, Université Paris I Panthéon-Sorbonne.

Iossa, E., & Martimort, D. (2011). *Post-tender corruption and risk allocation: Implications for public-private partnerships* (CEIS Tor Vergata, Research Paper Series, 9(195), issue 5).

Iossa, E., Spagnolo, G. & Vellez, M. (2007). Contract Design in Public-Private Partnerships. Report for the World Bank.

Jensen, M. C., & Meckling, W. II. (1976). Theory of the firm: Managerial behavior, agency costs and ownership structure. *Journal of Financial Economics, 3*(4), 305–360.

Kerf, M. (1998). *Concessions for infrastructure: A guide to their design and award* (World Bank Technical Paper no 399).

Kerr, S. (1975). On the folly of rewarding A, while hoping for B. *Academy of Management Journal, 18*, 769–783.

Kim, I. (1998). A model of selective tendering: Does bidding competition deter opportunism by contractors? *The Quarterly Review of Economics and Finance, 38*(4), 907–925.

Klein, M. (1998). *Bidding for concessions: The impact of contract design.* Washington, DC: The World Bank, online http://documents.worldbank.org/cura-ted/en/1998/11/441577/bidding-con cessions-impact-contract-design

Klein, B., & Leffler, K. B. (1981). The role of market forces in assuring contractual performance. *Journal of Political Economy, 9*(4), 615–641.

Klein, B., Crawford, R. G., & Alchian, A. A. (1978). Vertical integration, appropriable rents, and the competitive contracting process. *Journal of Law and Economics, 21*(2):297–326.

Kumbhakar, S., & Lovell, K. (2001). *Stochastic frontier analysis.* Cambridge: Cambridge University Press.

Laffont, J.-J. (2005). *Regulation and development.* Cambridge: Cambridge University Press.

Laffont, J.-J., & Martimort, D. (2000). Mechanism design with collusion and correlation. *Econometrica, 68*(2), 309–342.

Laffont, J.-J., & Martimort, D. (2002). *The theory of incentives: The principal agent model.* New Jersey: Princeton University Press.

Laffont, J.-J., & Tirole, J. (1986). Using cost observation to regulate firms. *Journal of Political Economy, 94*(3), 614–641.

Laffont, J.-J., & Tirole, J. (1993). *A theory of incentives in procurement and regulation.* Cambridge: MIT Press.

Lambert-Mogiliansky, A. (2010). *Endogenous preferences in games with type indeterminate players* (PSE Working Papers Halshs-00564895). HAL.

Le Lannier, A. (2010). *Difficultés d'exécution de la concurrence par comparaison. Une application au secteur de l'eau en Angleterre et au Pays de Galles.* Éditions universitaires européennes.

Leibenstein, H. (1966). Allocative efficiency vs X-efficiency. *American Economic Review, 56*, 392–415.

Lengwiler, Y., & Wolfstetter, E. (2006). Corruption in procurement auctions. In N. Dimitri, G. Piga, & G. Spagnolo (dir.), *Handbook of procurement* (pp. 412–432). Cambridge: Cambridge University Press.

Lévêque, J. (2005). *Réguler les chemins de fer sur une proposition de la nouvelle économie de la réglementation: la concurrence par comparaison.* Ph.D dissertation, Université Lyon 2 Lumière, Lyon, France.

Littlechild, S. C. (2002). Competitive bidding for a long-term electricity distribution contract. *Review of Network Economics, 1*(1), 1–38.

Manelli, A., & Vincenti, D. (1995). Optimal procurement mechanisms. *Econometrica, 63*, 591–620.

Martimort, D., & Sand-Zantman, W. (2006). Signalling and the design of delegated management contracts for public utilities. *The RAND Journal of Economics, 37*, 763–782.

Maskin, E., & Tirole, J. (1999). Unforeseen contingencies and incomplete contracts. *Review of Economic Studies, 66*, 83–114.

McAfee, R. P., & McMillan, J. (1987). Auctions with entry. *Economics Letters, 23*, 343–347.

Meeusen, W., & Van den Broeck, J. (1977). Efficiency estimation from Cobb-Douglas production functions with composed error. *International Economic Review, 18*(2), 435–444.

Ménard, C., Saussier, S., & Staropoli, C. (2003). L'impact des contraintes institutionnelles sur les choix contractuels des collectivités locales. In *Annuaire 2003 des collectivités locales* (pp. 109–118). CNRS Éditions.

Milgrom, P. R., & Weber, R. J. (1982). A theory of auctions and competitive bidding. *Econometrica, 50*(5), 1089–1122.

Morand, P. H., Mougeot, M., & Naegelen, F. (2001). UMTS: Fallait-il choisir un concours de beauté? *Revue d'économie politique, 111*(5), 669–682.

Moszoro, M. W., & Krzyzanowska, M. (2011). *Implementing public-private partnerships in municipalities.* IESE Business School-University of Navarra.

Moszoro, M. W., & Spiller, P. T. (2012). *Three isn't always a charm: Third-party opportunism, scrutiny, and the (in)efficiency of public contracts.* IESE Business School–Haas School of Business.

Naegelen, F. (1990). L'arbitrage qualité-prix dans les procédures d'appels d'offres. *Économie et Prévision, 96*, 95–105.

National Audit Office (2001). Managing the relationship to secure a successful partnership in PFI projects. Report by the Comptroller and Auditor General.

OECD. (2011). *Water governance in OECD countries: A multi-level approach.* Paris: OECD Publishing.

Piga, G. (2011). A fighting chance again corruption in public procurement? In T. Søreide & S. Rose-Ackerman (dir.), *International handbook on the economics of corruption* (Vol. 2). Edward Elgar.

Potters, J., Rockenbach, B., Sadrieh, A., & van Damme, E. (2004). Collusion under yardstick competition: An experimental study. *International Journal of Industrial Organization, 22*(7), 1017–1038.

Pouyet, J. (2002). Collusion under asymmetric information: The role of the correlation. *Journal of Public Economic Theory, 4*(4), 543–572.

Preston, J., Whelan, G., Nash, C., & Wardman, M. (2000). The franchising of passenger rail services in Britain. *International Review of Applied Economics, 14*(1), 99–112.

Resende, M., & Facanha, L. O. (2002). Privatization and efficiency in Brazilian telecommunications: An empirical study. *Applied Economic Letters, 9*, 823–826.

Robinson, H. S., & Scott, J. (2009). Service delivery and performance monitoring in PFI/PPP projects. *Construction Management and Economics, 27*(2), 181–197.

Rossi, M. (2001). Technical change and efficiency measures: The post-privatisation in the gas distribution sector in Argentina. *Energy Economics, 23*(3), 295–304.

Rossi, M. (2002). *Production Frontier analysis: Electricity distribution sector in South America.* M. Phil Thesis, University of Oxford.

Shapiro, C. (1983). Premiums for high quality products as returns to reputations. *The Quarterly Journal of Economics, 98*(4), 659–679.

Shleifer, A. (1985). A theory of yardstick competition. *RAND Journal of Economics, 16*(3), 319–327.

Sobel, J. (1999). A reexamination of yardstick competition. *Journal of Economics and Management Strategy, 8*(1), 33–60.

Spiller, P. T. (2008). *An institutional theory of public contracts: Regulatory implications* (NBER Working Paper 14152). National Bureau of Economic Research, Inc.

Tangerås, T. P. (2002). Collusion-proof yardstick competition. *Journal of Public Economics, 83* (2), 231–254.

Thanassoulis, E. (2000a). DEA and its use in the regulation of water companies. *European Journal of Operational Research, 127*(1), 1–13.

Thanassoulis, E. (2000b). The use of data envelopment analysis in the regulation of UK water utilities: Water distribution. *European Journal of Operational Research, 126*(2), 436–453.

Tirole, J. (1999). Where do we stand? *Econometrica, 67*(4), 741–781.

Williamson, O. E. (1975). Franchise bidding for natural monopolies – In general and with respect to CATV. *Bell Journal of Economics, 7*, 73–104.

Williamson, O. E. (1985). *The economic institutions of capitalism.* New York: Free Press.

Wilson, R. (1985). Reputations in games and markets. In A. E. Roth (dir.), *Game-theoretical models of bargaining* (pp. 65–84). New York: Cambridge University Press.

Yvrande-Billon, A. (2008). Concurrence et délégation de services publics. *Revue française d'é conomie, 22*(3), 97–131.

The Evolution of Financing Conditions for PPP Contracts: Still a Private Financing Model?

Frédéric Marty

1 Introduction

For public entities, resorting to PPPs[1] may be relevant not only because of the economic advantages it entails (integration of the construction and operations phases, innovation capacity of the private sector, incentive nature and performance orientation of the contract,...) but also for financial reasons. This may seem paradoxical, to say the least, since, in theory, having the private sector assume the debt leads to additional costs compared to a public financing model, realized in principle at a risk-free rate. Despite the difference in interest rates between public and private debt (Arrow & Lind, 1970; Rochet & Martimort, 1999), the financial net impact of PPPs can remain in favor of PPPs. Their initial disadvantage can be counterbalanced by certain benefits that mostly have to do with the predictability of the public entity's commitments and the incentive nature of the contractual structure.

In theory, a PPP protects the public party against cost overruns or delays in the construction and operation phases. Such cost and delay excesses are important hidden costs in traditional public procurement[2] (Domberger & Jensen, 1997). In a

---

[1] While most chapters in this book deal with different aspects of PPPs in the broad sense of the term (traditional procurement, concessions (user-pay PPPs), availability contracts (public-budget pay PPPs), this chapter mostly focuses on availability contracts (as most PFIs in the UK and Marchés de Partenariat in France), and the term "PPP" refers exclusively to them in this chapter.

[2] In a sample of infrastructure projects, Flyvberg (2009) assessed that cost overruns amounted to 20.4% in road projects and 64.7% in rail projects.

F. Marty (✉)
CNRS—Research Group on Law, Economics, and Management (GREDEG)—Université Côte d'Azur, Côte d'Azur, France

OFCE—Sciences Po., Paris, France

Sorbonne Business School, Paris, France
e-mail: Frederic.marty@gredeg.cnrs.fr

© Springer International Publishing AG 2018
S. Saussier, J. de Brux (eds.), *The Economics of Public-Private Partnerships*,
https://doi.org/10.1007/978-3-319-68050-7_4

PPP, the private contractor takes responsibility for these risks since payment flows associated with the contract are independent of its costs but are determined by the availability of the service and the satisfaction of quality and performance objectives assigned by the contract. A PPP enables the public authority to benefit from a fixed-price contract, at least in principle (Laffont & Tirole, 1993). In this respect, it can be considered that the additional financial costs compared to direct public financing are counterbalanced by such a cover. In this regard, additional financial costs can thus be viewed as an insurance premium[3] (Blanc-Brude, Goldsmith, & Välilä, 2009). However, these financial costs, and therefore the level of the premium, closely depend on the conditions of access to the loanable funds market. An increase in the risk premiums required by the investors or a higher cost of resources (due to a credit crunch phenomenon or to a tightening of the prudential rules applicable to banks or insurance companies) may drive this insurance premium to levels that are too high for such a cover to continue to make sense from an economic perspective. In other words, if the cost differential between private and public financing becomes too high, it is preferable for the public entity to limit itself to traditional public procurement and management schemes. It is more efficient for the public entity to remain its own insurer, i.e., to accept to cover itself the potential cost overruns and delays of traditional procurement.

PPP arrangements are also particularly sensitive to the situation in the loanable funds market, not only because of the scope of the investments required but also because of the financial engineering methods they involve. The latter are based on arrangements with strong financial leverage. A substantial proportion of debt (compared to equity) makes it possible to reduce the additional cost of private financing. Indeed, based on the model of British Private Finance Initiative contracts, PPP projects that are most substantial from a financial point of view use project finance techniques. Companies that have formed a consortium to pool the

---

[3]Nevertheless, with PPPs, the public entity cannot really be guaranteed that the payment flows will be predictable from the moment the contract is signed and stable over time. Firstly, contracts quite naturally include price adjustment clauses. Secondly, they are subject to frequent renegotiations (see Chapter "Renegotiating PPP Contracts: Opportunities and Pitfalls" in the second part of this book). Incidentally, the latter may be considered ambivalently. First, renegotiations may proceed from a phenomenon of contractual holdup. Once the threat of competition has been removed, the public entity's contractor may adopt an opportunistic behavior and exploit the gray areas of the contract (which can never be complete in the economic sense of the term) to renegotiate it to its own advantage (see Guasch, 2004). A frequently renegotiated fixed-price contract soon becomes a cost-plus contract, which essentially amounts to a double inefficiency for the public entity, with a risk premium *ex ante* and low incentive quality *ex post*. Renegotiations may also be associated with new requests from the public entity to bring about a change in the service. For the public entity, such requests can generate additional costs that may lead to reevaluate the economic appropriateness of the contract [25% of cost overruns in PPP projects in the construction phase are related to changes initiated by the public authority, according to a study by Standard & Poor's (2007)]. Nevertheless, they can be essential to satisfy the mutability requirement of the public service. Besides, renegotiations are fundamental in a long-term contract to maintain the economic equilibrium of the contract, which is a *sine qua non* condition for the efficiency of the partnership relation.

necessary expertise and financial resources to respond to a call for tenders create a joint company that will be awarded the contract. This *ad hoc* company (also called SPV for Special Purpose Vehicle) is dedicated solely to the contract. Although companies that are at the origin of the SPV (the sponsors) make equity investment, most of the resources of the SPV come from bank or bonded debt. In order to minimize financing costs, the proportion of debt financing must be maximized. Indeed, it is necessary to play on the leverage ratio (gearing) between equity and debt, since the cost of the latter is logically lower, as it is exposed to lower risks compared to those assumed by the shareholders. Indeed, not only is its rate of return fixed, but debt repayment has priority over equity in the event of liquidation. Giving priority to debt reduces the weighted average cost of capital and therefore the cost of private financing. However, the higher the proportion of debt is, the more its repayment. The debt service will absorb a substantial share of the SPV's revenue, thereby equally reducing its ability to cope with operational hazards. Thus, the probability of default increases in proportion to the leverage effect for a given level of risk. The ability to raise debt is thus limited by the investors' risk aversion. If the latter increases, the cost of PPP arrangements rises inexorably.

However, the cost of the debt that is subjected to the risk of default of the SPV—which is known as *project debt*—is limited by two mechanisms. First of all, debt is all the less costly as liquid assets have been abundant in the markets, because of exceptionally low interest rates due to the policy of the American Federal Reserve following the bursting of the dot-com bubble and the 9/11 terror attacks. Then, beyond this favorable macroeconomic context, financial and contractual engineering made it possible, until the 2008 crisis, to implement measures capable of reducing the special purpose vehicle's risk of default. Project finance techniques, which require substantial investment amounts due to the transaction costs incurred, often relied on payment mechanisms based on service availability rather than on user-pay mechanisms (tolls paid by end users for example), since the latter introduced a second type of risk, in this instance a demand-related risk. Here, the two main groups of PPPs become apparent once again, namely, contractual arrangements that fall largely into the category of availability-based contracts (as most PFIs in the UK) and concession arrangements (user-pay contracts).

In this chapter, we aim to trace the evolutions of financial arrangements used in PPP contracts over the last 20 years and to underline how sensitive they are to the conditions of access to the loanable funds market (Bensaïd & Marty, 2013). First, we will show how PPPs were initially developed in a favorable financial context, which allowed them to benefit from abundant and inexpensive funds. Additionally, project initiators could use financial tools limiting the additional cost of private funds compared to sovereign debt. The tightening of the conditions of access to credit following the financial crisis of 2008 had a noticeable impact on the conditions of financial close for PPP transactions. We will therefore assess the extent to which this challenging of the canonical model of PPP financing structures brought about a change in risk allocation between private and public partners. Finally, we will consider the future of the PPP financing model in light of the longevity of the current replacement of traditional bank financing by financing based on insurance funds, investment funds, or pension funds, in the context of regulatory evolutions.

2   A Private Financing Model Introduced in a Favorable Context

PPPs are contracts whereby a private operator takes responsibility for financing an infrastructure and gets its money back by way of an exclusive operation right. While their origin undoubtedly lies in the concession arrangements (called public service delegations) implemented in France since the sixteenth century, as illustrated by the case of the Canal des Deux Mers (Bezançon, 2004), their modern "rediscovery" is indisputably British.

This rediscovery hinges on a double dynamic. The first one has to do with the rise of new public management, especially in the Anglo-Saxon world (Skelcher, 2005). This approach considers that instead of focusing on controlling the regularity of resource consumption (inputs), the main emphasis should be on evaluating policy results (outcomes). As the service provided to the user is the essential dimension at stake, it does not matter whether it is produced by a public or a private entity, as long as its definition and the control of its delivery are carried out by the public authority. Considering the incentives to which private actors are subjected, it seems desirable, in terms of efficiency, to replace the interventionist State by a regulatory State (Marty, Trosa, & Voisin, 2006). The second dynamic that favored the development of PPPs has to do with the phenomenon of *fiscal stress* (Lüder, 1994). Public authorities are faced with a scissor-like movement, with on the one hand growing financing needs to satisfy a strong societal demand for public services and infrastructure and on the other the distinctly growing scarcity of resources available to them, especially because of the loss of taxpayers confidence in the authorities' ability to manage public resources efficiently. This results in lesser acquiescence to tax and a will to limit the public authorities' ability to raise debt, which is in direct contradiction to the ever-growing demand for public goods and services.

Thus, although this is admittedly simplistic, it would be possible to consider that PPPs respond to a logic of a public infrastructure privately financed and managed, in order to prevent the inefficiencies that are viewed as an integral part of public investment and public management. Therefore, it is also a question of preempting the incentive biases highlighted by new public economics in terms of investment project selection but also of cost control and guarantee that the quality and performance objectives will be met. The great public infrastructure projects of the 1980s, such as the Channel Tunnel, already illustrated that logic. The first British PPP, a bridge between Dartford and Thurrock (launched in 1987 and heralding the introduction of the PFI policy in 1992), can be considered in light of Margaret Thatcher's stance on the financing of the Channel Tunnel: *not a public penny.*

In its original sense, the British PFI was, as indicated by its very name, a *private financing initiative*. Indeed, PPPs fall into the category of contracts known as DBFO, which stands for *Design, Build, Finance, and Operate*.

Such private financing made it possible to introduce project finance into the public sphere (Lyonnet du Moutier, 2006). Although this financing technique cannot be found in all contracts, notably because of its excessive transaction costs for projects that only require limited investments, it constitutes an archetypal model highlighting the major characteristics of PPPs, namely, the global nature of the contract, the optimal risk sharing, long-term contractual commitment, and the implementation of financial and contractual engineering aiming to minimize the additional cost of private financing compared to public financing (Iossa & Martimort, 2015).

The first characteristic has to do with the global nature of the contract. PPPs are global contracts because of the pairing of the conception, construction, and operating phases (Hart, 2003) and also because of the fact that the contractor takes charge of financing the necessary investments. The second characteristic consists in contractual engineering that allocates risks in an optimal manner, each of them being assumed by the party that can bear it at the lowest cost, and from an incentive payment mechanism based on performance. Finally, the third characteristic relates to financial engineering techniques aiming to limit the additional cost of private financing compared to public financing. Indeed, we have noted that the latter is theoretically less costly since the State reputedly borrows at the risk-free rate, as it is supposed to be safe from any risk of default. . .

The analysis of these financial aspects of PPPs must be conducted starting from the tension lines between these last characteristics. The lower the additional cost of private financing compared to public financing, the more interesting it will be to have the private sector finance infrastructure through an incentive contract. If the additional cost is high, it will be more difficult for the potential gains associated with the incentive efficiency of the contract to cancel out this differential. Under such circumstances, limiting the additional cost of the PPP would imply that the public entity takes responsibility for a larger share of the risks, which would run counter to the microeconomic logic of the contract.

2.1 The Introduction of Project Finance Arrangements in the Public Sphere

When the situation in the financial markets is "normal," the cost of public debt lies below that of private debt. Consequently, if we distance ourselves from the misconception according to which PPPs are an easy budgetary solution allowing the debt associated with public investments to be borne by the private sector,[4] it

---

[4]For the public entity, private financing can also take on a significant interest in terms of budgetary equilibrium management. As observed by Dewatripont and Legros (2005): "*PPPs could be seen as*

appears that the efficiency gains derived from the incentive nature of the contract must counterbalance the additional cost of private financing. Symmetrically, it is possible to consider that the more limited the additional cost of private financing is, the more projects eligible for a PPP arrangement there will be. Minimizing the (additional) cost of private financing is thus the cornerstone of the PPP financial model.

Considering the fact that equity is exposed to higher risks because it is repaid last in the event of the company's liquidation, but that it is also more remunerative (meaning that the investors require a high internal rate of return on the invested capital), the idea is to minimize its share in the financial arrangement. The higher the share of debt is, the lower the weighted average cost of the invested capital will be. Thus, PPP arrangements are often characterized by an equity share lower than 10% and therefore a debt share higher than 90%. Nevertheless, it should be noted that in practice, PPP contract financing structures do not rely solely on equity and debt, which is exposed to the risk of the special purpose vehicle' default. Between this first category of debt, known as *project debt*, and equity, there are other types of intermediary debt, which do not take priority over project debt in the repayment order.

---

attractive for governments, which try to make their accounts good by (ab)using accounting rules that not correctly capture their assets and liabilities." Indeed, a PPP investment does not affect public accounts—in particular the level of debt—in the same way as an investment realized in the traditional way. Partnership arrangements can appear all the more attractive as they are likely to allow the entity not to consolidate (i.e., recognize) in public debt the amount of investments associated with the financed asset. In times of serious budgetary constraints, recording the infrastructure as an asset in the contractor's balance sheet, and subsequently recording the debt as one of its liabilities, can seem like a decisive advantage for the concerned public authority (Marty, 2007). Resorting to PPPs can therefore appear as a mechanism of public debt derecognition that is all the more expedient as the debt is high and subjected to a ceiling imposed by rules of budgetary discipline (Helm, 2010; Maskin & Tirole, 2008). However, the use of PPPs as an off-balance sheet instrument is only possible to the extent that budget and accounting regulations offer a favorable framework for implementing such derecognition strategies, and one where market operators accept that the asset and associated liability be recorded in the private contractor's accounting statement. The private operators' ability to record the debt in their balance sheet is therefore a first retraction force. A second one has to do with public accounting rules themselves, which must provide a regular, sincere, and faithful image of the public entity's net situation. Paradoxically, the adoption of the International Financial Reporting Standards (IFRS) by private stakeholders has favored a better recognition of the commitments associated with PPPs in public accounts. Indeed, private international accounting standards are based on a control criterion that leads all companies involved in PPP contracts not to recognize them in their accounts. Adjusting to the practices of private actors, combined with a will to translate commitments associated with PPPs, has led the authority in charge of establishing public accounting standards to adopt a standard reflecting the IFRS. In October 2011, the International Public Sector Accounting Standard Board (IPSASB) thus enacted a new standard on the accounting recognition of commitments made by public authorities as part of PPPs (*IPSAS 32—Service Concession Arrangements—Grantor*), established on that basis. As for the UK, it directly implemented the IFRS for the establishment of its public accounts, abandoning its initial accounting standards that proved to be far too favorable to derecognition strategies (Hodges & Mellet, 2012).

It is the case, for instance, of subordinated debt, which is often called "mezzanine debt." As it bears more risks, it is more remunerative than project debt. Subordinated loan can for instance be brought by the sponsors, especially those coming from the financial sphere (versus sponsors from the industrial sphere). Beyond the guaranteed remuneration, it is interesting for sponsors insofar as it reduces the volume of necessary debt. Indeed, it makes it easier to raise traditional debt by presenting potential lenders with more favorable debt/equity ratios, insofar as it is equivalent to quasi-equity. If the share of "normal" debt is lower, it is less likely that its service will not be honored (meaning that it will not be repaid at each due date), and the required interest rate will therefore be lower.

Project debt can come from two sources. First, it can be made up of loans granted by banks. This is the approach commonly used for contracts that only require moderately high investments and do not necessitate loans with very long maturity. However, bank loans are relatively costly, as an additional margin is debited by the credit institution in question. Bond loans can represent a less costly alternative in terms of rate. They also present the advantage of offering loans with significantly longer maturity. However, this requires concluding a public offering, which generates transaction costs that restrict this financing method to PPP transactions of large financial capacity.[5] In the UK, prior to 2008, half of the projects with a capital value exceeding 200 million pounds were financed in this manner. In the favorable financial situation that accompanied the development of PPPs between 2001 and 2008, one of the risks specific to bond loans—namely, the level of subscription to the bonds—was lifted through the use of *syndication* (underwrite and syndicate approach). Under such an arrangement, a financial stakeholder—a credit arranger—may subscribe to the entire issue of debt securities at once. It then sells the securities, taking responsibility for the risk related to bond subscription. This lead arranger provides the corporate issuer with a double guarantee in terms of rate and fund availability.

Beyond the question of the sources of debt, the financial structure of a PPP can take on different forms. Indeed, debt can either be issued by the firm that was awarded the contract or the debt can be issued by the special purpose vehicle (SPV) created for the purpose of the project (Delmon, 2010).

The first type of financing corresponds to a corporate finance. Debt is raised by the winning firm and not by the SPV. The risk premium required by external resource providers will not depend on the risk profile of the project itself but on that of the firm as a whole. If this option presents the advantage of reducing the required risk premium in some cases (to the extent that the firm can be seen as a diversified portfolio of projects and activities), it creates a few difficulties in the case of PPPs. First, it requires the firm to recognize all assets associated with contract performance and the corresponding liabilities in its balance sheet. This can burden its balance sheet with debt and therefore reduce its ability to raise new debt for other projects. Such a phenomenon results in increasing the financing cost

---

[5]If only because this capacity must be rated by financial rating agencies.

of firms operating in the PPP market (and therefore the cost of their tenders) or even in reducing the firms' ability to apply for future contracts. Now, for public entities, it is essential to ensure a sufficient degree of *competition for the market* to guarantee that PPPs can meet their objectives in terms of value for money, bearing in mind that, in such long-term contracts, *competition in the market* is by definition drastically limited (Mougeot & Naegelen, 2007).

As we have already noted, project finance constitutes a particularly attractive alternative for contracts with sufficient financial capacity. Debt is no longer raised by the firm that won the contract but by an entity created for the occasion [sometimes called *ad hoc body*, *special purpose vehicle* (SPV), or *special purpose entity* (SPE)]. This type of arrangement presents several interests in the case of a PPP (Yescombe, 2007). First of all, the global nature of the contract means that, in many cases, no single firm will have all the expertise required to provide all the services at stake. That is why consortia are formed to respond to calls for tenders. Once the contract is awarded, it is only natural for each member to take its share in a joint company. The object of the latter is naturally restricted to the implementation of the contract. It will not engage in any other activity and its existence will come to an end with the PPP contract. In the meantime, it will not engage in internal or external growth strategies, which may always entail poorly remunerative investments and divert the management team from its responsibilities in managing the initial project. Moreover, the fact that the structure is dedicated to a single project makes it far easier for the various stakeholders to control it both *ex ante* and *ex post*, especially external providers of financial resources. Unlike companies involved in several projects, *a fortiori* under financial arrangements of the corporate type (in which project debt is directly raised by the recipient of the contract), such a financing scheme guarantees perfect transparency regarding the cash flows associated with the contract.

These characteristics contribute to the efficiency of the monitoring that can (and must) be implemented both by the public contracting authority and by subscribers to the project debt, insofar as, in theory, the latter's sole guarantee of repayment are the financial flows associated with the proper execution of the contract. Indeed, project finance arrangements are known as *non*-recourse arrangements, in that external financiers have no guarantee for the repayment of their loan other than operational resources.[6] This risk constitutes a powerful incentive to invest enough

---

[6]It would actually be more fitting to use the expression "limited-recourse arrangement," in that the equity capital contributed by the sponsors constitutes a second source of guarantee. The higher the share of the latter in the pool of the special purpose vehicle, the lower the risk of default on debt service. The existence of additional guarantees, provided by sponsors, multilateral financial institutions, or the contracting public authority, is also likely to reduce the probability of the special purpose vehicle defaulting. As we will see in the next sections, the existence of such guarantees admittedly contributes to the reduction of the financing cost—by lowering the risk premium required by investors, but it equally reduces the external financiers' incentives to ensure the strength of the arrangement and the proper execution of the contract. The public authority will therefore be all the more exposed to risks of adverse selection and moral hazard.

resources to be able to assess the strength of the arrangement and business model of the contract *ex ante* and to monitor its execution *ex post*.

Despite the risks taken by lenders in such non-recourse financing arrangements with a strong leverage effect, these project finance techniques make it possible to raise abundant financial resources at a reduced cost. This financial structure makes it easier to implement the due diligence procedure, whereby lenders assess the *bankability* of the project, that is, the firm's ability to generate the necessary income flows to service its debt. Through this assessment, lenders evaluate the risks transferred by the contract to the special purpose vehicle and the ability of the latter to keep them under control throughout the operational phase. The volume and conditions of the financial contribution and especially the required interest rate (i.e., the risk premium) will depend closely on this assessment. The decisive nature of due diligence shows that the contractual risk allocation, as negotiated during the competitive dialogue phase, constitutes a key element not only in terms of efficiency of the public purchase (Engel, Fisher, & Galetovic, 2013) but also to obtain interesting financial conditions. Risk sharing is the cornerstone of the business model of PPPs. This model must not be driven by considerations of accounting off balance sheet treatment but by an allocation of each risk to the contracting party that can best manage it, cover it financially, or absorb it at the lowest cost. Optimal contractual risk allocation is key to minimizing the financing cost. Theoretically, it is reached when each risk is allocated to the party that is in a position to manage it (or insure it) at the lowest cost.

Two conclusions may be drawn from this. An excessive transfer of risk to the private sector is not in the public entity's interest, since it would be at least partly counterbalanced by an additional financial cost. In the same manner, the presence of external financiers serves the interests of the public entity. Indeed, the contract aligns the interests of external financiers with those of the public entity (Iossa & Martimort, 2015).

The ability of the vehicle created by the sponsors to honor its debt[7] also depends on its ability to guarantee the service payments without incurring penalties due to underperformance. The costs associated with controlling the risks of adverse selection and moral hazard, which the public entity must face in a long-term contract, are thus shared with subscribers to the debt securities (Dewatripont & Legros, 2005). However, this effect only comes into play if the funds are concentrated among a limited number of subscribers in order to avoid free-rider phenomena. It should also be mentioned that the presence of an important public investor or the granting of large guarantees by the latter could remove all incentive for investors to incur the—significant—costs of these due diligence procedures.

Thus, project finance techniques make it possible to reconcile the interests of each stakeholder. The public authority benefits from lower rates, which has the

---

[7]A second related advantage has to do with the fact that private investors will be less reluctant than a public decision-maker to reevaluate a project whose costs are becoming excessive (De Bettignies & Ross, 2009).

effect of reducing the annual cost of money (thus strengthening budgetary sustainability). It also draws an advantage from the outsourcing of part of the control costs to external financiers. The latter enjoys better financial security than in the case of corporate financing, because of the transparency generated by the setting up of the special purpose vehicle and the traceability of the ensuing cash flows. Finally, as far as sponsors are concerned, this arrangement makes it possible to preserve the financial debt ratios and to maximize the rate of return on the equity invested in the special purpose vehicle because of the leverage effect between equity and debt. Project finance also presented the advantage—at least until the financial crisis of 2008—of allowing the development of contractual and financial engineering capable of reducing the level of risk to which subscribers to the SPV-issued debt securities were exposed. This protection has an impact on the cost of a PPP. If the SPV has to bear a lesser amount of risk, then the probability of seeing it default on its debt service is lower, and therefore the required risk premium is lower too. The subsequent limitation of the financing cost is in the best interest of the sponsors—who can then maximize financial leverage—and of the public authority—who can minimize the additional cost of private financing and therefore the amount of its payment commitments.

A contractual arrangement can provide a first solution to isolate the SPV from the risk of defaulting on its debt repayment, namely, the technique of back-to-back contracts. In such a model, the SPV subdivides the service into different phases (such as construction, operation, and maintenance) and assigns each of them to a different specialized SPV (subcontracts). If one of these SPVs fails to provide the expected service on time (or at the expected cost), it will have to pay contractual compensation to the main SPV. This compensation must be at least equal to the penalties provided for in the main contract with the public entity (see Fig. 1).

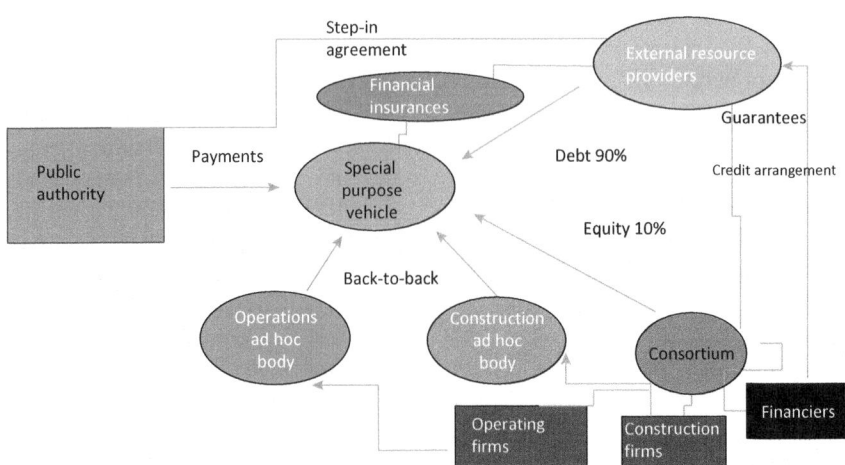

Fig. 1 Project finance arrangement with back-to-back contracts (used for the third unit of French prisons under availability contracts). Source: author

This way, the SPV is protected against the risk, insofar as lenders know that it will have the necessary resource flows to service its debt. Of course, such pass-through contracts rely on the subcontractors' ability to have the necessary funds available in order to pay liquidated damages of an amount equal to the penalties provided for in the main contract. This guarantee is in fact provided by the SPV's sponsors, who get involved jointly in the subcompanies corresponding to their field of expertise. For instance, group members from the building and construction industry will become involved in the SPV in charge of construction, while those specializing in facility management will become involved in the SPV in charge of operations. From a financial point of view, this arrangement helps isolate the various categories of risk assumed by the SPV and can thus reduce the level of required premiums at the global level (Faquharson, Torres de Mästle, Yescombe, & Encinas, 2011). Indeed, investors prefer financial assets characterized by one single category of risk for which their exposure is more easily measurable.

Another option consists in using a different contractual arrangement that reduces the risk perceived by capital providers: the step-in rights, which are the object of a direct agreement between the public entity and lenders. They are measures authorizing the main financiers to replace the contractor with another firm if and when underperformances lead them to question the SPV's ability to repay its debt (Christophe, Marty, & Voisin, 2007). However, such substitution measures imply that there are actors in the market who are able to take over operations, or even to complete construction, which leads to strong assumptions regarding the level of competition for the market and the absence of asset and technology specificity. Indeed, banks must be able to quickly find industrial actors capable of taking over operations (so as to limit transaction costs) and of guaranteeing the proper execution of the contract (so as to obtain the restoration of financial flows coming from the public authority).

Before the financial crisis, these contractual tools were supplemented by a set of financial devices. These made it possible to reduce even more the risk to which external resource providers were exposed. First, there were guarantee mechanisms such as surety bonds and performance bonds. The former were bonds issued by banks that supported the sponsors and guaranteed the repayment of the SPV's debt in the event of a delay in the construction phase. Before the crisis, 15–80% of risks associated with penalties for delay and of the potential loss of profit could be covered this way. We should bear in mind that in principle, in a PPP based on the British model, payments to the public entity are only triggered by service delivery. Throughout contract performance, the risks of default on debt service could also be covered by issuing performance bonds. If the resource flows of the SPV were not sufficient to cover the cost of debt repayment, these bonds could be used to fill all or part of the differential.

Risk faced by lenders could also be minimized by implementing credit enhancement techniques aiming at benefiting from lower interest rates. In the case of bond financing, a rating agency is mandated to give a financial rating to the issued securities. The rating is all the higher as the probability of the issuer failing to repay its debt is low. Therefore, the rating must be as close as possible to the AAA for the cost of debt to be minimal. Now, insofar as the firm bears some risks (otherwise, the PPP would be of no interest), it is unable to go into debt at the risk-free rate. It can nevertheless benefit from an attractive interest rate by resorting to the services of a financial actor that is rated AAA, thus allowing the SPV to enjoy a minimal interest rate (concept of wrapped bonds). This financial actor plays the part of an insurer. It guarantees that it will replace the debt issuer if the latter were to encounter difficulties repaying its debt. Thus, the risk of not getting repaid is no longer assessed in relation to the issuer but to the insurer (which is referred to as a monoline insurer). The premium that must be paid by the issuer is of course all the higher as the initial rating is remote from the AAA. In theory, the arrangement is interesting as long as it is assumed that the insurer enjoys an informational advantage over individual subscribers and is more capable of diversifying risks. Therefore, the profit realized through the reduction of the required risk premium more than counterbalances the payment of the insurance premium (Vinter, 2006).

2.2   Arrangements Facilitated by a Favorable Financial Context

Beyond the question of contractual and financial engineering, the development of PPPs benefited from a particularly favorable financial context, mostly between 2001 and 2008. The policy implemented by the American Federal Reserve after the bursting of the dot-com bubble and the 9/11 terror attacks resulted in the availability of abundant liquidities in the economy. This had the effect of reducing bond rates and therefore of limiting the cost of private financing.

Moreover, the growth of the portfolio of signed PPPs, especially those in their operating phase, had the effect of reducing the risk premiums required by investors for bonded debt issued by SPVs. The issued securities appeared as a particularly attractive category of assets because of their risk–return combination (Blanc-Brude, 2013). Besides, most of the project risks are generally concentrated in the initial construction and commissioning phases. Once these are completed, the risks associated with the operating phase are easy to control. Thus, securities issued by SPVs are particularly interesting for pension funds, which must have stable resource flows available to be able to honor their pension payment commitments. Before the crisis, the attractiveness of debt associated with PPPs favored refinancing operations. These made it possible to reduce the debt rate significantly as long as the operation occurred after the initial stage of risk removal. In PPP contracts, rules governing the distribution of profits associated with such refinancing between the public and private parties are usually included among the initial provisions.

Resorting to structures based on an SPV also generated capital fluidity, which led the initial sponsors to gradually transfer their shares to other investors, which in turn resulted in a significant increase in the internal rate of return of their investment. The UK saw the emergence of a secondary market of securities associated with SPVs, the evolution of which was likely to have a positive impact on the level of risk premiums required by all investors, whether equity investors or subscribers to project debt. This secondary market, which allowed the transfer of the SPVs' equity shares, also had the positive effect of increasing competition for the market, insofar as sponsors did not have to remain "stuck" within their pool throughout contract performance. They thus had the ability to engage and invest in other PPP contracts.

This favorable context was combined with a strong political will to support the development of PPPs, and this in spite of changes in power, as shown by the British case in 1997. The increasing tendency to resort to PPPs, such as could be observed in the UK until the end of the decade, can largely be explained by this political support that led some ministerial departments or local authorities to consider PPPs as the only game in town. Not only did the use of PPPs (availability contracts) make it possible to avoid recognizing the assets and corresponding liabilities in public accounts and to enjoy leeway with regard to the rules determining multiannual capital budgets, but it also allowed some public authorities to enjoy specific guarantee funds, or even additional subsidies. That is why the flow of signed PPPs represented as much as 10–15% of total public investment for several years (see Box 1).

Box 1: British PFIs: 1995–2011 Trends
The development of PPPs in the UK can be summarized in a few figures. Even if we exclude the three contracts initially concluded for the operation of the London underground, which represented a private investment (capital value) of 18 billion pounds, the total amount of private investments in PFIs represented around 62 billion pounds between 1995 and 2011. The budgetary burden associated with payments for PFIs in the performance phase amounted to 8.57 billion pounds for the 2011–2012 fiscal year and should reach 9.75 billion pounds in 2017–2018 (HM Treasury, 2011). As regards trends, Figs. 2 and 3, respectively, give the annual evolutions of the number of signed contracts and of the amounts of capital value between 1995 and 2011. From 1998 to 2007, the number of signed PFIs stabilized to reach a plateau of over 50 contracts per year (Fig. 2). The value of private investments increased until the brink of the crisis (Fig. 3), although one should bear in mind that the Royal Air Force contract relative to aerial refueling tanker aircrafts (FTSA contract) single-handedly represented a capital value of over 2.6 billion pounds in the spring of 2008.

Thus, the financial attractiveness of PPPs led to a distinct reduction in the additional cost of project debt relative to public debt, which rendered a very large number of public investments eligible for these arrangements. Major investments were realized in this form, from the contracts relative to the operation of London underground lines to the Royal Air Force's aerial refueling tanker aircrafts (NAO,

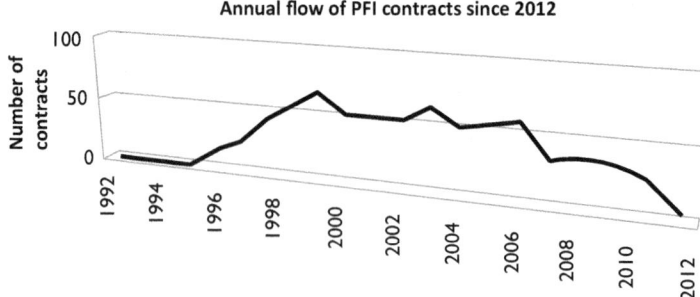

Fig. 2 Annual flow of signed PFIs, 1995–2011. Source: The author, based on data from HM Treasury (March 2012)

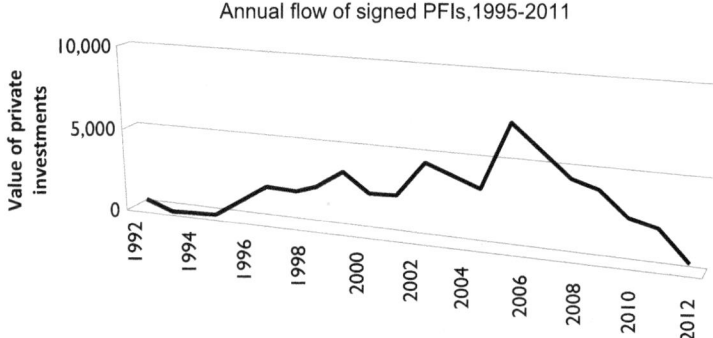

Fig. 3 Annual value of private investments in British PFIs. Source: The author, based on data from HM Treasury (March 2012)

2010a). The contract relating to these aircrafts, which was finalized just before the crisis during the summer of 2008, is particularly emblematic of the great PFI transactions before the sudden reversal of market conditions. Indeed, it resulted in an investment of some 2.69 billion pounds by the private partner. In order to minimize the financing cost, a separate competition was even organized to raise the necessary funds. This specific opening up to competition for the financial section, launched at the request of the public authority in the summer of 2007, concerned two billion pounds (Marty & Voisin, 2008). Consequently, the global nature of the contract no longer necessarily included financing, which was proof of the attractiveness of PPP arrangements for investors. Separating the "financing" section from the other components of the contract allowed the public authority both to reduce its costs by generating competition between numerous financial stake-holders and to receive valuable feedback from the markets about the economic equilibrium of the contract. Indeed, the risk premium required by financial investors theoretically constitutes a good reflection on the risks actually borne by the SPV.

Although the issue of a separate funding competition for PPP contracts is creeping up again, the financial context has undergone radical evolutions since the subprime crisis, which have had significant impact on contract financing.

3 After the Crisis of 2008: New Financial Conditions

The 2008 financial crisis and its aftermath—the European sovereign debt crisis in particular—deeply upset the financing conditions of public–private partnership contracts. Our objective, in this second part, is to highlight the fact that these changes are not only cyclical but structural (Sect. 3.1) and that they entail significant transformations in the general structure of PPP contracts, especially in terms of risk allocation (Sect. 3.2).

3.1 Far Less Favorable Conditions of Access to Financing

While until then the abundance of available liquidities and widespread reduction in risk premiums on debt had favored arrangements with strong financial leverage, the crisis resulted in a deleveraging phenomenon. In broad outline, the drop in the valuation of financial securities (due to growing uncertainty regarding borrowers' ability to service their debt) forces banks to depreciate their debt in their accounts. Indeed, the IFRS accounting standards order that these should be measured at their fair value, which can be their market value or the value established through financial measurement models. Insofar as financial solvency ratios compare credits outstanding with asset value, financial establishments must at best restrict the granting of new loans and at worse transfer some of their debt in the market in order to improve their balance sheet. Such transfers exacerbated the fall in prices, thus initiating a snowball effect that led to a credit crunch phenomenon. From the beginning, this phenomenon resulted in a contraction of bank loans for PPP projects but also in a marked increase in interest rates. In this context, the rise of interest rates required by financial investors is correlated far less with an increase in intrinsic project risks than with the increase in the price of bank liquidities (Hellowell, 2013). Moreover, this phenomenon takes on a structural nature when prudential rules applicable to the banking industry render long-term loans particularly costly (Basel III). Thus, the crisis resulted in a significant increase in spreads, i.e., the difference relative to the risk-free interest rate, as regards project debt but also, as we will see in the third section, debt for which repayment is guaranteed by the public authority itself. As far as project debt is concerned, the margin relative to sovereign debt (i.e., reputedly risk-free debt, at least until the crisis) went from 0.75 to 3% (i.e., from 75 to 300 basis points). Based on assessments from the British National Audit Office, insofar as the net benefit associated with resorting to PPPs amounts to 5–10%, the increase in financing costs by 20–33% can generate an additional cost of 6–8% on projects involving an important construction stage and therefore requiring heavy initial investments (NAO, 2011). Such an additional cost may lead to question the attractiveness of the PPP model for many public investment projects. These British evolutions were mirrored almost identically in France, with a spread on project debt ranging from 60 to 250 basis points between 2007 and 2009 (Dupas, Gaubert, Marty, & Voisin, 2012). Although interest rate differentials have decreased since the height of the crisis, the fact remains that the increase in the price of bank resources is not merely cyclical but turns out to be structural and that the difference relative to interest rates on public debt is heightened even more by public borrowing rates at a historical low (Helm, 2013).

These new financial circumstances result in clear pressures on debt. External resource providers are more and more watchful of the SPV's risk profile and require additional safety margins in terms of cover of the debt service. This rise in risk aversion can lead to an increase in interest rates on bank debt but also in a necessary reduction of its share relative to that of equity or other long-term financing sources. A consequence of this is a significant increase in financing costs, which leads to question the ability of PPP arrangements to achieve value for money. At the same time, replacing debt with equity would result in an excessive increase in the weighted average cost of invested capital and would question the very appropriateness of these contracts.

Even if these additional financing costs do not cancel out the efficiency gains associated with PPPs, the latter lead to an increase in the contracting public authority's payment flows. The public authority, in the context of heavy pressure on public accounts, is likely to question the budgetary sustainability of commitments associated with PPPs, which makes them very similar to ongoing budgetary commitments.

In the same way, the crisis deeply upset the conditions of access to the loanable funds market for SPVs. First of all, the assessment of project-specific risks is conducted in a far stricter way than before. The proposed rates reflect less and less the results of this risk assessment and more and more the constraints relating to the internal procedures of the lenders' investment committees. While at the international level some projects were canceled as a consequence of the crisis (such as a first project of seaward extension of the Monaco Principality over a dozen hectares, in 2008), others came back to traditional procurement schemes (the British Hartlepool NHS Foundation Trust, initially planned as a PFI, turned into a fixed-price construction contract of 450 million pounds). Above all, many projects suffered long delays in reaching financial close. Moreover, projects launched since then have significantly lower financial capacity. The growing share of brownfield projects (combining the renovation and operating phases) to the detriment of greenfield projects (involving new construction) can be analyzed in light of the increase in financing costs. Globally, one can also observe, especially in developing countries and emerging countries, a reduction in the relative share of projects based on concession arrangements—i.e., exposed to a demand risk—compared to arrangements for which payments largely come from the contracting authority, based on service availability or performance (public-budget pay PPPs, or availability contracts) (Cuttaree & Mandri-Perrott, 2010).

Investors' risk aversion is even more heightened by the disappearance of the financial guarantees of SPV-issued debt. As monoline insurers lost their AAA during the 2008 crisis because their financial reserves collapsed due to numerous guarantee calls, credit enhancement through market instruments has then become impossible. Therefore, capital providers require increasing guarantees from both sponsors and public authorities themselves, or even from the relevant Ministry in the case of public institutions such as hospitals or universities, for instance. Doubts about the very solvency of certain public entities drive lenders to demand more protective covenants.[8] *De facto*, this results in a re-internalization of part of the risks by the sponsors and public authority. Consequently, whereas project finance arrangements were traditionally nonrecourse arrangements, they become arrangements with recourse, since the contracting parties' financial exposure is no longer limited solely to equity contributions in the SPV.

For instance, external financing providers usually require of sponsors that they make commitments constituting additional guarantees in the event of adverse evolutions. These can take the form of contingent equity commitments, cost overrun guarantees, or completion guarantees. If unanticipated additional costs arise during the construction or operating phases, or if there are delays in construction, then sponsors commit to injecting new equity into the SPV to guarantee debt service. As for the public authority, it is increasingly required to provide revenue guarantees (Burger, Tyson, Karpowicz, & Coelho, 2009). Such guarantees are likely to compromise the incentive nature of the contract if the contractor is certain to have sufficient resource flows to service its debt and generate a reasonable rate of return on its invested capital.

Above all, the crisis resulted in an obvious transformation in the conditions of access to financing. The financial and contractual conditions of access to private financing are the arrangement parameters that are undergoing the most significant evolutions. Even beyond the cost of resources, the conditions of access to financing have undergone substantial evolutions.

The financing conditions offered by the private sector have experienced a major transformation with the generalization of market flex and market disruption clauses. Before the crisis, the various competing consortia guaranteed fixed-rate financing under conditions defined *ex ante*—thus facing the risk of unfavorable market evolutions during the long phase of contract negotiation and finalization. At the height of the financial upheaval, the private sector could no longer make such commitments. Incidentally, these entailed all the more risks as negotiations with the public entity lasted longer. Therefore, the legislator had to accept the fact that not only would financial bids be limited in time but that consortia would now be allowed to choose not to commit to fixed rates by introducing market flex clauses

---

[8]A covenant is a clause inserted in a loan agreement providing for anticipated debt repayment in case of nonfulfillment of the objectives assigned to the SPV.

in their bids. These led to formulating financial bids in terms of floating rates such as Euribor or Libor plus "x" basis points. Thus, the public entity assumes the risk of an increase in rates during the contracting phase. In the same way, market disruption or market-out clauses allow lenders to withdraw their offer if market evolutions go over a certain rate boundary defined *ex ante*.

Another noteworthy consequence of the change in the financing conditions of PPPs since 2009, which is behind the increase in financing costs, is the virtual disappearance of syndication and the multiplication of club deals. Before the crisis, it was often possible to benefit from syndication mechanisms (the underwriter and syndicate model) whereby a financial stakeholder, often one of the sponsors, subscribed to the entire debt issued by the SPV and then took responsibility for selling it in the market. This way, fund availability was established from the moment the contract was signed and the rate was certain. This mechanism has now become especially difficult, if not impossible to implement, since banks now only have liquidities that are both expensive and limited. Therefore, the syndication model has had to give way to the club-deal model. In the latter, financing is no longer provided by a single financial stakeholder but by a pool of banking establishments. The emergence of club deals is thus a consequence of the drastic reduction in the financial actors' individual commitment power (reduction in the average tickets). It may be necessary to call upon a pool of banks to provide all the capital required by large-scale PPP projects. This phenomenon inexorably results in an increase in financing costs. The reason for this is not only an irreversible alteration of funding competition but also the fact that the financing conditions applied by all banks (especially in terms of rate) are then determined by the marginal bank whose contribution is essential to reach financial close (see Box 2). Banking margins increase mechanically.

Box 2: Club Deals in British PFIs Signed in 2010
In the UK in 2010, the drop in average tickets for PFI transactions led to maximal capital injections of 25–50 million pounds. Thus, the financing of the Kirkcaldy hospital, which required the injection of 187 million pounds, could only be realized through the formation of a club deal including four banks that each contributed 42.5 million pounds (NAO, 2010b). In the same way, no <16 banks were involved in financing the PFI relating to the M 25 motorway, each of which contributed between 25 and 60 million pounds (NAO, 2010c).

One last consequence of the crisis on PPP contract financing should be highlighted, namely, the appearance of the mini-perm phenomenon, or the necessary refinancing of debt when the contract is ongoing, due to the unavailability of funding with sufficient maturity (Dupas, Marty, & Voisin, 2013). The rise in lender risk aversion and market illiquidity means that markets have difficulties granting loans that last as long as PPP contracts, which are inherently long-term contracts when their objects are real estate projects or public service infrastructure. It follows that debt refinancing is necessary in the course of contract performance. These refinancing operations are not new at all. The very long duration of some concession contracts already made it necessary to resort to such operations before the crisis. Likewise, some British PFIs had been subjected to such refinancing over the last decade (NAO, 2006).

The difference lies in the fact that these operations occurred in a far more favorable financial context, marked by falling rates, and in a situation that was specific to the PPP contracts in question, that is, at a time when the initial risks (of construction and commissioning) had been removed. In that situation, the refinancing operation led to clear reductions in the debt rate. What was at stake then was the sharing of benefits among the contracting parties.

Despite this change in the financial context, an "early" refinancing of the initial debt can also be considered to work as a "claw back provision," especially if the initial raising of capital was done under unfavorable financial circumstances. However, if the situation in the markets gets worse in the meantime, if the project encounters difficulties or if trust in the public authority's ability to honor its payment commitments deteriorates, it is not certain that the refinancing will be realized at a more attractive rate, or even that all the necessary debt can be raised. As a consequence, a new risk must be taken into account when drawing up contractual clauses. Insofar as there is no insurance mechanism left in the market to provide financial cover, the public entity and sponsors must share responsibilities in order to face up to the risk of refinancing during contract performance.

Thus, the financial crisis that began in 2008 challenged the PPP model by causing the reappearance of a significant additional cost of private financing and by leading to a reallocation of risks between public and private contracting parties. Insofar as the tools provided by contractual and financial engineering no longer make it possible to cover the largest part of risks, the public entity largely takes over responsibility for these risks. Thus, not only is there now a limited number of projects still eligible (financially) for PPP arrangements, but it is less easy for the public entity to decide to resort to these from an insurance perspective, insofar as it increasingly has to act as last-resort guarantor for the repayment flows of the SPV-issued debt.

3.2 New Contract Balances Based on Risk Reallocation

Thus, public authorities are faced with a dilemma. Project arrangements of the kind that preexisted the crisis would now result in significant additional financial costs. Therefore, less projects would be eligible for PPP arrangements and these would have to be replaced by traditional procurement and financing methods. However, this would be tantamount both to renouncing the potential efficiency gains associated with PPPs and, above all, to financing the investments in question with public funds exclusively, at a time when budgetary leeway is tending asymptotically toward zero. Thus, the necessary perpetuation of the model was brought about by a series of public supports aiming to reduce the risks weighing on subscribers to the SPV-issued debt, or even to limit the very share of this debt in the financing scheme of the transaction (Helm, 2013).

Indeed, there are two major approaches to limiting the cost of private financing and making it easier to subscribe to the SPV-issued debt. The first one has to do with a financial contribution from the public entity to the financial arrangements and the second one with its assuming a growing share of the risks in order to minimize the risk of default on debt service.

First of all, the financial close of PPP transactions is made more easily reachable by a series of public initiatives resulting in a marked relaxing of requirements regarding the conditions of financial contribution. In calls for tenders, applying consortia are no longer required to provide, as early as the tender submission stage, a comprehensive financing plan adhering to strict conditions, in particular in terms of fixed rates. Bids offering partial financing (often combined with market flex clauses, as we have seen) are now accepted. For this reason, the public entity runs the risk of discovering that its potential contractor is unable to raise the necessary funds at a very late stage in the negotiations, which makes it very difficult to go back because of the elapsed time and incurred costs. Symmetrically, refusing such bids would lead, in a difficult financial context, to a drastic reduction in the degree of competition for the market.

In the same way, refinancing risks are shared between public and private parties, so as to accommodate both the public entity's profit sharing in the event of a favorable evolution in market conditions and the limitation of risks faced by the contractor (Dupas et al., 2013). As shown in Fig. 4 below, which comes from a KPMG report (2009), the repartition of cost variations is differentiated according to a series of thresholds. Refinancing benefits are shared based on a 50/50 rule; additional costs are assumed by the private contractor up to 100 basis points; beyond this threshold, increases are shared, with a growing share being borne by the public party.

As a corollary, it is in the public entity's best interest to participate financially in the arrangements, in spite of the budgetary pressures it must face. Indeed, the higher

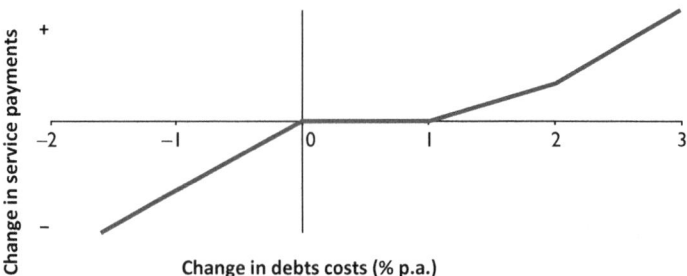

Fig. 4 Rules governing cost and benefit allocation in contractual provisions relating to mini-perms (source: KPMG, 2009, p. 14)

the share of debt, the lower the additional financial cost of the PPP. The aim is therefore both to reduce debt costs (which are all the higher as the SPV is facing substantial risks) and to increase the share of debt in the financing scheme as much as possible. Now, mechanically, the higher the share of debt, the less favorable the debt service coverage ratio will be. Indeed, a high percentage of debt implies that a large share of resources generated by the operation should be dedicated to debt repayment. Therefore, the public entity must assume a part of the risks which would previously have been borne by the private contractor and limit the weight of "project debt."

A first solution consists in financial contributions coming from the public entity itself or from national or international financial institutions (see Box 3). Such contributions can be in the form of equity (public–private cofinancing model), of subordinated debt, or of traditional loans granted at market conditions. These mechanisms have the effect of improving the SPV's financial ratios and so of reducing its financing need and cost.

The change of direction in British policy from PFIs to "PF2s," initiated by a Treasury report published in December 2012 (HM Treasury, 2012), illustrates this evolution. The aim is to reduce the share of project debt, especially bank debt (see Fig. 5), by favoring the entry in the pool of long-term investors, such as pension funds, long-term investment funds, or even sovereign wealth funds, but also by allowing public equity participation, or even by authorizing the subscription to all or part of the SPV's debt, in particular during its refinancing operations. The objective is to take advantage of the low cost of public resources compared to private funds, but also to reinforce control over the SPVs themselves, which have often been criticized for being insufficiently transparent and for granting excessive returns on capital invested by sponsors.

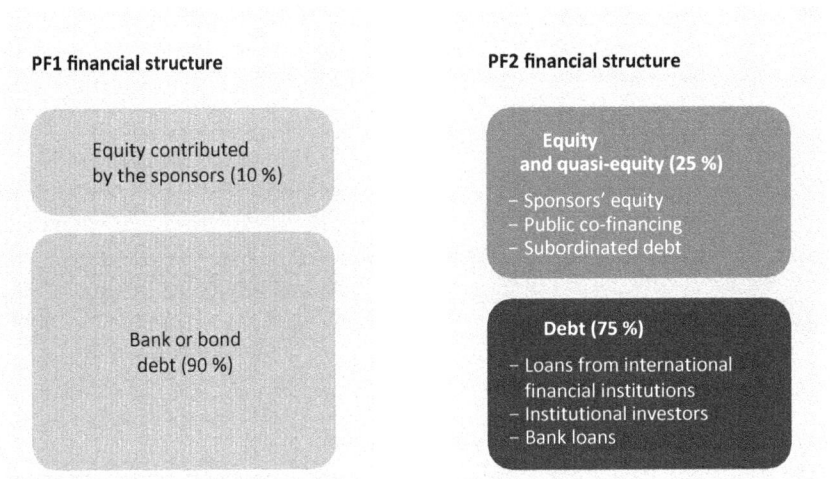

Fig. 5 Evolution of the financing structures between PFIs and PF2s

It should be noted that the rates applied in early 2013 on the project debt of British PFIs ranged from 6.25 to 7.5%. The weighted average cost of capital invested as part of these transactions [estimated based on a leverage effect of 10/90 and on the rates of returns required by equity investors (National Audit Office, 2012)] therefore ranged from about 7.13–8.25%. Simultaneously, the British government raised 20-year debt at <3.5% (Hellowell, 2013).

Public participation can therefore reduce the SPV's financing need and thus the financial cost of the transaction.[9] In the same way, the resulting reduction in financial leverage (the PF2 counts on a 10–25% increase in equity share) makes it possible to reassure the SPV's lenders, insofar as they constitute a safety cushion in case an underperformance of the SPV should result in a reduction in operating revenue flows. However, it is necessary to question the incentive effect which this public participation can have both *ex ante* and *ex post* for third-party financiers. Indeed, the presence of a shareholder with theoretically extensive resources and who cannot accept a default from the firm in charge of the contract (the public entity acts as last-resort guarantor) can lead them to adopt a free-rider behavior and therefore reduce their incentives to invest in due diligence and monitoring procedures at a suboptimal level. Finally, there is also the issue of a possible conflict of interest for an entity that will be both shareholder and customer of the SPV (de Brux & Marty, 2014).

A second solution, less costly in terms of public funds, would be to grant guarantees on debt service payments or on the collection of a minimal revenue flow during contract performance. Such guarantees—which may require the drafting of comfort letters[10]—have the effect of reducing the risk premium required by subscribers to the debt issued by the SPV. Indeed, the debt subscribers have the guarantee, which is provided by the public authority, that the SPV will have sufficient resources available to face up to repayment deadlines (this technique is known as debt underpinning).

However, although this mechanism allows the public entity to limit the financing cost and thus to facilitate the budgetary sustainability of the PPP, it also results in the re-internalization of a substantial share of the risks. Because of this, gains associated with the incentive nature of the PPP contract are potentially reduced (the public entity's payment is guaranteed, whether the contractor honors its

---

[9]Here, the British case is characteristic. Net public investment now only represents 1.5% of the GDP for fiscal year 2014–2015, against 3.3% in 2009–2010. Forecasts for 2019–2020 predict that this effort will represent 1.2% of the GDP, a rate which is admittedly higher than in 1997–1998 (0.5%) but still far below the needs for investment in British infrastructure. This low level of public investment, despite very low long-term interest rates, has to do with objectives of public debt control. The British government's ambition is that investment projects designated as having priority (Infrastructure Pipeline 2014) will be financed up to 64% by private investors, 14% through cofinancing, and only 23% by public funds (Rhodes, 2014).

[10]These are letters of intent whereby banking establishments or auditing companies recommend subscribing to a firm's debt. They vouch for the sincerity of the financial data provided by the firm in question.

commitments or not) and a new budgetary risk arises (if the guarantees are called). We can more or less consider that the public authority replaces mechanisms of credit standing enhancement of the debt raised by SPVs, which disappeared with the 2008 crisis.

Box 3: Guarantees and Direct Official Support: British and French Examples

Starting from 2009, many states set up additional guarantee mechanisms to provide selected consortia with loans—at market conditions—so as to enable them to reach financial close. In principle, this is not to be considered as State aid, which must be the object of prior notification to the European Commission, insofar as conditions governing the allocation of loans are identical to those applied by a private investor (in terms of risk/return combination).[11] The TIFU—Treasury Infrastructure Finance Unit—was therefore created in the UK. It was intended to transfer its debts as soon as the situation in financial markets would allow it. The only time it was called upon was for the GMW PFI contract (Great Manchester Waste), for which it provided the 120 million pounds necessary to the close of a 582 million contract.

Lenders were provided with other types of guarantees in relation to revenue risks. It is the case, for instance, of the guarantees provided for transport infrastructure by the European Investment Bank as part of the LGTT program (Loan Guarantee Instrument for Trans-European Transport Network Projects). For example, the EIB supported the SEA high-speed line (HSL) project (South Europe Atlantic), which in 2011 was subjected to a concession arrangement, not only by way of this guarantee mechanism (to the amount of 200 million euros) but also through a contribution of one billion euros out of a total investment of 7.8. The debt raised with banks amounts to 2.4 billions, i.e., 31% of the debt to which the EIB subscribed at 8%, and the sponsors' equity contributions to 774 millions, i.e., 10% of the necessary funds. The remaining four billions (51%) came from both future revenue and subsidies. The amount of public financing represented 50% of the total investment amount. The guarantee by virtue of the LGTT covered 6.6% of the project debt, which was already covered up to 80% by the State in accordance with reflationary measures introduced in February 2009 (EIB, 2011). Between 2008 and July 2011, the LGTT European program thus

(continued)

---

[11]The absence of government aid is of course debatable in that the contribution of public funds may be seen as a *sine qua non* condition for the contract to reach financial close. This official support can be analyzed as a way to render projects eligible for private investment. It would thus be a way to make up for a market failure. However, the private investor's criterion in a market economy can be all the more easy to satisfy as the mere simultaneity of public and private investments under the same conditions of risk and profitability is viewed as a sufficient criterion.

Box 3 (continued)

supported six PPP transactions in the transport industry, in France, Germany, Spain, and Portugal, for a cumulative amount of ten billion euros. However, *ex post* assessments of the program have led to qualify its actual incentive effect on supported projects (EIB, 2014).

A similar logic was implemented at the French level through the intermediary of the Caisse des Dépôts et Consignations (CDC), a State-owned bank, in favor of PPPs in the field of infrastructure, in the rail industry in particular (Quinet, 2012). The loans thus granted, capped at 25% of the debt (with the exception of the contract relating to the Nîmes-Montpellier bypass, which was the object of a dispensation whereby the rate was increased to 50%), make it possible to benefit from resources with a far longer maturity than bank loans and far lower rates than the margins of 200–300 basis points usually applied (see Table 1 below).

Table 1 CDC financing

Project	Loan from the CDC (m€)	Share in the bank financing scheme	Maturity (years)	Rate (%)	Margin over Euribor (in bp)
High-speed line (HSL) SEA—Tours-Bordeaux (concession, 2011)	757	25	40	4.62 (then 5.48)	51 (then 137)
HSL BPL—Le Mans-Rennes (availability contract, 2011)	254	25	25	4.22	30
HSL CNM—Nîmes-Montpellier (availability contract, 2012)	521	50	25	3.61	90

Source: Quinet (2012)

It should also be noted that in addition to project debt, a second type of debt may be used, namely, debt for which service payments are guaranteed by the public authority. In broad outline, the contractor's financing needs are reduced by facilitating the transfer of its claim on the public entity and by increasing the value of the claim in question through a pay-to-bearer commitment. Indeed, contracting firms can transfer their claims on the public entity to financial stakeholders. The transfer price will naturally depend on how much time is left until the due date, but also on the uncertainty associated with its efficiency, insofar as payment flows should not be taken for granted in an incentive contract. If the service is not provided or the quality and performance objectives are not met, the public authority will not pay at maturity. This risk no longer exists if the latter commits to repaying the debt seller in any case—and if it turns against its own contractor *ex post*.

The existence of a guaranteed debt indubitably causes a problem of incentive. Indeed, it is necessary for the SPV to remain sufficiently *at risk* to prevent any problem of moral hazard. A trade-off appears between minimizing the (additional) cost of private financing and preserving the incentive qualities of the contract, the terms of which are substantially affected by the crisis.

It is thus a mechanism of *accepted debt assignment*, which in France is regulated by the Dailly law. This refers to the share of debt for which the public authority committed to making payments to the bearer, even if it means asking the SPV to pay back the amounts afterward. As a result of the crisis, the threshold for acceptance of debt assignments was raised to about 80% of the financing and investment shares of repayment flows. Insofar as this debt no longer bears the risks associated with contract performance, its rate is far more attractive than that of project debt. Not only has the limit for accepted debt assignments increased substantially since 2008, but, in many cases, project debt itself has disappeared, arrangements being closed using only equity, public subsidies, and Dailly debt (Dupas et al., 2012).

However, it should be noted that although this debt has virtually replaced project debt in the French case, it has also known an increase in spreads that is unexpected for a debt that is theoretically risk free, reaching 180 basis points in 2009. In September 2012, these spreads amounted to 200–250 basis points. The level of this risk premium, which reflects not only the markets' mistrust of sovereign debt but also the increase in bank refinancing costs, especially under the influence of compliance with "Basel III" prudential ratios, raises several issues. First of all, the only reason it is still bearable is because interest rates are at a historical low. An increase in rates could have far-reaching consequences as regards the level of applied risk premiums. Then, the hardening of these financing conditions affects local authorities in particular, for which access to financing is far more difficult and expensive.

As illustrated by Table 2 below, taken from Quinet (2012), these interventions nevertheless have the effect of reducing the risk borne by investors, limiting the need for costly bank resources, and thus reducing the global cost of private financing. In this respect, they have made it possible to ensure the continued existence of the PPP model, despite the crisis.

The limitation of the share of "project debt" of banking origin in the debt itself is all the more necessary as the banks' ability to provide long-term financing was paradoxically hindered by the strengthening of prudential rules (Basel III criteria). Thus, regulatory responses to the crisis result in promoting a type of market-based financing of PPPs that is closer to the American model than to the French precrisis model, in which financing was mostly bank based. In theory, bond financing should not be self-evident, insofar as many financial instruments of credit standing enhancement have disappeared with the crisis. Besides, the risk profile of PPPs is quite specific. Indeed, risks are concentrated in the infrastructure construction and commissioning phases and are very limited once the infrastructure is fully operational. Therefore, investors such as pension or insurance funds, which seek stable

Table 2 Impact of guarantee mechanisms on the financing cost of PPPs

	Public protections	Weighted average cost of capital invested in the project
WACC of the concession without official support		6.5%
Protection of the SPV against traffic risk	Transition from a concession arrangement to an availability contract (payment based on availability)	−80 bp
Protection of lenders during the operating phase	Acceptance of debt assignments (Dailly)	−80 bp
Public loans to reduce the share of bank loans	Loans from savings funds (capped at 25%)	−40 bp
WACC in availability contract with official support		4.5%

Source: Quinet (2012)

and predictable resource flows rather than a high rate of return, may be tempted to contribute only during refinancing phases.

The current efforts of public authorities aim to favor investments by such actors from the initial phase, by providing, as we have seen, guarantees that replace the old market instruments or by creating specific institutional measures. It is the case for instance of the Pension Infrastructure Platform (PIP) in the UK, which was subjected to a memorandum of understanding between the Treasury and pension funds to secure their investments in public infrastructure. The idea is to create a support structure to enable these funds to invest in PF2 projects by providing resources in expertise to assess their risks, among other things. The aim is to bridge the gap between the British situation, where pension funds only invest 1% of their assets in infrastructure, and the situation in Australia and Canada where they invest 8–15% (House of Commons, 2013). In March 2013, the British platform provided its guarantee to ten investors for an investment amount of one billion pounds (Rhodes, 2014). Through such mechanisms, the public partner takes responsibility for the construction risks, which investors may be reluctant to assume (Helm, 2013).

Aside from pension funds, long-term financing can come from insurers. Again, the idea is to compensate for banking establishments' commitment limitations and to direct household savings toward infrastructure financing (OECD, 2014; Quinet, 2012). These arrangements also imply support from public authorities, in order to improve the rating of the debt issued by SPVs to make them eligible for the investment criteria of insurance funds. Such financing schemes have assumed growing importance in the close of PPP transactions, as shown for instance by the case of the L2 ring road in the French city of Marseille in the autumn of 2013. However, they are challenged by the implementation terms of the Solvency II rules, which might, like the situation of banking establishments, hinder insurers' long-term investments. Even more generally, so-called *patient capital* investments in public infrastructure in general and in PPPs in particular are determined by the evolution of the European statutory framework (on this topic, see the European regulation on long-term investment funds, adopted on 17 April 2014). In this respect, experiments relating to project bonds, initiated jointly by the European Commission and European Investment Bank, and to debt funds (i.e., securitization mechanisms), already recommended by the European Commission (2014), possibly foreshadow the implementation of the Juncker plan (Dupas, Marty, & Voisin, 2015). We should bear in mind that the 315 billion euro investment plan will only come in the form of public funds to the amount of six billion euros. Guarantees provided by the Commission will amount to 15 billions and loans from the European Bank to 63 billions. For the most part, financing will come from the private sector.

4 Conclusion

What consequences do these evolutions have on the economic model of PPPs? Theoretical debates about PPPs have often revolved around the two issues of their intrinsic efficiency (Bennett & Iossa, 2006) and of their possible budgetary opportunism (Maskin & Tirole, 2008). To put it briefly, a PPP can only satisfy the value for money criterion, namely, creating value for a public investor, if and only if the gains derived from its incentive nature exceed the additional cost of private financing. Optimal risk allocation results from a balance between transfers of risks to the contractor and risk premiums required by financial resource providers. In the favorable financial context in which PPPs initially developed, it was possible to transfer a significant amount of risks to the contractors without it resulting in exorbitant financial costs. With the crisis, the financial cost of PPPs increased substantially and structurally. Now, either the SPV raises a debt strained by higher rates or it increases the share of equity. In both cases, the weighted average cost of invested capital increases, at the risk of jeopardizing the viability of the partnership arrangement.

All solutions implemented in European countries involved a re-internalization of part of the risks by the public authority. Such re-internalization can be achieved using contractual clauses themselves (risk allocation between the parties, sharing or capping measures for the risks assumed by the private sector) or participation or financial guarantees mechanisms aiming to reduce the risks borne by external resource providers.

From a certain point of view, this re-internalization process, especially in the form of debt service guarantee clauses, exposes the public sector to additional budgetary risks. These risks are all the more unwise as they are contingent commitments imperfectly transcribed into public accounts. Such risks could contribute to an increase in the markets' mistrust as regards the public authority's solvency. From a different point of view, one may also consider that the financial context of 2001–2008 constituted a highly specific parenthesis and that current arrangements rest upon bases that are far more reasonable in terms of the decision to use a PPP and above all in terms of risk allocation (Marty & Voisin, 2006).

It is therefore possible to give a different reading of these ongoing evolutions. Admittedly, the public guarantees thus provided represent budgetary risks, but they are increasingly well recognized in public accounts (the new standards established by the *International Public Standard Accounting Board* on *Service Concession Arrangements* and the procedures of provisions for liabilities associated with the guarantees included in the Chilean finance acts both pertain to this logic). Then, risk re-internalization is also achieved through the close monitoring of markets. Indeed, as debt issued as part of PPPs is more or less guaranteed by the public authority, the financial rating of the debt raised by the SPV depends on that of its public counterpart... Consequently, the public authority is given incentives to ensure that the risks taken are reasonable compared to its own budgetary situation, and so, simultaneously, to guarantee risk allocation in the contract itself. In addition, public–private cofinancing schemes are legitimate for large-scale infrastructure projects characterized by a social return that is higher than the one an economic operator can capture. In this respect, purely private financing schemes may prove to be illusory and a stronger public involvement may be viewed as a return to normal financing conditions in the presence of externalities. However, the question of the appropriateness of resorting to private financing could be raised again when long-term public rates are extremely low in real terms and profits derived from a global contract including financing are challenged. Defending the option of a purely public financing of PPP contracts would mean forgetting the incentive gains associated with the involvement of external financiers whose interests are aligned with those of the public entity and who are capable of reducing the informational advantage enjoyed by the administration's contractor (Marty & Voisin, 2008). Thus, as highlighted by Iossa and Martimort (2015): *"Bundling private finance and operation is optimal when outside financiers have access to some informative signal on the operator's effort level. The power of incentives unambiguously raises and aggregate welfare improves with respect to public finance."*

The impacts of the crisis on the financing conditions of PPPs thus have ambivalent effects. They favor realism in risk allocation and project design. They emphasize the interest of avoiding negotiation phases that are too long (to avoid negative evolutions in financial markets) and highlight the necessity to provide for renegotiation phases so as to allow for the evolution of a contract's financial arrangements.

References

Arrow, K. J., & Lind, R. (1970). Uncertainty and the evaluation of public investment decisions. *American Economic Review, 60*(3), 364–378.

Bennett, J., & Iossa, E. (2006). Building and managing facilities for public services. *Journal of Public Economics, 90*, 2143–2160.

Bensaïd, J., & Marty, F. (2013, November). Pertinence et limites des partenariats public-privé: une analyse économique. *Prisme, 27*. Paris: Centre Cournot, 77 p. Online http://www.centre-cournot.org/?wpfb_dl=139

Bezançon, X. (2004). *2000 ans d'histoire du partenariat public-privé pour la réalisation des équipements et services collectifs* (285 p). Paris: Presses de l'École nationale des Ponts et Chaussées.

Blanc-Brude, F. (2013, January). *Towards efficient benchmarks for infrastructure equity investments. A review of the literature on infrastructure equity investment and directions for future research* (86 p). EDHEC-RISK Institute.

Blanc-Brude, F., Goldsmith, H., & Välilä, T. (2009). A comparison of construction contract prices for traditionally procured roads and PPPs. *Review of Industrial Organisation, 35*(1 & 2), 19–40.

Burger, P., Tyson, J., Karpowicz, I., & Coelho, M. D. (2009). *The effects of the financial crisis on public-private partnerships* (IMF Working Paper, no 09/144, 24 p).

Christophe, J., Marty, F., & Voisin, A. (2007, April). Le financement des contrats de partenariats public-privé. *Contrats Publics – L'actualité de la commande et des contrats publics*, pp. 28–35.

Commission européenne. (2014). *Communication sur le financement à long terme de l'économie européenne*. COM(2014) 168 final, 27 March.

Cuttaree, V., & Mandri-Perrott, C. (2010). *Public-private partnerships in Europe and Central Asia – Designing crisis-resilient strategies and bankable projects* (140 p). World Bank.

De Bettignies, J. E., & Ross, T. (2009). Public private partnerships and the privatization of financing: An incomplete contract approach. *International Journal of Industrial Organization, 27*, 358–368.

de Brux, J., & Marty, F. (2014). IPPP – Risks and opportunities: An economic perspective. *European Procurement and Public-Private Partnership Law Review, 2014-2*, 113–125.

Delmon, J. (2010). *Partenariats public-privé dans le secteur des infrastructures* (156 p). PPIAF, World Bank.

Dewatripont, M., & Legros, P. (2005). Public-private partnerships: Contract design and risk transfer. *European Investment Bank Papers, 10*(1), 121–145.

Domberger, S., & Jensen, P. (1997). Contracting out by the public sector: Theory, evidences, prospects. *Oxford Review of Economic Policy, 13*, 67–78.

Dupas, N., Gaubert, A., Marty, F., & Voisin, A. (2012, January). Les partenariats public-privé post crise financière. Évolution des conditions de financement des contrats et répercussion sur l'allocation des risques. *Gestion et Finances Publiques, 1-2012*, 51–59.

Dupas, N., Marty, F., & Voisin, A. (2013, January–March). Maturité des financements et contrats de partenariats public-privé: les enjeux du refinancement à mi-parcours. *Politiques et Management Public, 30*(1), 113–130.

Dupas, N., Marty, F., & Voisin, A. (2015, March–April). Investisseurs en capital patient et financement de long terme des infrastructures publiques. *Gestion et Finances Publiques, 3–4*, 107–113.

Engel, E., Fisher, R., & Galetovic, A. (2013). The basic public finance of public-private partnerships. *Journal of the European Economic Association, 11*, 83–111.

European Investment Bank. (2011, July). *Loan Guarantee Instrument for TEN-T Projects – Mid-term review 2011*. Luxembourg.

European Investment Bank. (2014, April). The *Loan Guarantee Instrument for TEN-T Projects (LGTT) – An evaluation focusing on the role of the EIB in the implementation of the instrument.* Operations Evaluation Synthesis Report, Luxembourg.

Faquharson, E., Torres de Mästle, C., Yescombe, E. R., & Encinas, J. (2011). *How to engage with the private sector in public-private partnerships in emerging markets?* (178 p). PPIAF, The World Bank.

Flyvberg, B. (2009). Survival of the unfittest: Why the worst infrastructure gets built – And what we can do about it. *Oxford Review of Economic Policy, 25*(3), 344–367.

Guasch, J.-L. (2004). *Granting and renegotiating infrastructure concessions*. Washington, DC: World Bank.

Hart, O. (2003). Incomplete contracts and public ownerships: Remarks and application to public-private partnerships. *The Economic Journal, 113*(486), C69–C76.

Helm, D. (2010), "Infrastructure and Infrastructure Finance: the Role of the Governement and the Private Sector in the Current World", European Investment Bank Papers, *Public and Private Financing of Infrastructures - Policy Challenges in Mobilizing Finance*, pp.8-27

Hellowell, M. (2013). PFI redux? Assessing a new model for financing hospitals. *Health Policy, 113*(1–2), 77–85.

Helm, D. (2013). British infrastructure policy and the gradual return of the state. *Oxford Review of Economic Policy, 29*(2), 287–306.

Her Majesty Treasury. (2011, March). *PFI signed projects*.

Her Majesty Treasury. (2012). *A new approach to public private partnerships*. London.

Hodges, R., & Mellet, H. (2012). The UK private finance initiative: An accounting retrospective. *British Accounting Review, 44*, 235–247.

House of Commons. (2013, October). *Infrastructure policy* (note no SN/EP/6594).

Iossa, E., & Martimort, D. (2015). The simple microeconomics of public-private partnerships. *Journal of Public Economic Theory, 17*(1), 4–48.

KPMG. (2009). *Financing Australian PPP Projects in the global financial crisis* (24 p). KPMG.

Laffont, J.-J., & Tirole, J. (1993). *A theory of incentives in procurement and regulation*. Cambridge: MIT Press.

Lüder, K. (1994). The 'contingency model' reconsidered: Experiences from Italy, Japan and Spain. In E. Buschor & K. Schedler (dir.), *Perspectives on performance measurement and public sector auditing*. Bern: Paul Haupt Publishers.

Lyonnet du Moutier, M. (2006). *Financement sur projet et partenariats public-privé* (317). Paris: EMS.

Marty, F. (2007, October). *Partenariats public-privé, règles de discipline budgétaire, comptabilité patrimoniale et stratégies de hors bilan* (working paper OFCE, no 2007-29, 48 p).

Marty, F., & Voisin, A. (2006). L'évolution des montages financiers des PFI britanniques: La montée des risques. *Revue française de finances publiques, 94*, 107–120.

Marty, F., & Voisin, A. (2008, February). *Partnership contracts and information asymmetries: From competition for the contract to competition within the contract?* (Working paper OFCE, no 2008-06, 29 p).

Marty, F., Trosa, S., & Voisin, A. (2006). *Les partenariats public-privé*. Paris: La Découverte, "Repères".

Maskin, E., & Tirole, J. (2008). Public-private partnerships and government spending limits. *International Journal of Industrial Organization, 26*(2), 412–420.

Mougeot, M., & Naegelen, F. (2007). Was Chadwick right? *Review of Industrial Organisation, 30* (2), 121–137.

National Audit Office. (2006, April). *Update on PFI debt refinancing and the PFI equity market*. HC 1040, session 2005–2006.

National Audit Office. (2010a, March). *Ministry of defence – Delivering multi-role tanker aircraft capability*. Session 2010–2011.

National Audit Office. (2010b, July). *Financing PFI projects in the credit crisis and the Treasury's response* (34 p). HC 287, session 2010–2011.

National Audit Office. (2010c, November). *Procurement of the M25 – Private finance contract* (37 p). HC 566, session 2010–2011.

National Audit Office. (2011, April). *Lessons from PFI and other projects* (31 p). HC 920, session 2010–2012.

National Audit Office. (2012, February). *Equity investment in privately financed projects* (36 p). HC 1792, session 2010–2012.

OECD. (2014, May). *Institutional investors and long term investment – Project report* (32 p).

Quinet, A. (2012). Le financement des infrastructures. *Revue d'économie financière, 4-2012*, 201–219.

Rhodes, C. (2014, December 9). *Infrastructure policy* (note sn/EP/6594). House of Commons.

Rochet, J.-C., & Martimort, D. (1999). Le partage public-privé dans le financement de l'économie. *Revue française d'économie, 14*(3), 33–77.

Skelcher, C. (2005). Public-private partnerships and hybridity. In E. Ferlie, L. E. Lynn, Jr., & C. Pollitt (dir.), *The Oxford handbook of public management* (pp. 347–370). Oxford: Oxford University Press.

Standard & Poor's. (2007). *Anatomy of construction risk: Lessons from a millennium of PPP experience*. London: Standard & Poor's.

Vinter, G. D. (2006). *Project finance: A legal guide*. London: Thomson, Sweet & Maxwell.

Yescombe, E. R. (2007). *Public-private partnerships: Principles of policy and finance*. London: Butterworth-Heinemann.

Part II
An Empirical Analysis of PPPs

The Relative Efficiency of Competitive Tendering

Laure Athias and Lisa Chever

1 Introduction

The selection of private partners, as part of traditional public procurement contracts, concession contracts (user-pay PPPs), or availability contracts (public-budget pay PPPs), is generally done by introducing competition for the market between operators, defined as the auctioning of the right to serve the market.

Theoretical arguments in favor of this selection method have largely been developed in the literature since the rediscovery by economists of the principle of "competition for the field," initially put forward by Chadwick (1859) and taken over by Demsetz (1968). Indeed, competition for the market, or *ex ante* competition, is seen as a way to introduce market mechanisms in sectors exhibiting natural monopoly characteristics, which is claimed to be beneficial for customers/users in terms of service prices and quality, as well as in terms of the bidders' reactivity to demand.

Moreover, competitive calls for tenders are seen as the most transparent award mechanism, i.e., the one granting the less amount of discretionary power to public authorities and, consequently, reducing risks of corruption and favoritism. This is the reason why European directives largely encourage public administrations to use open tendering procedures. The open tender has thus become, both in practice and in the academic world, the reference procedure, both most widely used and most studied.

L. Athias (✉)
University of Lausanne, IDHEAP, Lausanne, Switzerland
e-mail: laure.athias@unil.ch

L. Chever
Associate research fellow at Sorbonne Business School, Paris, France
e-mail: lisa.chever@gmail.com

© Springer International Publishing AG 2018   113
S. Saussier, J. de Brux (eds.), *The Economics of Public-Private Partnerships*,
https://doi.org/10.1007/978-3-319-68050-7_5

From one country to another, as well as from one industry to another, there are substantial variations in the implementation of calls for tenders. For instance, criteria used to select the winner are very varied: one may choose to select the lowest tenderer (which corresponds, in economics, to the concept of "first-price auctions"), the second lowest tenderer ("second-price auctions"), or the average price. Overall, the most widely used method seems to be the "best-value auction" or "cost-effective bid," which includes criteria of price but also of quality. The open call for tenders thus seems to go from a simple mechanism based mostly on price to a more complex mechanism including qualitative dimensions.

This evolution is a direct echo of increasingly strong criticisms from a number of academic studies regarding the efficiency of open calls for tenders. Indeed, a growing part of the empirical literature highlights the difficulties in organizing competitive calls for tenders and taking advantage of the theoretical benefits of competition for the market. Problems relating both to requirements definition and forecast and to information asymmetries between contractors and public authority are likely to entail deferred costs: a renegotiation of the initial agreement or a reduction in the quality of the goods or service provided. Such difficulties may lead public authorities to resort to alternative award methods, which do not rely exclusively on competitive mechanisms. For instance, procedures involving a negotiation phase would allow, on the one hand, to better apprehend the qualitative dimensions of transactions and, on the other hand, to improve mutual feedbacks.

The aim of this chapter is to draw up an assessment of the results obtained in the empirical literature regarding award procedures. After outlining the various award methods available to public authorities in the first part, we will attempt, in the second part, to describe the factors that are likely to alter the efficiency of competitive calls for tenders. Finally, the third part will introduce the results found in the literature on the relative efficiency of the various methods for selecting private operators.

2 Descriptive Analysis of the Various Methods for Selecting Private Operators

There are different ways of selecting a private partner. In Europe, these various methods are largely defined by the European directives[1] responsible for standardizing the award rules of the different member States. Overall, this statutory framework tends to encourage open tendering procedures, which are thought to be both more transparent and more efficient. Indeed, a classical finding of auction theory, which for a long time formed the frame of reference for the analysis of PPP award, establishes the existence of a positive correlation between award efficiency and the

---

[1]The so-called special sectors directive 2004/17 on contracts relating to the water, energy, transport, and postal services sectors. Directive 2004/18 for "classical" public works, supply, and service contracts.

number of bidders (Bulow & Klemperer, 1996). In general, public authorities nevertheless have a certain degree of latitude in adapting the award procedure to the object up for auction.

2.1   A Variety of Procedures

Based on statistics derived from European databases, we can distinguish eight types of procedures.[2] Figure 1 indicates the frequency of use of each type of procedure between 2008 and 2012, in the award of contracts subjected to the two directives that used to regulate public procurement (2004/17 and 2004/18). Clearly, public buyers resort most massively to open tendering procedures (designated by the acronym OPE in Fig. 1): they were used to award over three-quarters of all contracts this way.

Then come the restricted procedures, followed by negotiated procedures (with or without publication, i.e., with or without the prior publication of a notice to inform potential bidders of the call for tenders). The definition of these three procedures is given in European Directive 2004/18[3]:

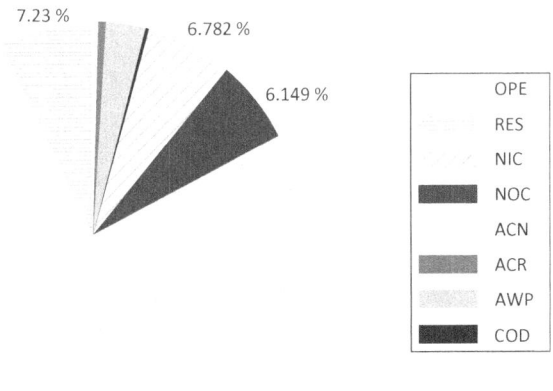

Fig. 1 Share of the various award procedures used in the EU in 2008–2012 (in terms of number of contracts). Source: Chong et al. (2014)—Statistics based on 600,026 contracts regulated by EU directives and listed in the European TED database, in 2008–2012. *OPE* open procedure; *RES* restricted procedure; *NIC* negotiated procedure with prior publication; *NOC* negotiated procedure without prior publication; *ACN* accelerated negotiated procedure; *ACR* accelerated restricted procedure; *AWP* award without prior notice; *COD* competitive dialogue

---

[2]These statistics are computed using the TED database (Tenders Electronic Daily), developed from projects published in the Official Journal of the European Union.

[3]See pages 14 and 15 of the European Directive 2004/18 on public procurement.

1. "'Open procedures' means those procedures whereby any interested economic operator may submit a tender";
2. "'Restricted procedures' means those procedures in which any economic operator may request to participate and whereby only those economic operators invited by the contracting authority may submit a tender";
3. "'Negotiated procedures" means those procedures whereby the contracting authorities consult the economic operators of their choice and negotiate the terms of contract with one or more of these,"

Thus, unlike open procedures, negotiated procedures allow the parties to discuss the project before the contract is awarded; as for restricted procedures, they make it possible to limit the number of bidders.

However, the prevalence of open procedures is less significant if we look at the distribution of procedures when contracts are weighted by their value. The frequency of use of open tendering procedures then drops to 50%. This decrease seems to result from a substitution effect: indeed, given the changes in proportion between graphs 1 and 2, we can see that public authorities tend to favor negotiated and restricted procedures for contracts with high value (Fig. 2).

A parallel can be drawn between this substitution effect and recommendations from the theoretical literature (introduced in Chapter "An Economic Analysis of Public–Private Partnerships" of the first part of this book) according to which the more complex the goods or services to be provided,[4] the less suitable open

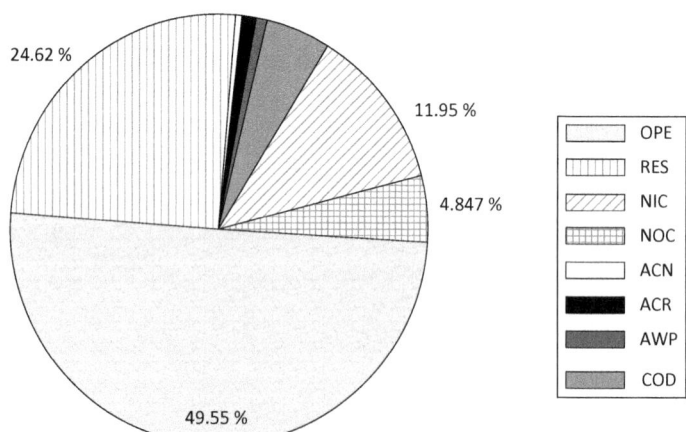

Fig. 2 Share of the various award procedures used in the EU in 2008–2012 (computed in terms of contract value). Source: Chong et al. (2014)—Statistics based on 600,026 contracts regulated by EU directives and listed in the European TED database, in 2008–2012. *OPE* open procedure; *RES* restricted procedure; *NIC* negotiated procedure with prior publication; *NOC* negotiated procedure without prior publication; *ACN* accelerated negotiated procedure; *ACR* accelerated restricted procedure; *AWP* award without prior notice; *COD* competitive dialogue

---

[4]In theory, goods or services of substantial proportions will be more complex on average than goods or services of modest proportions.

tendering procedures will be to select a provider. In addition, the number of firms that are likely to provide the goods or services probably decreases with the size of the contract up for auction, thus reducing the benefits of open procedures.

2.2   Degrees of Competition and Types of Procedure

The degree of competition can be approximated by the number of tenderers. It varies depending on the type of procedure and the economic sector under consideration. According to the statistics listed in the TED European database, over the period 2008–2012, the average number of bidders was 5.5 for open procedures, 6 for restricted procedures, 4.8 for negotiated procedures with publication, and 1.6 for negotiated procedures without publication. Nevertheless, giving a direct interpretation of these figures is a delicate task. Indeed, on the one hand, the number of tenderers may be influenced by the choice of procedure; on the other hand, the choice of procedure itself may be influenced by public authorities' forecasts as to the number of bidders. In the analysis of economic issues in general and of PPP auctioning in particular, one often comes across situations in which the direction of causality is ambiguous. Economists then talk about an endogeneity problem. Their empirical analysis involves resorting to specific data analysis techniques, which will be mentioned in the third part of this chapter.

Information relating to the number of tenderers is not generally disclosed to the public, so that it is not possible to obtain exhaustive data for each industry. Thanks to the work of sector regulatory authorities and to the opening of databases to researchers, we can nevertheless provide a few additional figures regarding the apparent levels of competition in various industries.

Thus, in the French water industry, the *Observatoire des services publics d'eau et d'assainissement* (2013) reports that in 2009, competitive tendering procedures generated an average of 3.8 applications and 2.7 tenders.[5] On a more qualitative level, we can observe that, in about 80% of cases, contracting authorities feel that they *"enjoy genuine competition."* Here, it seems quite relevant to approximate competitive intensity by the number of bidders, since contracting authorities are more likely to state that they perceive genuine competition when the number of tenderers is high (Table 1).

In the construction industry, several academic works provide information about the number of bidders in various countries. Chong, Klien, and Saussier (2014) study the 77,188 public works contracts awarded between 2005 and 2007 in France and

---

[5]Calls for tenders are generally organized into two phases. The first one is the application phase, which consists in the firms sending documents relating to their specific characteristics (turnover, number of employees, past experiences, etc.). The second one is the tendering phase, which consists in sending the qualitative and price-related elements corresponding to the need advertised by the contracting authority. Thus, the number of applications cannot be superior or equal to the number of tenders.

Table 1 Impression of competition and number of tenders and applications in the French water industry in 2009

Impression of competition	Yes	No
Average number of applications	3.8	2.7
Average number of tenders	3	1.3

Source: *Observatoire des services publics d'eau et d'assainissement*—Impact of competitive tendering procedures on water and sanitation services in 2009 and 2010

indicate that public buyers received more than six tenders on average. Bajari, Houghton, and Tadelis (2014) focus on a sample of 819 motorway construction projects in California over the 1999–2005 period and find that, on average, 4.47 bidders submitted a tender. Once more, the simple variations observed between sectors or countries may be ambivalent and fail to provide, alone, any clear information about the degree of competition. As an example, the work of Coviello and Mariniello (2014), focusing on 31,610 Italian public works contracts awarded between 2000 and 2005, shows that auctions generated an average of 36.1 bidders per project! At first glance, one could be tempted to conclude that the Italian construction industry is extremely competitive. In reality, other factors seem more likely (or at least, as likely) to explain this figure (see Box 1).

Box 1: Open Auctions and Competitive Incentives: The Case of Average-Price Auctions in Italy

The ability of calls for tenders to stimulate competitive forces is highly dependent on the way in which firms react to the incentives they are given. Average-price auctions, analyzed by Conley and Decarolis (2013), constitute a striking example of auctions giving rise to strategic behaviors on the part of tendering firms.

The particularity of average-price auctions is that the winner is selected by an algorithm. This algorithm results (more or less) in the contract being awarded to the firm that submitted the tender with the price that is closest to the average (of all proposed prices).

This type of procedure, although marginally used, is still present in several countries, including Chile, China, Colombia, Italy, Japan, Peru, Malaysia, Switzerland, Taiwan, and the USA.

Conley and Decarolis (2013) focus more particularly on firms' strategic behaviors in Italy, where average-price auctions were used massively from 1999 to 2006 (the implementation of European directives then limited their use). According to the authors, this type of auction introduces a "collusive mechanism": insofar as the winner is the one that submitted the bid closest to the average, the authors suspect that it is in the firms' interest to coordinate their entry and prices in order to influence the said average and thus manipulate the auction result. If the rationality of such a strategy is effective, this

(continued)

Box 1 (continued)

type of auction should be characterized by a high number of bids: "piloting" bids (which aim to pilot the average) and "real" bids (which try to get as close as possible to the average). Simple descriptive statistics support the authors' argument: whereas contracting authorities receive an average of seven bids when resorting to first-price auctions, they receive an average of 51 with average-price auctions! Additionally, the econometric tests realized by Conley and Decarolis confirm the idea that groups of firms have repeatedly colluded to coordinate their participation.

In the end, many factors are likely to affect the level of competition. Therefore, it is not a parameter on which public authorities may rely on consistently. Although open competition is very efficient to award goods or services with simple characteristics in a context where there are many potential bidders, this procedure is not always easy to implement. In the next section, we propose to focus on the limitations associated with the implementation of open competitive tendering procedures.

3 Difficulties in Implementing Open Calls for Tenders

The economic literature on the choices of selection methods has highlighted the fact that many factors are likely to alter the efficiency of open competition.

3.1 Uncertainty and the Cost of Participating in Calls for Tenders

The efficiency of the tendering mechanism depends first and foremost on the buyer's ability to specify the object of the call for tenders accurately. Indeed, potential tenderers may be discouraged from participating in an ill-specified call for tenders because of the cost of information retrieval they would have to bear in order to respond to it. Yet the task is not an easy one for public authorities dealing with calls for tenders for public goods or services contracts. Indeed, they have to consider not only quantitative criteria, such as the proposed price, but also more qualitative criteria such as sustainability, safety, environmental impact, aesthetics, etc. They are thus faced with many questions: based on which criteria should contracts be awarded? How can tenders involving both quantitative and qualitative dimensions be compared? Thus, specifying the contract terms, and consequently determining what exactly is expected from the selected operator, is not an easy task, which can entail prohibitive costs of operator selection for public authorities and participation-related costs for operators. As an example, in their work on the reform of British railways, Preston, Whelan, Nash, and Wardman (2000) estimated the median cost of preparing a tender submission for applicants at 0.75 million pounds. In France, in the urban public transport industry, the "competition stimulation fund" (which was created in return for the authorization of a merger between two major operators, namely, Veolia and Transdev) provides for the payment of a compensation to nonselected applicants ranging from 50,000 to 300,000 euros, depending on the turnover of the network. Besides, a study conducted by the UK National Audit Office (NAO, 1998) indicates that PFI contracts are characterized by a higher degree of complexity than traditional short-term contracts relating to the provision of a service or infrastructure. The study stresses the fact that, during the tender procedure, such complexity generates transaction costs that are particularly high and often underestimated by public authorities. The study mentions the example of the real estate development project of the Newcastle NHS department (1999), for which the costs associated with contract conclusion had initially been estimated at 397,000 pounds, before being reevaluated 6 months later at 1.7 million pounds, to reach a final amount of 4.4 million pounds, that is, over 11 times the initial amount. Over half of this cost overrun (2.6 million pounds) can be explained by the fees of consulting firms in the financial and legal fields. Likewise, another study conducted by the British National Audit Office, published in 2004, indicates that conclusion costs for the PFI contract relating to the development of the London underground had first been valued at 150 million pounds before finally reaching 455 million pounds, that is over three times the budgeted amount. This cost overrun is due in large part to the reimbursement of costs incurred by the bidders (in the range of 275 million pounds).

Similarly, Warren (2014) shows both theoretically and empirically that the degree of contract completeness may depend not on the complexity of the underlying project but on the availability of public officers. Thus, overloaded public officers tend to opt for a lower degree of contractual completeness and, consequently, to resort less often to competitive calls for tenders. And the marginal effect is significant: an increase in 10% of the number of contracting public officers increases the probability of resorting to an open competitive procedure by 10% and lowers the probability of resorting to a restricted procedure by 33%. This has to do with the fact that an imprecise specification of the object up for auction, i.e., of the contract terms, may affect the expected benefits of the opening up to competition[6]: on the one hand, because it may dissuade potential applicants from taking part in the auction, for fear of the contract being renegotiated and of finding themselves subjected to the public authority's opportunism (Zupan, 1989a, b), and on the other hand, because it may lead applicants to include high risk premiums in their tenders. In their study on motorway construction and maintenance contracts in California, Bajari et al. (2014) show that applicants to calls for tenders take contractual

---

[6]Warren (2014) claims that public officers anticipate such effects and therefore do not choose the open procedure.

incompleteness into account in their proposals, and they estimate that risk premiums included by applicants to cover the potential costs of contract adaptation represent on average 10% of the total value of their tenders. Another disadvantage of these uncertainties is that the selected operator may not be the most efficient but the most opportunistic or optimistic. In that case, one talks about a problem of adverse selection.

3.2 Uncertainty and Adverse Selection

The opening up to competition "for the market" may be subjected to problems of adverse selection of various kinds. Once the operator is selected and the contract concluded, the relationship between the public authority and the operator in place is one of bilateral monopoly. As highlighted in the first part of this book, this relationship of dependency creates holdup opportunities for both contracting parties, which may result in renegotiations that are costly and unjustified from a social point of view. Now, such opportunistic renegotiations may challenge the efficiency of an *ex ante* competitive call for tenders. Indeed, if bidders anticipate that such renegotiations might allow them to prevent any loss *ex post*, they are given an incentive to submit abnormally low tenders, i.e., tenders containing promises that will be difficult to keep, for the sole purpose of winning the contract.[7] Thus, the operator with the best lobbying and renegotiation capacities will win the call for tenders, even though it is not the most efficient candidate. This problem of adverse selection will be all the more significant as the contract in question is subjected to uncertainty problems (for instance, when service obligations are ill-specified).

Thus, this issue of adverse selection results in abnormally low bids. Both the press and empirical studies suggest that this is a frequent phenomenon, in developed countries as in developing countries. For instance, on November 9, 2011, French newspaper Le Monde ran as a headline: "Abnormally low tenders are in a bad state" ("*Les offres anormalement basses prennent du plomb dans l'aile*") on the occasion of the signature of a charter between the French Building Federation (*Fédération française du bâtiment*) and the Association of French Mayors (*Association des maires de France*) to detect and handle abnormally low tenders (ALTs) in public procurement. This charter starts from the observation that "these ALTs have become legion in the building and construction industry" and recommends using a mathematical method to try and detect ALTs based on the average of received tenders. For instance, it indicates that tenders that are over 20% below this average should be dismissed. One of the main advantages of this charter is also to protect public authorities at the origin of the call for tenders (also known as the project

---

[7]This type of strategic behavior on the part of tenderers is known as a "low-balling strategy."

owner) against any legal recourse on grounds of corruption or favoritism in the event of a rejection of the lowest tenders. In this regard, the Italian experience provides valuable lessons. Between 2000 and 2006, some public authorities switched over from a selection method of the private firm based on the tender with the price that is closest to the average of all tenders (See Box 1) to a selection method based on the best price. Decarolis (2014) uses this change to assess the effect of these two open competition procedures on winning bids, as well as on performance criteria (compliance with costs and deadlines). He finds that, although best-price auctions do allow public authorities to obtain substantially lower prices, they also have a significant negative impact on the *ex post* performance of contracts.

Hence, Guasch (2004) observes that, out of a sample of over 1300 infrastructure concession contracts concluded between 1985 and 2000 in Latin America, 50% of road concessions and 70% of water contracts are renegotiated *within the 2 years following their signature*. According to the author, this is a strong signal that tenders submitted by operators do not constitute a genuine commitment. More particularly, he gives the example of the concession for the airport in Lima, awarded in 2001. The award criterion was the percentage of gross revenue to be paid to the State. The winner (a consortium between the operator of the Frankfurt airport and a local partner) proposed to pay 47% of its gross revenue to the State and also committed to investing over one billion dollars and to building a second landing strip as from the 11th year of the contract (the total duration of which was 30 years). Such a tender thus implied that with 53% of its gross revenue, the operator would be able to cover its operating costs, amortize its investments, and obtain a return on its investments... But shortly after the contract was awarded, the consortium asked to renegotiate it and won its case: in late 2003, the investment requirements were revised downward, as well as the percentage of revenue to be paid to the State every year.[8]

Competitive calls for tenders may also be subjected to another problem of adverse selection, when the contract up for tender is characterized by uncertainty as to future demand or future operating conditions (and this despite the fact that public authorities' expectations are clearly defined). Indeed, such uncertainty is generally not assessed in the same manner by participants to the call for tenders. It is then possible that the opening up to competition will result in selecting the most optimistic candidate rather than the most efficient one, which can lead to what is known as the "winner's curse" if the selected operator goes bankrupt *ex post*. It is then in the interest of rational bidders to internalize this winner's curse effect by bidding less aggressively when the number of tenderers increases. This is what is demonstrated in Hong and Shum's study (2002), described in Box 2 below. Athias and Nunez (2008, 2015) also highlight the internalization of the winner's curse in a study focusing on 49 toll road concessions awarded throughout the world. Based on

---

[8]See also Williamson (1976), who provides, through the study of cable TV in Oakland city, a detailed example of the difficulty of eliminating abnormally low tenders and of the consequences on contract execution.

the relative deviation between traffic forecasts included in the winning tenders and real observed traffic, the authors show that operators bid less aggressively when they expect strong competition (i.e., they include a risk premium corresponding to the number of bidders, so as to avoid the winner's curse). But they also show that this behavior is less pronounced in countries with a weak institutional framework, where it is easier to renegotiate so as to avoid suffering losses *ex post*, which highlights the opportunism of tenderers. The efficiency of open competitive tendering is thus challenged when bidders are asymmetrically informed about the uncertain future conditions of realization of the contract behind the call for tenders, i.e., when bidders internalize the winner's curse. Consequently, in such a context, a limited number of tenderers, or even a bilateral negotiation, can enable the public authority to obtain lower tenders.

Box 2: Hong and Shum (2002)

One of the objectives of Hong and Shum's article (2002) is to assess the effect of the number of bidders on the price included in the winning tender during calls for tenders for construction projects issued by the New Jersey department of transportation in the years 1989–1997. Their results clearly indicate that the internalization of the winner's curse is particularly strong for auctions relating to motorway works. As illustrated in the figure below, the average procurement cost strictly increases with the number of bidders. The more numerous the bidders, the more each bidder internalizes a risk of winner's curse, and is therefore driven to submit a tender that is not too aggressive in order to protect itself. For instance, in this study, median costs increase by about 15% when the number of bidders rises from three to six.

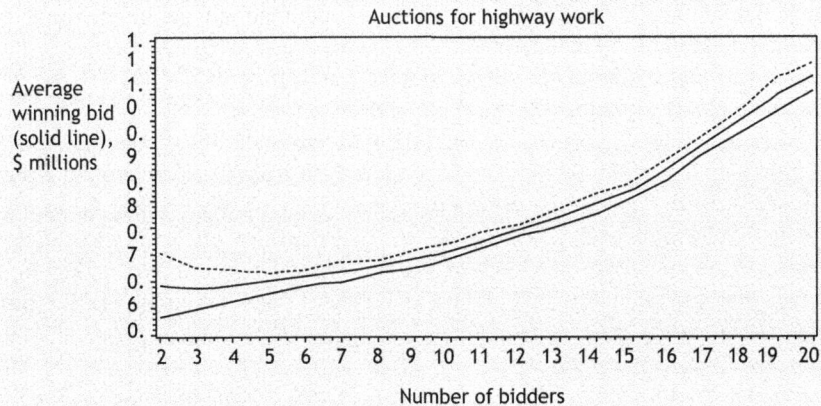

Source: Hong and Shum (2002)

3.3 Multidimensional Auctions and Transparency

Whether it is deliberate or not, adverse selection appears as a recurring issue with which public authorities struggle to cope. One of the solutions suggested in the literature consists in taking explicitly into account qualitative dimensions in tender evaluation by setting up a multidimensional auction. Nevertheless, the few empirical studies on the topic emphasize the excesses that arise from this type of auction. Based on data about road and railway concessions in Latin America, Estache, Guasch, Iimi, and Trujillo (2009) thus show that, on the one hand, resorting to multidimensional auctions significantly increases the risk of contract renegotiation and that, on the other hand, this type of auction is often chosen for noneconomic reasons (for instance, in order to use social criteria aiming to reduce unemployment), thereby diverting the auction from its initial objective. In addition, when the criteria for selecting applicants to participate in an auction are multiple but not clearly expressed, the contracting authority enjoys substantial leeway and it is difficult for candidates to anticipate the result of the selection process. To remedy this uncertainty, they may be tempted to corrupt, influence, or lobby the authorities in order to drive them to use their discretionary power in a way that is favorable to them. Additionally, to avoid being at the mercy of the buyer's opportunism, bidders may seek to collude, thus generating price inflation.

In this regard, the work of Tran (2008) is highly interesting. The author was given access to the unofficial records of an Asian firm, featuring not only the public goods or services supply contracts won by the firm (562 contracts in total over the 1997–2006 period) but also the bribes paid by the firm for each contract (out of the 562 contracts, all but three involve the payment of a bribe). As it happens, over the 1997–2006 period, the rules applied by the government to select private firms changed: prior to 2000, the government was under no obligation to resort to competitive calls for tenders; in 2001, best-value auctions (which correspond to multidimensional auctions) became mandatory, before giving way, in 2004, to best-price auctions. This context allows the author to assess the effect of the government's various selection procedures on the firm's propensity to corrupt. The results are surprising: the reform of 2001 did not reduce the bribes paid by the firms; it even increased them (by about nine percentage points of equipment cost) in the case of restricted calls for tenders! In contrast, the 2004 reform did reduce corruption (relative to the situation following the 2001 reform). These results thus highlight the fact that open tenders only reduce corruption when the public authorities' discretionary leeway is limited.

Ohashi (2009) studies the Japanese public works contracts awarded by the Mie government from March 2001 to March 2004, in which firms must be qualified to take part in a tender. Before mid-2002, the selection of qualified firms was based on criteria of size, as well as on other factors that were explicitly left to the discretion of the buyer. However, as of mid-2002, the right to participate in an auction became determined according to objective technical and financial characteristics. The results show that the use of a more transparent selection procedure caused an 8%

reduction in tender prices, thus suggesting that collusive or corruptive practices were associated with less transparent procedures.

Taking into account candidates' reputation in the procedure may also be viewed as a particular type of multidimensional auction, where a firm's past performances are used to evaluate its current tender. In the USA, the legislation encourages the setting up of databases on the evaluation of firms' past performances in public contracts and the dissemination of such information. In contrast, the European directives adopt a radically different stance: a firm's reputation may not be used to evaluate its current tender (see Box 3). The ambivalent theoretical and empirical results about the benefits of an increase in public buyer's discretionary power probably explain the coexistence of these two paradigms. On the one hand, Yvrande-Billon (2009) analyzes 191 calls for tenders organized between 1995 and 2006 in the French sector of public urban transport. The article focuses on the determinants of low market turnover, incumbent operators being renewed in 84% of cases. The author shows in particular that resorting to low-transparency procedures based on the vague and arbitrary principle of *intuitu personae*, by which public authorities take into account the "identity" of the candidate to discriminate between operators, significantly increases the probability of the incumbent operator being renewed.[9] At first glance, taking into account the operator's reputation and the efficiency of the opening up to competition seems to be negatively correlated. However, the study emphasizes that *"one of the avenues of research to be pursued would consist in analyzing the evolution of incumbent operators' behavior so as to assess whether they exploit their "first-mover" advantage to appropriate a larger share of the rent."* On the other hand, Pacini and Spagnolo (2011) study how the introduction of a system for rating private operators' past performances impacts the price and quality of public services. The public company that was part of this experiment is Italian and manages energy sale and distribution services, water services, and public lighting. In September 2007, a rating system was therefore introduced, based on the rewarding of past performances by granting a bonus when a new contract is awarded. The mechanism was announced and presented several times, in order to inform potential firms as well as possible about its principles. The results suggest that although the mechanism has a neutral effect on prices, it nevertheless increases the quality and safety of services (which are assessed by auditors based on a total of 124 criteria).

---

[9]It should be noted that the contracting authority's wish to renew the partnership with the same partner may be explained by a search for efficiency. See for instance the policy implemented to this effect by the city of London in its calls for tenders for London bus transportation (Amaral, Saussier, & Yvrande-Billon, 2009).

Box 3: The Ban on Taking into Account Operators' Past Performances in a Call for Tenders: An Example
In May 2009, a French public buyer, dissatisfied with the past performances of one of its operators, chose to exclude its application from a call for tenders. The operator in question decided to appeal on the grounds that its application had no reason to be rejected on the basis of the arguments put forward by the public buyer. At the end of the procedure, the administrative court ruled in favor of the firm.[10] Indeed, past bad performances cannot be grounds enough to exclude a firm's application in traditional public procurement. To be able to do so, the buyer must demonstrate that the technical, professional, and financial abilities mentioned in the application are likely to generate mistakes that have already occurred in the past!

In the end, the opacity generated by resorting to multidimensional criteria may be used by public authorities or firms to skew competition. Nevertheless, it would seem that, when combined with enhanced transparency, discretionary leeway is more likely to be used in the service of economic efficiency [see the previously outlined results of studies by Ohashi (2009) and Pacini and Spagnolo (2011)]. Indeed, it is not surprising that, as transparency is enhanced, firms gradually gain access to information allowing them to better control the integrity of the procedure: discretionary excesses are then more likely to be detected, and their occurrence should consequently decrease. Incidentally, the virtues of transparency were highlighted in relation to other dimensions of the opening up to competition: two (complementary) studies by De Silva, Dunne, Kankanamge, and Kosmopoulou (2008) and De Silva, Kosmopoulou, and Lamarche (2009) show that disclosing the estimated cost of a project reduces errors of prediction and allows for better calibrated tenders. Besides, this would improve the survival of new entrants, which are more exposed to winner's curse problems since the information they have about the (real) value of awarded objects is more fragmentary.

Nevertheless, like multidimensional auctions, transparency is not without danger (see Box 4). As observed by the French Competition Authority [Autorité de la concurrence (2000), p. 6], "*the a priori publication of selection criteria and their hierarchy [...] can have anticompetitive effects. [...] Notifying tenderers of the selection criteria is particularly likely to favor collusion [since] "ground rules" that are precise and known in advance to tenderers allow the latter to understand the award conditions. Whether the successful tenderer is systematically the lowest tenderer or the firm whose tender is "most advantageous economically" based on the published criteria, a cartel would then allow its members to designate among themselves, in coordination and unknown to the public buyer, who will submit the lowest tender or the one that is "most advantageous economically", and who will*

---

[10]Order 2-06-09 Perfect Nettoyage. Available at the following address: http://static. marchespublicspme.com/file/documents/ordonnance-2-juin-2009-perfect-nettoyage.PDF

submit "cover" biddings, which are higher and do not meet one or more of the award criteria—or meet them more imperfectly." Therefore, the French Competition Authority's recommendation is, *"on the one hand, that the awarding authority should define its need precisely and, on the other hand, that the organizations in charge of monitoring contract award procedures should be able to ensure that the award is based solely on the respective merits of the tenders in relation to the expressed need"* (Autorité de la concurrence (2000), p. 7).

Box 4: Procedure Transparency: From Theory to Practice

One anecdote illustrates the paradox which contracting as well as legal authorities must face daily as to the merits of disclosing or not information about the organization of the procedure. The *Moniteur* from October 2nd, 2009 reports that *"a firm excluded from a European call for tenders for road enlargement works wished to be granted the disclosure of financial documents pertaining to the tenders."* The article also reports that *"the detailed tender price, that is, the schedule of rates and prices of the selected firm* (as it happens, it was a call-off contract, editor's note), *is in principle available to the public in so far as it is an integral part of the contract."* Nevertheless, the difficulty in this instance consisted in assessing the extent to which the disclosure of this type of information was likely to contravene the authorities' obligation to preserve the firms' commercial secrecy. In the end, *"the Commission d'accès aux documents administratifs* [Commission on access to administrative documents] *remarks that in the case in point, the fact that a new consultation could be initiated in the short run, including certain unit cost items featured in the schedule of rates and prices requested by the excluded firm, was not sufficient to characterize a risk of interference with competition, given the "specificity" of the works project in question."*

In the end, the implementation of calls for tenders is particularly susceptible to problems of adverse selection and regularly encounters them. Public authorities have levers at their disposal which they can choose to activate, within the limits of the legal constraints to which they are subjected, in order to face up to such problems. Multidimensional auctions (which consist in taking explicitly into account the quality of tenders or the reputation of bidders) is one of these levers, but as we have seen they are not always advantageous. However, combined with a higher degree of transparency, it would seem that the discretionary leeway they confer on the public party is more frequently used in the service of economic efficiency. Nevertheless, transparency itself is likely to generate some detrimental effects: on the one hand, the reduction of uncertainty it may entail reduces errors of prediction by tenderers, but on the other hand, a deeper understanding of the "ground rules" makes it easier to organize collusive strategies, and the disclosure of extensive information (too extensive?) about tender characteristics could compromise commercial secrecy.

An open call for tenders is thus difficult to implement when the object up for auction is not standardized. It is then likely to be sidelined in favor of other award procedures, which endeavor, explicitly and in an organized manner, not to take advantage of the sole intensification of competition.

4   Open Calls for Tenders and Alternative Award Methods: Choosing a Procedure

As highlighted in the previous section, open tenders have many limitations that challenge their efficiency, and therefore their optimality, compared to other possible award methods.

Although Goldberg (1976) and Williamson (1976) had already emphasized the potential dangers of too high levels of competition, it is only with the theoretical works of Manelli and Vincenti (1995), and then Bajari and Tadelis (2001), that those dangers were rigorously formalized. From then on, several empirical studies attempted to analyze the performances of alternative procedures, which may consist either in restricting competition to a limited group of tenderers, or, more radically, in initiating a negotiation with a single firm.

4.1   Open or Restricted Call for Tenders?

Recent empirical contributions[11] focus on calls for tenders in which a limited number of participants are invited to submit a tender. If these works are still too few to allow us to apprehend the advantages and limitations of such a strategy in a rigorous manner, they nevertheless shed light on its potential benefits and the conditions for its efficiency.

Through a database of 3362 works contracts awarded in various Italian provinces from 2000 to 2005, the work of Coviello and Giancarlo (2014) compares the performances (both *ex ante* and *ex post*) of open and restricted calls for tenders. Indeed, the sample of contracts presents the following original characteristic: the award mechanism changes discretionally depending on the reserve price of the contract. Hence, below a certain threshold (300,000€), the buyer can resort to a restricted call for tenders for which it must invite at least 15 firms to submit a tender, whereas above this threshold it tends to more systematically use more open procedures. Thus, assuming that contracts located just below and just above the threshold have similar unobservable characteristics, the researchers identify the causal effect of the award mechanism on a number of indicators likely to reflect the

---

[11]The articles mentioned in this section are still in the exploratory phase, and their results are therefore likely to evolve.

quality of the award. This assessment technique is known as regression disconti-nuity and makes it possible to address the endogeneity problems that would otherwise require the use of instrumental variables, which are often hard to find. As regards *ex ante* indicators, the authors focus first of all on the effect of the award mechanism on the number of received tenders (which may naturally differ from the number of candidates) and on the winning rebate (i.e., the percentage of reduction in the price of the winning tender compared to the reserve price). The award procedure seems to have no effect on either of these outcomes. In contrast, it has a radical impact on the probability of selecting a firm from the same province as the contracting authority: when resorting to an open call for tenders, the buyer reduces by 72% the probability of contracting out to a local firm.

Then, the authors study the effect of the award mechanism on cost overruns borne by the buyer and on the duration of the works. If the implemented procedure is neutral in relation to the first criterion, it seems however that restricted auctions reduce the time it takes for the works to be delivered.

In the end, it appears that restricted tender procedures are likely to improve the efficiency of the award process and that the dogma according to which more competition is always preferable does not always stand the test of facts. Neverthe-less, the benefits one may hope to derive from restricted calls for tenders are markedly dependent on the way in which they are implemented, or, in other words, the way in which the firms invited to submit a tender are selected.

The study by Chever, Saussier, and Yvrande-Billon (2014) tells us a little more on this topic of the implementation of restricted tender procedures. Based on an original database of 180 recurrent contracts relating to simple services, the authors investigate the way in which a restricted tender procedure is implemented by a public buyer (the main public operator of social housing in Paris). In this procedure, a minimum of three candidates, selected from a list of prequalified firms, are invited to submit a tender. For each call for tenders, the authors have information on (1) the identity of all prequalified firms, (2) the tenders submitted by all invited bidders, and (3) the winning tenderer. This allows them to assess the effect of invited bidders' characteristics on the competitiveness of received tenders. Their findings suggest that bidders are not selected randomly: in particular, past performances are a major determinant in the probability of being invited to bid. Additionally, using a two-step Heckman model, the authors show that this reasoned invitation may allow the buyer to save money, as the invited firms' unobservable characteristics are correlated with a reduction in the price of submitted tenders. Thus, reducing the competitive intensity, even for simple contracts, limits the *ex ante* transaction costs while maintaining competitive pressure.

4.2   Open Tenders or Negotiation?

Empirical studies investigating the advantages of negotiating with a single firm are more numerous, but their contradictory findings do not yet allow us to settle the debate for good.

Bajari et al. (2014) study a sample of 819 Caltrans contracts[12] awarded through open calls for tenders from 1999 to 2005. The authors show that candidates anticipate future adaptations by including a substantial risk premium in the price of submitted tenders. The reduction in adaptation costs thus appears as a fundamental issue in public procurement. Therefore, it seems that open tenders are not systematically the most efficient mechanism; when awarding a complex contract, they could be overshadowed by procedures allowing for better dialogue between the parties to discuss elements of uncertainty.

This idea that uncertainty must or should be a determinant of the choice of a selection procedure has also been the object of empirical analyses. The main findings, outlined below, reveal differences between private and public buyers, which point to the fact that the latter still have substantial room for improvement.

Let us focus first on the case of private buyers. Using a database on construction projects awarded in California from 1995 to 2000, Bajari, McMillan, and Tadelis (2009) develop and test hypotheses pertaining to the characteristics that are likely to affect the choice of the award mechanism. In the sample under study, 50% of contracts were awarded through direct negotiation with a firm: as private buyers do not share the same legal constraints as public buyers, they are free to choose the procedure they deem most efficient and can therefore resort more massively to negotiated procedures. The first hypothesis is that complex projects should be negotiated, whereas simpler projects are more likely to be awarded through competitive bidding. To test this hypothesis, three types of variables—which are supposed to capture the complexity of the projects—are used as determinants of the choice of procedure: the value of the project as estimated by the buyer, the floor area of the construction project, and the number of trade divisions involved. The econometric results show that the three variables are indeed associated with a higher probability of resorting to negotiated procedures.

The second hypothesis is that, in an environment where there are few available bidders, the likelihood of resorting to auctions will decrease. To test this assumption, the authors assume that if the volume of work undertaken within the past 6 months increases (in the county under study), firms will have lower available capacities and will therefore be less likely to submit a bid.

Consequently, the number of bidders should be lower and (based on the hypothesis being tested) the use of negotiated procedures more frequent. The assumption is confirmed by an econometric test.

Finally, the authors' third hypothesis is that the use of a negotiated procedure results in the selection of contractors with the best reputation and largest experience. The underlying idea is that if the buyer is faced with reputable constructors, it will have more incentives to start a negotiation with them in order to benefit from their expertise. Two variables are used to test this assumption: the first variable takes the value 1 if the firm appears more than once in the sample under study (0 otherwise), and the second variable takes the value 1 if the firm had previously

---

[12]California Department of Transportation.

appeared in the sample under study (0 otherwise). The econometric study does show a positive correlation between each of these two variables and the choice to resort to negotiated procedures.

Chong, Staropoli, and Yvrande-Billon (2013), as for them, investigate the determinants behind the choice of procedure using a French database of public works contracts awarded in 2007. Their findings reveal that public buyers seem to be more concerned about issues of legal security and compliance than economic efficiency. Indeed, contrary to the theoretical recommendations and findings from the work of Bajari et al. (2009), they find that calls for tenders are favored for the award of costly long-term projects. The authors interpret this finding as a consequence of the fact that public buyers are frequently suspected of favoritism and corruption and protect themselves against such suspicions by resorting to the least discretionary procedures possible.

Nevertheless, Lalive and Schmutzler (2011) question the superiority of direct negotiation procedures to award complex projects. The authors study the effect of the liberalization of regional railway services in Germany, implemented in 1996. Before the reform, contracts were awarded following a negotiation with the incumbent supplier, whereas since the reform, local authorities can choose between negotiation and auction. The authors collected data in 1993 and 1994 (prior to the reform) as well as in 2003 and 2004 (after the reform) on a total of 551 regional railway lines. They have data on the characteristics of these lines: frequency of service before and after the reform, geographical distance to the nearest city with at least 100,000 inhabitants, number of inhabitants of the largest city served by the line, etc. After endogenizing the choice of procedure (using in particular geographical data on line characteristics, but also data on frequency of service before the reform), the authors assess the impact of the award mechanism on procurement price and service frequency. They find that auctions improve the frequency of service by 16% and reduce the transfer price by 25%. Thus, according to this study, negotiations seem to be less efficient than auctions. The authors nevertheless stress how such results could be explained by the fact that the service under consideration is not overwhelmingly complex.

5 Conclusion

When the service to be provided is complex, future conditions are uncertain and the expertise of the public party is limited, open competition may prove to be difficult to implement, or even inefficient (problems of adverse selection). Other mechanisms for selecting private operators have emerged in practice and given rise to empirical studies investigating their efficiency. These studies indicate that negotiated procedures, restricted calls for tenders, or an increase in the public authority's discretionary leeway may turn out to be preferable to an open call for tenders under certain conditions, especially under conditions of transparency.

References

Amaral, M., Saussier, S., & Yvrande-Billon, A. (2009). Auction procedures and competition in public services: The case of urban public transport in France and London. *Utilities Policy, 17,* 166–175.

Athias, L., & Nunez, A. (2008). Winner's curse in toll road concessions. *Economics Letters, 3* (101), 172–174.

Athias, L., & Nunez, A. (2015). Effects of uncertainty and opportunistic renegotiations on bidding behaviour: Evidence from toll road concessions. In *The economics of infrastructure provisioning: The changing role of the state* (pp. 285–314). Cambridge: MIT Press.

Autorité de la concurrence. (2000). Avis 00-A-25 relatif à un projet de décret portant réforme du code des marchés publics.

Bajari, P., & Tadelis, S. (2001). Incentives versus transaction costs: A theory of procurement contracts. *RAND Journal of Economics, 32*(3), 387–407.

Bajari, P., McMillan, R., & Tadelis, S. (2009). Auctions versus negotiations in procurement: An empirical analysis. *Journal of Law, Economics, and Organization, 25*(2), 372–399.

Bajari, P., Houghton, S., & Tadelis, S. (2014). Bidding for incomplete contracts: An empirical analysis. *American Economic Review, 104*(4), 1288–1319.

Bulow, J., & Klemperer, P. (1996). Auctions versus negotiations. *American Economic Review, 86* (1), 180–194.

Chadwick, E. (1859). Results of different principles of legislation and administration in Europe of competition for the field, as compared with competition within the field of service. *Journal of the Royal Statistical Society, 22*(A), 381–420.

Chever, L., Saussier, S., & Yvrande-Billon, A. (2014). *The law of small numbers: Investigating the benefits of restricted auctions for public procurement* (working paper).

Chong, E., Staropoli, C., & Yvrande-Billon, A. (2013). Auction versus negotiation in public procurement: Looking for empirical evidence. In E. Brousseau & J.-M. Glachant (dir.), *The manufacturing of markets: Legal, political and economic dynamics.* Cambridge: Cambridge University Press.

Chong, E., Klien, M., & Saussier, S. (2014). *The quality of governance and the use of negotiated procurement procedures: Some (un)surprising evidence from the European Union* (working paper).

Conley, T., & Decarolis, F. (2013). *Detecting bidders groups in collusive auctions* (working paper).

Coviello, & Giancarlo. (2014). *The effect of discretion on procurement performance* (working paper).

Coviello, D., & Mariniello, M. (2014). Publicity requirements in public procurement: Evidence from a regression discontinuity design. *Journal of Public Economics, 109,* 76–100.

De Silva, D. G., Dunne, T., Kankanamge, A., & Kosmopoulou, G. (2008). The impact of public information on bidding in highway procurement auctions. *European Economic Review, 52*(1), 150–181.

De Silva, D. G., Kosmopoulou, G., & Lamarche, C. (2009). The effect of information on the bidding and survival of entrants in procurement auctions. *Journal of Public Economics, 93* (1–2), 56–72.

Decarolis, F. (2014). Awarding price, contract performance and bids screening: Evidence from procurement auctions. *American Economic Journal: Applied Economics, 6*(1), 108–132.

Demsetz, H. (1968). Why regulate utilities? *Journal of Law and Economics, 11,* 55–66.

Estache, A., Guasch, J., Iimi, A., & Trujillo, L. (2009). Multidimensionality and renegotiation: Evidence from transport-sector public-private-partnership transactions in Latin America. *Review of Industrial Organization, 35*(1), 41–71.

Goldberg, V. P. (1976). Regulation and administered contracts. *Bell Journal of Economics, 7*(2), 426–448.

Guasch, J. (2004). *Granting and renegotiating infrastructure concession: Doing it right.* Washington, DC: The World Bank.

Hong, H., & Shum, M. (2002). Increasing competition and the winner's curse: Evidence from procurement. *Review of Economic Studies, 69*(4), 871–898.

Lalive, R., & Schmutzler, A. (2011). *Auctions vs negotiations in public procurement: Which works better?* (working paper).

Manelli, A., & Vincenti, D. (1995). Optimal procurement mechanisms. *Econometrica, 63*, 591–620.

National Audit Office. (1998). *PFI: Construction performance.* Report by the Comptroller and Auditor General, HC 576 Session 1997-98. London: The Stationery Office.

Observatoire des services publics d'eau et d'assainissement. (2013). Impacts des procédures de mise en concurrence dites "Loi Sapin" sur les services d'eau et d'assainissement en 2009 et 2010.

Ohashi, H. (2009). Effects of transparency in procurement practices on government expenditure: A case study of municipal public works. *Review of Industrial Organization, 34*(3), 267–285.

Pacini, R., & Spagnolo, G. (2011). *Vendor rating on product quality: A case study.* Work in Progress, Italian Treasury and SITE, Stockholm.

Preston, J., Whelan, G., Nash, C., & Wardman, M. (2000). The franchising of passenger rail services in Britain. *International Review of Applied Economics, 14*(1), 99–112.

Tran, A. (2008). Can procurement auctions reduce corruption? Evidence from the internal records of a bribe-paying firm. Mimeo.

Warren, P. (2014). Contracting officer workload, incomplete contracting, and contractual terms: Theory and evidence. *RAND Journal of Economics, 45*(2), 395–421.

Williamson, O. E. (1976). Franchise bidding for natural monopolies: In general and with respect to CATV. *Bell Journal of Economics, 7*(1), 73–104.

Yvrande-Billon, A. (2009). Appels d'offres concurrentiels et avantage au sortant: une étude empirique du secteur du transport public urbain en France. *Revue d'économie industrielle, 127*, 119.

Zupan, M. A. (1989a). The efficacy of franchise bidding schemes in the case of cable television: Some systematic evidence. *Journal of Law and Economics, 32*(1), 401–456.

Zupan, M. A. (1989b). Cable franchise renewals: Do incumbent firms behave opportunistically? *RAND Journal of Economics, 20*(4), 473–482.

Renegotiating PPP Contracts: Opportunities and Pitfalls

Jean Beuve, Aude Le Lannier, and Zoé Le Squeren

1 Introduction

Many examples highlight the central place held by renegotiations in public–private partnership contracts (PPPs) in France: renegotiations of highway concession contracts, early termination of the contract for a central hospital between the cities of Évry and Corbeil-Essonnes and the private Eiffage group, political deadlock, renegotiations and termination of the contract between the State and the Ecomouv' consortium for the implementation of an environmental tax (the *écotaxe*), tensions surrounding the delays in the delivery of the new "French Pentagon" by the firm Bouygues... These arrangements are all PPPs concluded between municipalities (or the national State) and private operators, and all have been the object of more or less antagonistic renegotiations. Such renegotiations, frequent and sometimes contentious, are highly common when dealing with complex and long-term contracts, concluded between a public and a private party. This is indubitably not only the case for French governments but for every government that concludes long-term agreements with private firms [see for instance Domingues and Sarmento (2016) for evidence of renegotiation of European transport concessions].

J. Beuve (✉)
University of Paris I Panthéon-Sorbonne, Paris, France
e-mail: jean.beuve@univ-paris1.fr

A. Le Lannier
ARAFER and associate research fellow at IAE Paris—Sorbonne Business School, Paris, France
e-mail: aude.lelannier@arafer.fr

Z. Le Squeren
IAE—University of Lille I, Lille, France
e-mail: zoe.lesqueren@gmail.com

© Springer International Publishing AG 2018
S. Saussier, J. de Brux (eds.), *The Economics of Public-Private Partnerships*,
https://doi.org/10.1007/978-3-319-68050-7_6

Table 1 Percentage of PPP contracts renegotiated per country and per industry

Geographical area	Industry	% Renegotiated contracts	Average time of the first renegotiation	References
Latin America and the Caribbean	All industries	68	1.8 years	Guasch (2004)
	Electricity	41	2.1 years	
	Transportation	78	2.9 years	
	Water	92	1.3 years	
United States	Transportation	40	–	Engel, Fisher, and Galetovic (2011)
France	Urban parking	74	3.8 years	Beuve et al. (2013)
France	Motorways	50	–	Athias and Saussier (2010)
United Kingdom	All industries	55	–	NAO (2001)

Source: Estache and Saussier (2014)

PPP contract renegotiations are not a recent phenomenon, and they are an integral part of the life of such contracts. During the operational phase of these agreements, the parties are almost systematically faced with unforeseen events forcing them to renegotiate the terms of the initial contract. Several empirical studies, conducted in various countries and industries, illustrate this "usual" nature of PPP contract renegotiations (see Table 1).

Most of the time, renegotiations are interpreted as a sign of failure of the contractual relationship, in particular because of the deadline extensions and cost increases they usually generate. As an example, empirical studies conducted using British data indicate that only 30% of public service infrastructure were delivered within the time initially allotted and that 73% of projects presented cost overruns during the construction phase (HM Treasury, 2003), which suggests that these contracts have been repeatedly renegotiated.[1] On the same subject, analyses conducted in the USA report averages of 25% of cost overruns and 22 months of delays in delivery, against only 28% of projects delivered in compliance with the terms of the initial contract.[2]

However, looking at renegotiations with an objective eye is more difficult than it seems because of their ambivalent nature. PPP renegotiations should therefore not be criticized in a systematic way, but this phenomenon should rather be considered as a complex one, which deserves to be studied carefully. Indeed, if renegotiations can be the scene of opportunistic behaviors from stakeholders, they are nevertheless unavoidable and often beneficial because of the specific characteristics of PPP contracts.

---

[1]Data from infrastructure construction projects, British National Audit Office (2003).

[2]Data from the United States Government Accountability Office (2009), which include 96 large-scale supply projects in the field of defense in the USA.

First of all, PPP contracts are inherently incomplete: they cannot include a precise description of all contingencies that may arise during their implementation (Hart, 1995; Saussier & Farès, 2002; Williamson, 1985). Indeed, PPPs are long-term arrangements (those contracts commonly last for several decades) relating to complex projects that often include the construction of an infrastructure, as well as its operation and maintenance. As shown in the theoretical and empirical literature, contractual incompleteness increases with contract duration and project complexity (Masten & Saussier, 2000; Bajari, MacMillan, & Tadelis, 2009); these incomplete contracts therefore have to be renegotiated, to adapt the terms of the initial agreement to contingencies revealed *ex post*. Such unforeseen events may be exogenous (economic crises, technological innovations, legislative changes, etc.) or result from internal needs of the contractual relationship (evolution of needs for more efficient service management or inadequate design of the initial contract).

Secondly, PPPs are traditionally used for projects requiring substantial investments. These investments in specific assets[3] give rise to a *"fundamental transformation,"* that is, to a transition from a competitive relationship to a situation of bilateral dependency between the signatory parties (Williamson, 1985). This situation may encourage renegotiations for two reasons. On the one hand, it can favor opportunistic renegotiations: private operators and public authorities may both try to renegotiate the terms of the contract to their own advantage, knowing that the other party is "trapped" by the relationship. On the other hand, it makes contract termination more complex. Indeed, neither the private partner, which has invested in specific assets, nor the public authority, which has incurred substantial costs to award the contract (and which is responsible for the continuity of public services), is inclined to terminate the arrangement. Therefore, parties generally prefer to renegotiate the terms of the initial contract rather than put an end to it in a way that generates conflicts.

Thus, given the specificities of PPP contracts, their renegotiations are an essential topic, which should be studied carefully. Indeed, PPP contract renegotiations can be a source of efficiency because of the necessary contractual adaptations they enable or conversely a source of inefficiency due to opportunistic behaviors. They therefore generate both risks and opportunities for contractors and more generally for all parties involved in these contracts (i.e., consumers, citizens, etc.). The central role of the renegotiation process in "public–private" contracts has recently been acknowledged in the European directives on "Public procurement" and "Concessions" from February 2014. While before then, the European directives only supervised public contract award, the new directives define rules for their potential renegotiations (see Box 1).

This chapter first describes the different types of opportunistic behaviors which can arise in PPP contracts (Sect. 2.1). Such behaviors are an argument in favor of designing more rigid contracts, or using extracontractual mechanisms aiming to

---

[3]Assets are specific when they are difficult to redeploy toward other users or customers without incurring costs.

limit the occurrence of renegotiations (Sect. 2.2). We will then present "desirable" renegotiations, which allow parties to adapt the terms of the contract to contingencies revealed *ex post* (Sect. 3.1). These renegotiations are an argument in favor of designing more flexible contracts, which nevertheless require an appropriate regulatory and institutional framework (Sect. 3.2).[4]

Box 1: The European Directives of February 2014

The European directives on "Public procurement" and "Concessions" of February 2014 attach special importance to renegotiations, which illustrates the significance of this phenomenon for the proper execution of these contracts.

For public procurement contracts, the directive stipulates that contractual modifications are allowed when they are not considered substantial, that is, when their value is inferior to 10% of the initial contract value for service and supply contracts, and to 15% for works contracts. Modifications are also authorized in two cases: when the parties encounter unforeseen technical constraints (material difficulties of an exceptional nature that were unforeseeable when the contract was signed, and the cause of which is external to it) and when such adaptations have been provided for in the contract in the form of clear, precise, and unequivocal price revision clauses or options. However, such modifications are only authorized provided that any increase in price is not higher than 50% of the value of the original contract, this 50% limitation applying to the value of each modification and not to their combined value when several successive modifications are made to the same contract.

As regards concessions, the directive indicates that contracts may largely be modified under similar circumstances and in the same proportions as public contracts (recitals 75 and 76 and article 43 of the Directive on Concessions, February 2014).

These directives expand the possibility to renegotiate public procurement and concession contracts. Indeed, until February 2014, the thresholds below which renegotiation of these contracts was allowed (without resorting to a reopening up to competition) were not defined clearly in the legislation, but case law decreed that renegotiations were allowed only when any increase in price was between 15 and 20% of the initial contract value, depending on cases. The new directives thus give a more important place to the renegotiation process by defining a new threshold of 50% when renegotiation is deemed essential to the proper running of the contract (see abovementioned

(continued)

---

[4]The opposition between "good" and "bad" motives for renegotiations can be linked to the conceptualization matrix of PPP renengotiation causes made by ITF (2017). In this approach, the endogenous and exogenous factors of renegotiations (as seen in relation to the specific PPP project under consideration) are crossed with objective and subjective (or alternativeley more technocractic/more political) factors.

Box 1 (continued)

conditions). Thus, these directives take into account the fact that renegotiations are sometimes necessary because of the incomplete nature of contracts and of the "fundamental transformation": additional clauses may be included in the event of unforeseen circumstances or when additional services have become necessary and a change of contractor (i.e., of private operator) is impossible or would cause significant inconvenience. Thus, these directives integrate the complex reality of renegotiations.

2 Renegotiations and Opportunistic Behaviors

The economic literature often highlights the potential opportunistic behaviors that can arise with PPP renegotiations (Sect. 2.1). This risk of opportunism may lead the parties, and in particular public authorities, either to set up contracts that are more rigid or to rely on operators' concerns for their reputation (Sect. 2.2).

2.1 The Different Kinds of Opportunism

In the economic literature, opportunism is defined as *self-interest seeking with guile* (Williamson, 1985, p. 47). Agents behave in an opportunistically when they take advantage of the contractual incompleteness, inherent to public–private contracts, for their personal benefit and sometimes to the detriment of the other agents. Most studies highlight the opportunism of private partners (Sect. 2.1.1). However, public authorities may also act opportunistically (Sect. 2.1.2) and, according to more recent theories, third parties also have the possibility to influence the public party or the contract to their own advantage (Sect. 2.1.3).

2.1.1 Private Operator Opportunism

In a PPP contract, private party opportunism corresponds to rent-seeking behaviors: the operator seeks to renegotiate the contractual conditions *ex post* in order to increase its profit (for instance, through price increases, reductions in the quality of the service or investments). It is relatively easy for the private operator to conduct such renegotiations, because it enjoys a higher power of negotiation than the public party. This higher bargaining power is due to its better expertise, better information control, and higher level of resources.

First of all, private operators often have a larger experience of both contracting and the renegotiation process. This asymmetry in knowledge and skills is even deeper if the public entity is a small municipality with limited financial and human resources. This shortage of expertise of the public party has been highlighted, in the case of public procurement, in a recent study by the French Union of Public Purchasing Groups (*Union des groupements d'achats publics*, UGAP). This study highlights that 61% of public buyers joined procurement offices by switching services within the same public authority (that is, *via* internal staff mobility), and they actually have no experience in this field. In other words, only 39% of public procurement officers have completed a training program leading to a diploma in procurement (16%) or a course to become a buyer (23%). Finally, over two-thirds of buyers recognize that they do not have a good knowledge of the economic and industrial fabric, and almost half of them declare that they never engage in economic or technological watch.[5]

Secondly, when a public authority assigns the construction or management of an infrastructure to an operator, it very often withdraws from its daily management and therefore detains less information about the project. This effect is strengthened by the turnover of public advisors and employees, which limits the "institutional memory" of the public party, and *de facto* reduces its ability to efficiently supervise and control contracts that often span over several decades.

Finally, private operators generally enjoy far more substantial resources than public authorities. An information report published by the French Senate in July 2014 thus indicates that local and regional authorities do not have sufficient internal resources to negotiate contracts with major private groups, which are usually backed by several advisors. In this report, the relationship between local authorities and operators is therefore described as asymmetrical (Sueur & Portelli, 2014). However, such asymmetry is not limited to PPPs at the local level. A report from the French Court of Audit (*Cour des Comptes*) on highway concessions also condemns the fact that the bargaining power of Ministry in charge of transportation is too low, compared to the one of powerful highway concession companies backed by major groups (Cour des Comptes, 2013).

Thus, there is a triple asymmetry in terms of expertise, information, and resources, which favors the private party. The latter can then initiate opportunistic renegotiations aiming to appropriate a larger share of the rent generated by the deployment of specific assets ("holdup" phenomenon). Although these contractual revisions may be detrimental to the public party, the latter can hardly refuse to renegotiate, because the private partner can then threaten to withdraw from the PPP contract. Now, selecting a new partner would incur high transaction costs, which would be all the higher as competition is weak and the number of eligible operators is low (Kerf, 1998), and this threat to withdraw from the contract thus diminishes

---

[5]Survey conducted by the UGAP and the magazine *Décision Achat* in 2011, to which 370 officers in charge of the procurement services of various public authorities responded.

the public party's power (Iossa, Spagnolo, & Vellez, 2007). Therefore, the public authority is relatively inclined to accept requests for contractual renegotiation, even when they are potentially opportunistic, and even more if there is a risk of service interruption, which runs contrary to the principle of public service continuity (Williamson, 1976).

This private party opportunism was highlighted in Guasch's empirical study (2004) investigating over 1300 concession contracts in Latin America and the Caribbean. Out of all contracts under study, he shows that 61% of renegotiations were initiated by the private operator, against only 26% by the public party and 13% by mutual consent between the parties. In 60% of cases, these renegotiations resulted in price increases and investment reductions favorable to the private party (see Box 2). Thus, even if the author acknowledges that some renegotiations allow for more efficient contract management, he underlines the fact that they most often lead to a decrease in users' welfare. Renegotiations therefore tend to reduce, or even cancel out, the expected benefits of competitive award procedures for PPP contracts.[6]

Indeed, opportunistic renegotiations hinder the efficiency of the opening up to competition for the market. This mechanism may then be disrupted by aggressive bidding (also called "low-balling strategies"), a situation where the operator willingly submits a low tender to win the contract, anticipating future renegotiations. Thus, the opening up to competition no longer results in selecting the best candidate (that is, the lowest tenderer in terms of prices or the best tenderer in terms of the general quality of the tender) but the one that is most confident in its power of renegotiation. This type of behavior is perfectly illustrated by Alcazar, Abdala, and Shirley (2002) in the case of a water-sector concession in Buenos Aires. Indeed, the selected operator of that concession was unable to ensure the financial equilibrium of the contract without renegotiating its terms *ex post*.[7] Athias and Nunez (2008) also find a similar result in their analysis of highway concessions. Using an original dataset of 49 concession contracts in several countries, the authors investigate how operators establish their traffic forecasts, which constitute the base of their tenders. Their findings indicate that operators are all the more inclined to submit low tenders (that is, to deliberately overestimate the traffic forecasts) as they anticipate a strong

---

[6]See Chapter "The Relative Efficiency of Competitive Tendering" of the second part for award procedures.

[7]The operator had signed a loan agreement requiring that a debt/net worth ratio be reached. Now, this ratio could only be reached through a price increase or a reduction in the investments provided for in the contract, which seems to imply an anticipation of renegotiation on the part of the private partner.

probability of being able to renegotiate the contracts, thus making sure that they win the contract while avoiding potential losses *ex post*.

Box 2: The Outcome of Renegotiations

In his book published in 2004, *Granting and Renegotiating Infrastructure Concession: Doing It Right*, Guasch analyzes over 1300 concession contracts concluded since the 1980s in countries of Latin America and the Caribbean. His study focuses on several industries: transport (road and railway networks, airports, ports), energy (electricity), water (supply and treatment), and telecommunications. By collecting and analyzing all the information available on these contracts and their successive renegotiations, the author establishes descriptive statistics on the outcome of renegotiations and finds that 30% of contracts under study were renegotiated, 2 years on average after their signature. This renegotiation rate even rises to almost 55% in the transport industry and to almost 75% in the water and sanitation industry. The table below highlights the beneficial nature of these renegotiations for private operators (price increase, investment reductions, drop in fees, etc.).

% of renegotiations resulting in this outcome	
Extension of deadlines in investment requirements	69%
Shortening of deadlines in investment requirements	18%
Price increase	62%
Drop in prices	19%
Rise in the number of cost items included in the automatic increase of prices	59%
Extension of concession duration	38%
Reduction in investment requirements	62%
Drop in fees paid by the operator to the public party	31%
Increase in fees paid by the operator to the public party	17%

Many additional, more recent and confirmative informations about rengotiations outcomes are provided in the 2017 report of the International Transport Forum (ITF 2017).

2.1.2 Public Entity Opportunism

Opportunistic renegotiations of the terms of initial agreements are not the preserve of private operators. The contractual incompleteness inherent to PPP contracts can also be exploited by public authorities.

First of all, public authorities may decide to resort to PPPs for other reasons than economic efficiency. "Wrong reasons" (electoral objectives, desire to reduce budgetary constraints in the short term) may thus encourage public actors to sign this type of arrangement. For instance, Chong et al. (2013) use French data on the construction industry to highlight the existence of a "red ribbon" effect, that is, the fact that political decision-makers favor projects that are scheduled to be completed in the 2 years preceding an election.

Engel, Fischer, and Galetovic (2009) also study this effect. They postulate that the public authority in place is more likely to be reelected if substantial infrastructure expenditure has been realized during its term of office. It is thus in the authorities' interest to renegotiate their PPP contracts in order to increase the volume or value of works, without, however, being forced to "bear" the additional costs associated with these renegotiations (indeed, these costs are then largely recorded in the budget of future administrations). Renegotiations are thus viewed as a way to circumvent budgetary rules. In order to test this assumption, the authors use data on renegotiations conducted as part of 50 concession contracts awarded in Chile between 1993 and 2006 for the construction and operation of roads, airports, prisons, water reservoirs, and public transport infrastructure. First of all, what emerges from their analysis is that total investments for these concessions rose from 8.4 billion dollars to 11.3 billions through 78 renegotiations. Yet, only 35% of these additional costs were assumed by the public authority taking part in the renegotiation. The authors then investigate "abnormal" contractual modifications, that is, those arising at the beginning of the contract and those responding to easily foreseeable events. Their analysis brings to light two types of renegotiations. On the one hand, renegotiations aiming to add extra works *via* "supplementary contracts," negotiated bilaterally with operators (that is, without advertising the project or opening it up to competition). These additional clauses us allow to increase infrastructure expenditure quickly, so that the authorities in place could obtain results that are visible to the voters as elections approached. On the other hand, some renegotiations result from the fact that the operators' traffic forecasts were too optimistic, thus leading the latter to ask for a revision of the fixed-price contract. In such cases, the government agreed to grant the operators a toll revenue equivalent to what they would have obtained if the traffic forecasts turned out to be correct. If the operators' revenue was insufficient, renegotiations allowed for extensions in contract duration (going as far as ten additional years), in order to allow operators to obtain the anticipated returns. As a last resort, if the time extension did not allow them to generate this revenue, the government went as far as to commit to paying the difference in revenue to the operator. Thus, these modifications deeply modified the initial contractual design, incidentally transferring the financing of current infrastructure to future administrations. The authors therefore conclude that, although these renegotiations are different from a "holdup" (the public party does not renegotiate the contract to its own advantage and to the detriment of the private operator), they nevertheless correspond to an opportunistic behavior on the part of the public party which seeks to maximize its chances of being reelected.

Le Squeren and Moore (2015) also highlight the presence of a political cycle for the renegotiation of public–private partnerships, using French data on the parking industry. Their study shows that contracts concluded between French municipalities and a private operator are on average more likely to be renegotiated when municipal elections are approaching, and these pre-electoral renegotiations especially modify visible items (particularly end-user fees, and the remuneration of the parties). This suggests that local public authorities manipulate end-user prices through contractual renegotiations in order to maximize their chances of being reelected, while lowering the royalties that must be paid by the operator to the city, so that the company will accept the renegotiation more willingly.

But public party opportunism may also manifest itself to the detriment of the private party. Indeed, the public authority enjoys strong discretionary power in that it can modify the "ground rules" unilaterally (for instance, in the case of a government, by making a certain type of contract illegal or by banning any price increase; in the case of a local authority, by deciding to lower end-user prices). Faced with the risk of this kind of opportunistic behavior, private operators may refuse to realize the necessary investments, or ask for a financial compensation before setting up these investments (even when they were provided for in the contract). This example was illustrated by Guasch (2004) in the case of water concessions in Tucuman (Argentina), awarded in 1994. The author underlines the threats of price reductions formulated by the government once the operator had made the investments, combined with media campaigns encouraging users not to pay their bills. After applying reduced prices for a while, the operator put an end to the concession because of financial difficulties associated with these pressures from the public partner. Guasch (2004) also illustrates this kind of situation in the case of the Venezuelan oil sector, where the introduction of a decree on nationalizations completely modified the rules for private operators in the industry. Indeed, in May 2007, the public oil company took control of all projects in the sector, after private operators had invested several billion dollars to develop their activities, thus driving them to bankruptcy. Public party opportunism is all the more likely to arise when the political and institutional environment is unstable.[8]

It is important to underline that PPP contracts can be subjected to both opportunism from the private party (see Sect. 2.1.1) and public party opportunism at the same time. Guasch, Laffont, and Straub (2008) thus investigate 307 concession contracts in Latin America and show that their renegotiations can be the result of both a "holdup" from the private operator and political cycles (see Box 3).

Box 3: The Determinants of Renegotiations

In their 2008 article, Guash, Laffont, and Straub conduct an econometric analysis of the determinants of renegotiations. Using a database made up of 307 concession contracts in the water and transport industries in Argentina, Brazil, Chile, Colombia, and Mexico (1989–2000), the authors attempt to explain the occurrence of renegotiations. Over the period under study, 162 out of the 207 contracts were renegotiated at least once. The results of the econometric assessments indicate that:

The probability that a concession contract will be renegotiated increases:

- When the contract provides for a minimum income guarantee for the operator

(continued)

Box 3 (continued)

- When it is a price-cap contract[9]
- With the time elapsed since the contract was awarded
- With the level of investment requirements
- When the contract includes arbitration clauses
- In the years following an election
- During periods of economic recession

The probability that a concession contract will be renegotiated decreases:

- When the institutional quality is higher (rule of law, absence of corruption, bureaucratic quality)
- When there is a regulatory body distinct from the public party
- During periods of economic expansion

In this article, the authors show that political cycles and economic crises have a very strong impact on the occurrence of renegotiations. They also highlight the risks of private party opportunism. They therefore advocate setting up independent regulatory bodies before concluding concession contracts, in order to reduce the risks of opportunistic behavior.

2.1.3 Third-Party Opportunism

More recent theories (Moszoro & Spiller, 2012; Spiller, 2008) also highlight the importance of opportunistic behaviors from third parties to PPP contracts. Indeed, opportunism may come not only from the signatory parties (private operator and public authority) but also from interest groups or political groups: since PPP contracts relate to the provision of a public service and commit public funds, they affect the whole society. As emphasized by McCubbins and Schwartz (1984), the interest taken by third parties can prove useful when the public party deviates from the political agenda initially announced: they then assume a supervisory role. Nevertheless, they can hinder the proper running of PPPs when they seek to pursue their own interests instead of the general interest. For instance, the private operator's competitors could benefit from the termination of the contract, just like the public party's political rivals. It is thus in the third parties' interest to question the integrity of the public party as part of a public–private contract when they are in competition with the latter in a "political market" (Spiller, 2008).

This type of opportunistic behavior can have various consequences on the political and economic spheres. Criticisms from third parties may lead to the replacement of one of the parties, that is, the public authority or the private operator. Such a replacement would not be justified economically, as it would only be done to

---

[9]For a distinction between price-cap and cost-plus, see Chapter "Regulatory Instruments for Public-Private Partnerships" of the first part on PPP regulation.

satisfy the interests of a self-interested third party. This may lead to public service disruption, but also, in less extreme cases, to imbalances in the relationship between the parties, which can be detrimental to the proper running of the contract.

The French example of political conflicts which canceled the introduction of an environmental tax (the *écotaxe*) provides a good illustration of how the political interests of external parties to the contract may hinder its proper running. In 2008, the Grenelle Environment Forum validated the setting up of a specific tax on heavy goods vehicles, with the double objective of encouraging the use of less polluting means of transport and of involving this sector in the maintenance of transport means and infrastructure. This *écotaxe*, which then enjoyed unanimous support both on the left and on the right of the political spectrum, nevertheless raised a number of technical and financial challenges: ability to tax a certain type of trucks only on certain roads, installation of portals, organization of a system compatible with possible future European electronic tolls, etc. The French State then decided to set up a PPP and a call for tenders was issued in March 2009. The Ecomouv' consortium won the auction in 2011 and then undertook the first investments, hiring 200 people for the management center and planning to begin implementation in 2013. However, transport operators as well as many local elected representatives questioned several aspects of the contract: collection operators, road network concerned by the measure, etc. Protests intensified in May 2013 when 60 right-wing members of Parliament filed an appeal before the Constitutional Council against the government's flat-rate project and then in October 2013 when the Breton "red caps" demonstrated violently and demanded the complete withdrawal of the *é cotaxe*. The government then decided to suspend its implementation and to open a commission of inquiry in order to break the deadlock. It was not until June 2014 that the outcome of the renegotiations between Ecomouv', the government, and the third parties (transport operators, red caps) came to be known. The scope of applicability of the tax was then divided by four (with only one route in Brittany). Finally, in October 2014, the *écotaxe* PPP contract was purely abandoned, and the French government had to pay almost 1 billion Euros to compensate the Franco-Italian company in charge of the project. Third-party opportunism therefore led first to a major renegotiation of the terms of the initial agreement, before leading to a complete abandoning of the project.

2.2 Solutions to Limit Opportunism

Setting up rigid contracts makes it possible to limit the occurrence of renegotiations and thus the risks of opportunistic behaviors (Sect. 2.2.1). In addition, reputational concerns limit the risks of private party opportunism, which is an argument in favor of contract combination strategies (Sect. 2.2.2).

2.2.1 Rigid Contracts

In order to discourage "bad" renegotiations initiated by opportunistic partners, the solution may be to set up contracts that are both more complete and more rigid. A complete contract, one that would define precisely all contingencies likely to arise *ex post* as well as the parties' commitments and obligations in all situations, would *de facto* make it possible to lower the number of renegotiations significantly. This would substantially reduce opportunities for the parties (private operators, public authorities, third parties) to take advantage of contractual incompleteness and the ensuing renegotiations to serve their personal interest. In addition, contracts can be made more rigid by limiting the possibilities of contractual interpretation and modification *ex post*. The objective is then to leave as little latitude as possible for renegotiation. However, one should keep in mind that a rigid contract is not necessarily complete, and *vice versa* (see Box 4).

Several studies highlight a positive correlation between the likelihood of observing opportunistic behaviors and contractual rigidity: the more the parties anticipate this risk of opportunistic behavior, the more they tend to set up rigid contracts. Empirically, the degree of PPP contract rigidity is often analyzed in relation to the price adjustment mechanisms provided for in the initial contract. In their respective studies on military equipment contracts in the USA and highway concession contracts in France, Crocker and Reynolds (1993) and Athias and Saussier (2010) use this variable to assess the level of contractual rigidity chosen by public authorities. Thus, a rigid contract sets the price *ex ante* and does not authorize any form of *ex post* renegotiation, whereas a flexible contract does not determine a price *ex ante* but postpones setting the price to a later date, when the information necessary for its determination is known to the parties. These two studies demonstrate the effect of past experience on the level of contract rigidity. Athias and Saussier (2010) show that price adjustment mechanisms tend to be less rigid when the parties have already had several contractual relationships in the past, while Crocker and Reynolds (1993), using a more qualitative measure, find a positive correlation between the number of past conflicts and the level of contract rigidity. Thus, when the parties "know each other" and risks of opportunistic behaviors are low, contracts tend to be less rigid; on the contrary, when past relationships were characterized by a high number of conflicts, contracts tend to be more rigid.

More recent works also underline a positive correlation between contract rigidity and the potential opportunism of third parties (see Sect. 2.1.3). Beuve, Moszoro, and Saussier (2015) propose a different way to measure rigidity[10] and find that, in the car park industry, contracts concluded by municipalities where political contestability is high tend to be more rigid. Indeed, the local council in place will

---

[10]The authors use the following measure of contract rigidity: they introduce rigidity categories (certification, evaluation, litigation, penalties, contingencies, design and termination) and proceed to a machine-reading of these dimensions in contracts. These categories capture relevant contractual clauses that lower the likelihood of being challenged by opportunistic third parties.

try to avoid contract renegotiations that could be costly in terms of image if political competition within the municipality is stiff. These results thus indicate that contractual rigidity can be used as protection against a high risk of third-party opportunism.

However, two disadvantages of setting up rigid contracts should be highlighted. On the one hand, such contracts are particularly expensive. Indeed, drafting them entails additional transaction costs both for the public party (*ex ante* information retrieval, detailed drawing up of specifications, etc.) and the private party (because these contracts may imply longer and more complex tender submission procedures), which could cancel out the potential advantages of a rigid contract. On the other hand, rigidity may hinder contract adaptability to changes in the environment (statutory, technological, financial, etc.), such evolutions being unavoidable in long-term contracts (see Sect. 3).

Box 4: Contractual Completeness and Contract Rigidity

A contract is said to be incomplete when it does not give an exhaustive description of all contingencies that may arise during its implementation phase and of the parties' commitments and obligations for each of these contingencies. Contractual incompleteness is due, on the one hand, to the cost of drawing up contingent contracts and, on the other hand, to the fact that the information is non-verifiable by third parties, judges in particular (Grossman & Hart, 1986). Indeed, when drawing up the contract, it is almost impossible—and very costly—to provide for all events that may arise after it is signed. Moreover, it would be useless to write such a contract (a complete contract), because it would only be "understood" by the two signatory parties. Thus, third parties—and judges in particular, in the event of a dispute—are not qualified enough or do not have the information necessary to understand all clauses of a complete contract. An analogy is sometimes made with what is known as flexible contracts, as opposed to rigid contracts. Rigid contracts aim to leave as little latitude as possible for *ex post* renegotiation. Their objective is to define as many contractual dimensions as possible beforehand, whether in relation to price clauses, investment requirements, fee amounts, etc. In this respect, they are close to the definition of complete contracts. In contrast, flexible contracts deliberately authorize *ex post* renegotiations, which are supposed to allow for the adaptation of the contract to events that only become observable in the course of the contractual relationship. Thus, periodic review clauses, price review clauses, or integration clauses are various means implemented to make contracts flexible, that is, adaptable to a changing economic environment.

2.2.2   Reputational Effects

In the particular case of private operator opportunism, another way to limit potential opportunistic behaviors is to rely on the private parties' concern for reputation. Indeed, opportunistic behaviors damage operators' reputation, which can dissuade public authorities from granting them contracts in the future. The works of Zupan (1989a, b) and Prager (1989) on cable TV concessions in the USA highlight this effect. The results of their empirical studies show that the operators in place did not take advantage of the numerous possibilities for opportunism permitted by the "competition for the market." They preferred to retain, or even improve, their reputation capital rather than adopt an opportunistic behavior generating benefits in the short run but compromising their relationships with their current and future partner(s). Using a database of 3516 cable TV concession contract renewals, Zupan (1989b) compares the terms of trade (e.g., number of channels, usage fee, channels dedicated to community programs, price bases, range of prices for each service provided) of the renewed contracts with those of the initial contracts. His findings indicate that even though incumbent operators have a stronger bargaining power (they have better knowledge of the project and have already developed specific assets as part of the previous contractual relation), there is no difference between the renewed and initial contracts. He explains this result by the operators' desire to preserve their "reputation capital." The same argument is put forward by Gil and Marion (2013) in their study focusing on 5120 road construction and reparation contracts between 1996 and 2005 in California. Indeed, their econometric results show that firms submit tenders that are all the more interesting as they anticipate more opportunities of future contracts.

However, the effects of opportunistic behaviors on private operators' reputation are not always deterrent enough, as they evidently depend on public parties' ability to detect and punish deviant behaviors (Guasch, 2004). It is therefore necessary to set up incentive mechanisms encouraging parties to use renegotiations in order to adapt contracts to their environment and to contingencies revealed *ex post*, instead of behaving opportunistically. This can be achieved through the prospect of winning future contracts if the operator behaves appropriately during the ongoing contracts. However, this type of incentive mechanism implies leaving a certain amount of discretionary power to the contracting authority in PPP award procedures. Thus, the high renewal rates in the water and urban transport industries in France should not necessarily be interpreted as a consequence of a lack of competition or of possible collusive behaviors between operators but may also result from cooperative behaviors among actors.

Another possible strategy for local authorities consists in signing several PPP contracts for various public services with the same operator (for instance, a single operator to manage the water and transport services). Thus, the risk of nonrenewal (in the event of opportunistic behavior) hangs over several contracts, and the operator has more to lose by adopting noncooperative strategies during renegotiations. In their analysis of the water sector in France, Desrieux, Chong, and Saussier (2013) show that prices applied for drinking water are lower when the operator is also in charge of sanitation (net result of the synergistic effects between the two kinds of activities). By extension, we can assume that these operators would also be less inclined to engage in opportunistic renegotiation strategies.

3 Renegotiations as a Way to Adapt Long-Term Contracts

Although the renegotiation process may be hindered by opportunistic behaviors, PPP efficiency depends on the parties' ability to foster the adaptability of these contracts (Sect. 3.1). To take up such a challenge, some solutions have been highlighted, and some others remain to be explored. We will therefore expose how contractual and institutional designs can work in favor of efficient PPP contract performance (Sect. 3.2).

3.1 Necessary Renegotiations for Proper Contract Performance

Although the major part of the economic literature considers that renegotiations result from actors' opportunism, the high rates of renegotiation in PPPs cannot be limited to this type of strategic behavior. On account of the specific characteristics of PPP contracts mentioned in the introduction of this chapter, renegotiations are unavoidable and may even sometimes determine the viability and proper performance of the contract. It is precisely the case when the initial contract needs to be reviewed because of initial errors in its design (Sect. 3.1.1), of exogenous shocks that are difficult to foresee (Sect. 3.1.2), or of an evolution in the public party's needs (Sect. 3.1.3).

3.1.1 Renegotiations and Contractual Maladaptations

A distinction should be made between changes in circumstances provided for in the initial contracts and those that are not. The majority of risks associated with a project are generally described in the PPP contract, which therefore specifies the risk sharing between the two parties. For instance, risks associated with project financing or geotechnical conditions are most often assumed by the private partner. In fact, any modification in circumstances affecting these elements (deterioration of financial conditions resulting in an increase in financing costs or project refinancing costs, discovery of unfavorable geotechnical conditions, etc.) is the responsibility of the private partner and may not give rise to a renegotiation of contractual clauses. However, under the combined effect of environmental complexity and the bounded rationality of economic actors, the initial contract cannot anticipate every risk. In the same manner, some opportunities may arise during the implementation of the contract, allowing for an improvement in the quality or execution of the service or infrastructure. For instance, technological progress may allow the operator to implement improvements requiring the renegotiation of certain contractual provisions. When faced with unforeseen risks or opportunities, renegotiations are then considered as necessary to mitigate maladaptation costs, inherent to long-term contracts, and "realign" the contract with its economic environment. It is difficult, however, to differentiate changes in circumstances that can be anticipated from those that cannot (see Box 5).

Box 5: The Velib' Case

Launched in July 2007, the Velib' program constitutes, to this day, the largest bike-sharing network in the world. In order to have the private sector finance such an operation, the city of Paris concluded a 10-year public contract with Somupi, a subsidiary of the JCDecaux group specializing in urban advertising. The initial contract provided for the installation of 1451 stations around Paris. The JCDecaux group was to bear alone the costs of setting up, operating, and maintaining the system, while revenues (subscriptions and rentals) would be collected by the city of Paris. In return, the private operator would be remunerated through the operating revenues derived from the 1600 advertising panels in the city. But the terms of the contract had to be largely renegotiated in 2009.

First of all, the Velib' operation was a victim of its own success. Thus, 196 stations turned out to be too small and had to be extended. In addition, faced with the success of the program, the city of Paris decided to expand the network and to equip 30 adjoining towns with 300 additional stations. Finally, the call center had to be extended in order to cope with the numerous user requests. The city thus agreed to pay a flat-rate allowance of 2.6 million euros to the operator for these additional expenses. Moreover, the initial contract had largely underestimated the number of bicycle thefts and degradations. Thus, as of June 2009, there were almost 8000 stolen bicycles and over 18,000 damaged ones. Faced with such additional costs (bearing in mind that one Velib' costs JCDecaux 610 euros), the city agreed to give the operator 400 euros for each bike that had to be replaced, when 4–25% of the fleet was damaged.

Finally, because some of the quality indicators were not fully satisfactory (for instance, as regards bicycle safety or cleanliness), renegotiations resulted in the setting up of financial incentives for the operator. The latter also had to pay financial penalties, even though the total amount provided for in the

(continued)

Box 5 (continued)

contract could not be paid, as its level would have completely destabilized the contract. Penalty reductions and incentive measures were thus granted by the city. Consequently, JCDecaux now receives 35% of marginal revenue if annual revenues exceed 14 million euros and 50% of marginal revenue if they exceed 17.5 million euros.

The city of Paris and JCDecaux both agree that it would have been impossible to anticipate such circumstances, as the Velib' operation is the first bicycle sharing network on such a scale. Considering the numerous aspects not provided for in the initial contract, we can wonder, however, if some of them (for instance, the success of the program) could not have been anticipated.

Such PPP maladaptation issues were highlighted in the work of Guasch. Among the various industries investigated by Guasch in his 2004 book, the case of Mexican highways is very eloquent in this respect. In the early 1990s, the Mexican government awarded 52 highways renovation and operation contracts to private operators through a tender procedure. Due to a lack of expertise and information, the public authority's choices led to a contractual design that was particularly unsuitable. First of all, most concessions were awarded to the operators that had committed for the shortest concession durations. This award criterion, which is highly debatable in view of economic theory (the long duration of concession contracts is theoretically justified by the need to amortize the investments to which the concessionaire agreed), makes it more difficult to reach the financial equilibrium of the contract. Secondly, the government provided operators with forecasts in terms of traffic volume that were extremely optimistic, leading operators to base the financial equilibrium of their tender on erroneous information. Finally, the state banking system granted loans to operators without conducting any detailed analysis of the structure and viability of the projects to be financed. The combination of these three "mistakes" resulted in the Mexican government having to restructure the financing of highways by means of a public refinancing of 80% of the concession contracts. Faced with this type of contractual maladaptation, renegotiation is no longer associated with opportunistic behavior from the parties but corresponds to a way of adapting the contract and rectifying past errors in judgment.

3.1.2 Renegotiations and Exogenous Shocks

Renegotiations may also arise from external events that were impossible to foresee during contract drafting. The econometric results of the analysis conducted by Guasch et al. (2008) indicate for instance that the probability of renegotiating concession contracts increases during phases of economic recession and decreases during phases of economic expansion (see Box 3). According to Bajari and Tadelis (2001), problems associated with PPPs have to do first and foremost with the existence of "exogenous shocks." The authors illustrate their observation using the case of the Getty Center Art Museum in Los Angeles, a construction contract that had to be renegotiated multiple times because of the site particularities (related to the subsoil) and above all due to unforeseen events (earthquake, modifications in the legal framework), which would have been virtually impossible to anticipate. Here, once more, the parties had to renegotiate the initial agreement to adapt the contract to a new environment.

The case of the international airport in Phnom Penh (Cambodia), studied by de Brux (2010), provides an interesting example of renegotiations which followed an exogenous shock and that proved to be beneficial for every stakeholder. In 1995, when the 20-year concession contract relating to the construction and operation of the airport was signed, the parties were unable to foresee two major events that later deeply disrupted the economic and institutional environment of the contract: the Asian crisis and the military coup of 1997. Cambodia was then faced with a massive outflow of capital from the country as well as with a brutal interruption of air traffic, which put the concessionaire at high risk of bankruptcy. Although the contract had provided for the possibility of contract termination in case of force majeure, the parties decided to renegotiate its terms and found a compromise allowing them to make up for part of the concessionaire's losses, while ensuring that the Cambodian financial situation did not deteriorate further. The concession was then extended for an additional 5 years (to a total duration of 25 years) and a "compensation account" was created to make up for the losses sustained by the private partner. Afterward, traffic increased quickly, so that revenue sharing among the partners was readjusted in favor of the government. In this example, renegotiation thus appears to be beneficial to both parties by allowing the contract to adapt to its new environment.

3.1.3   Renegotiations and Evolution Needs

Aside from issues of maladaptation and a lack of anticipation of exogenous shocks, a simple evolution in public buyers' needs can be at the origin of contractual renegotiations that benefit the parties. Indeed, if the public authority wishes to modify the service provided by the private operator, it can decide to renegotiate the initial conditions of the contract in order to adapt it to its new needs (provided that it does not modify the general structure of the contract). For instance, the public party may wish to extend the scope of the project (serving a larger number of users for a water, electricity, or road network, etc.) or to increase its quality (adding an elevator in a car park, reducing the number of interruptions on the electrical grid, using more environment-friendly materials, etc.).

Such a situation was illustrated by de Brux (2010), through the case of the contract between the city of Marseille and a French private firm (the *Société marseillaise du tunnel Prado-Carénage*, SMTPC). In the 1990s, the SMTPC was selected by the city of Marseille for the concession of a tunnel connecting the

Carénage basin to the avenue of Prado, for a duration of 30 years (expiration date in 2025). It is the first French example of an urban toll tunnel aiming to limit traffic in the city center. However, in the 2000s, problems of traffic congestion in another neighborhood (around the train station) intensified dramatically and the city therefore decided to connect this geographical area to the tunnel *via* an additional section. Through an amendment to the contract added on July 26th, 2005, the concession for the new tunnel (Louis Rège) was awarded until 2025. The amendment stipulated that the city would be in charge of preparatory work and of building the foundations for the new tunnel, while the private operator would be responsible for building and maintaining the road and safety facilities of the tunnel. This renegotiation was conducted without the city needing to compensate the operator financially due to the expected increase in traffic in the existing tunnel. However, renegotiations had to be conducted with the lenders (in order to define a new financial model) and with the shareholders of the SMTPC (in order to make sure of the evolution of dividend payments, although part of the additional works was self-financed). It was possible to conduct such renegotiations because the new contract was indeed beneficial to both parties. This example shows how renegotiating a PPP contract may be an opportunity to respond to an evolution in the public party's needs while being beneficial to all stakeholders.

3.2 Contractual and Institutional Solutions

Several mechanisms can be set up in order to give PPP contracts the adaptability that is necessary for their performance. These mechanisms have to do with the contracts themselves (Sect. 3.2.1) but also with the institutional and competitive framework in which they are concluded (Sect. 3.2.2).

3.2.1 Flexible Contracts

Although, as highlighted in the previous section, drawing up a rigid contract can protect the parties against possible opportunistic behaviors, it can also prove to be detrimental when it prevents the contract from adapting easily in reaction to potential mistakes in the initial design, evolutions in needs, and exogenous shocks. The necessity to favor this type of beneficial renegotiation can thus justify the existence of more flexible contracts, that is, contracts allowing for *ex post* adjustments, as and when the parties acquire relevant information. The contractual design initially selected can thus allow for better adaptability of these long-term contracts.

According to existing empirical studies on the topic, choosing the optimal level of contract flexibility results from an arbitration between rigidity, in order to limit the risks of opportunism (see Sect. 2) and flexibility, in order to favor renegotiations that are beneficial to both parties. As previously mentioned, such flexibility is often analyzed in relation to price adjustment mechanisms. Thus, the works of Crocker and Reynolds (1993) and Athias and Saussier (2010) indicate that when the relationship is characterized by greater uncertainty (uncertainty about environmental and technological evolutions for the military equipment contracts described by Crocker and Reynolds, and about traffic forecasts in the highway concession contracts studied by Athias and Saussier), contracts tend to be more flexible.

This need for flexibility in PPPs was also highlighted by Ménard, Saussier, and Staropoli (2003) in a study focusing on the water sector in France. Based on a sample of 73 contracts, the authors compare distribution contracts concluded in 1999 between operators and local authorities with their previous version, signed before the French decentralization law of 1982. They observe that the new contracts more often include price review clauses and that when these clauses are present both in the old and the new contract, their trigger threshold was revised downward. Thus, these different empirical studies are a perfect illustration of the positive nature of renegotiation as a mechanism allowing the parties to adapt the contractual arrangements to a changing environment and highlight the need for adaptability in PPP contracts. However, it should be noted that there is no unified definition of flexible contracts. Thus, a flexible contract is not necessarily a contract containing price review clauses. The adjustment variable may also be contract duration, as described in Engel, Fischer, and Galetovic (2010) (see Box 6).

Choosing the contractual design implies reflecting *ex ante* about mechanisms for contract adaptations arising *ex post*, as well as about termination options in case the partnership is not able to reach its term. Since a flexible contract implies *ex post* adaptations based on new information, it is essential to ensure that the parties have access to the same information, in other words to avoid asymmetries leading to opportunistic behaviors as described in Sect. 2.1. The public party should therefore monitor and assess the private partner's performance throughout the duration of the contract. Monitoring and assessment tools must be provided for in the contract, in order to facilitate communication and guarantee efficient interactions between the parties (see Chapter "The Evolution of Financing Conditions PPP Contracts: Still a Private Financing Model?" of the first part on PPP regulation). Such tools can only be efficient if the public party has the expertise and resources needed to use them. Therefore, the setting up of such tools must be combined with competence and expertise of public officers in charge of monitoring PPP contracts, especially in terms of risk management, financing, and private accounting. This expertise of the public entity is all the more necessary to monitor complex contracts (concessions, availability contracts). Then, the public authority must understand and control the information provided by the contractors but must also be able to have an overall view of the economic and technical issues related to the projects. This can facilitate contract adaptability while reinforcing the bargaining power of the public party. In addition, by regularly monitoring operators, the public authority gives them incentives to attach special importance to their reputation, which strengthens the mechanism introduced in Sect. 2.2.2.

Box 6: Least Present Value of Revenue Auctions

A flexible contract can be a contract with a duration that varies according to the level of demand associated with the project, as described by Engel et al. (2010).

Least present value of revenue auctions (LPVR) enable the public authority to award a contract to the operator offering the least present value of total revenue from end-user fees. The contract then comes to an end when the amount of revenue provided for in the contract is reached. Unlike price, contract duration is not established *ex ante*, although a maximum duration may be specified. Thus, if demand is low, the contract will last longer than in case of high demand, as it will take longer for the operator to collect the revenue provided for in the contract.

By indexing partnership duration on the demand associated with the project, this type of arrangement reduces the risk to which the operator is exposed and therefore the risk premium it requires. It also makes it possible to limit the risks of opportunistic behaviors leading to "bad" renegotiations, as the two parties came to an agreement *ex ante* about the level of revenue to be reached.

However, practitioners are sometimes skeptical about this arrangement as uncertainty about loan duration may put banks and investors at risk.

3.2.2 Institutional and Competitive Regulation

Sometimes, renegotiations can therefore be a desirable phenomenon, which seems to plead in favor of setting up flexible contracts. However, an institutional framework of high quality is necessary to conclude flexible contracts, because opportunistic behaviors must then be discouraged.

Weak institutions damage the credibility of public authorities and can thus encourage opportunistic behaviors leading to a misappropriation of resources or a decrease in the quality of the goods or services provided. A weak institutional framework also reinforces the risks of opportunistic behaviors by the public entity. Indeed, in the absence of government control systems, it is easier for the latter to modify the "ground rules" unilaterally. Guasch (2004) thus reports that the occurrence of renegotiations can be reduced significantly by the presence of an independent regulatory authority. In his study investigating over 1300 concession contracts, the author notes that, although the observed rates of renegotiation are particularly high in the transport sector (55%) and the water sector (74%), these rates decrease by 20–40% when a regulator is in charge of managing the contracts.[11] The existence of a national authority provided with independent resources and *ad hoc* expertise can indeed make it possible to conduct benchmarking analyses and to

---

[11]This result was confirmed by a later study of Guasch et al. (2008).

disseminate their results, in order to reduce information asymmetries and thus limit opportunistic behaviors by the parties (see Chapter "The Evolution of Financing Conditions PPP Contracts: Still a Private Financing Model?" of the first part on PPP regulation). A study by Athias and Saussier (2010) supports this result. In their analysis of highway concession contracts in various countries, the authors use an aggregate indicator of governance developed by the World Bank (Kaufmann, Kraay, & Mastruzzi, 2004) to define the level of institutional quality, and they show that the stronger the institutional framework is, the more flexible the contracts tend to be.

All these empirical findings thus confirm that the quality of the institutional framework constitutes an important counterweight to the opportunism of contracting parties. Moreover, the existence of a regulator reduces issues of information and expertise asymmetry mentioned previously, especially in the case of small and middle-sized local and regional authorities.

A more active promotion of competition for the market may also limit opportunistic behaviors. Thus, Chong, Huet, and Saussier (2006) show that while the credibility of penalties partly depends on contractual clauses, it is also associated with the structure of the sector. Through their analysis of the French water sector, these authors demonstrate that competition between private operators and public undertakings renders the threat of a return under state control credible and strongly influences the behavior of private operators. Similarly, the regulator of London bus transport deliberately decided to keep a public body operating in the sector in order to reestablish contract termination as a credible threat (Amaral et al., 2009).

Whether through flexible contracts or better competitive and institutional regulation, the various ways to improve the performance phase of PPP contracts can only be investigated and assessed by conducting more precise scientific research on the subject. Indeed, this chapter highlighted the fact that the many empirical works that investigate the determinants of renegotiations are only too rarely able to clearly distinguish the motivations of the parties behind these renegotiations. For instance, it is often very difficult to detect opportunistic behaviors by studying PPP contract renegotiations. Knowing that such behaviors are detrimental to the quality of the relationship between signatory parties, a careful analysis of the effect of renegotiations on this relationship would constitute an interesting area for further research. Although some studies (for instance, Guasch, Laffont, & Straub, 2007) begin to shed light on the subject, most empirical works use data from countries with weak institutions. Oxley and Silverman (2008) thus remark that future empirical works are essential to perfect our knowledge and understanding of renegotiations and their consequences.

In particular, these studies will have to determine whether renegotiations allow for a joint evolution toward greater efficiency or constitute the demonstration of opportunistic behavior by one of the partners. This should be done by *"explicitly connecting renegotiation to (actual or perceived) performance effects, and to unpacking more disaggregated detail about which types of provisions are renegotiated in the presence of which triggering factor"* (Oxley & Silverman, 2008, p. 231). The challenge at stake here is thus to move beyond the limits of the existing literature to characterize the effect of renegotiation on performance more precisely. Beuve, de Brux, and Saussier (2013) conducted one of the first empirical analyses on the subject and investigated the effect of renegotiations on the contractual relationship between French municipalities and an urban car park operator (see Box 7). However, this type of empirical research is rare, as it requires a direct access to PPP contracts and their renegotiations. This is an argument in favor of greater transparency of information regarding PPP contracts throughout their duration (from their award through their operational phase and until their potential renewal).[12]

Transparency allows anyone to monitor the actions of the public entity in order to make sure that they comply with the principles of free access (the right to be aware of the needs expressed by the public entity) and equal treatment (ban on discrimination at every stage of the procedure). If such transparency has an immediate cost for public authorities, as well as for private operators, this cost can be more than counterbalanced by beneficial effects. Indeed, transparency can increase the level of competition (as information is *de facto* accessible to a larger number of potential tenderers during calls for tenders), and it can also help discourage deviant practices (monitoring contract award and renegotiations can act as an incentive to implement good practices, and as a deterrent against the opportunism of both public and private parties). However, it should not encourage opportunism by third parties, which could hinder the proper running of PPP contracts (see Sect. 2.1.3).

Saussier and Tirole (2015) suggest that a simple and inexpensive way of improving transparency in the case of renegotiations would be to introduce a specific dispute proceeding for public procurement contracts. This quick "amendment summary" procedure would be similar to pre-contractual and contractual summary proceedings. The amendment summary procedure would thus allow any third party (elected representative, company, citizen, etc.) to request the cancelation of an amendment. However, it would only be possible to make such requests in the event of a failure to comply with legal rules (for instance, regarding the calculation of legal thresholds, modifications of the object of the contract, fraud, etc.). The objective of such a measure would thus be to foster transparency while limiting abusive appeals that could slow down adaptations or be the result of opportunism by interested third parties. The authors also suggest that information transparency more generally constitutes an essential issue in public policy evaluation. A wide and quick dissemination of information regarding the award and performance phases of all public procurement contracts is therefore necessary. Today, there is a substantial disparity between countries as regards the accessibility of such information. A study by the OECD[13] points to major shortfalls in this area (accessibility of

---

[12]See the report for the European Parliament regarding the project of directive on Concessions by Stéphane Saussier (2012), advocating greater transparency in the performance phase of PPPs. This directive was passed in early 2014, without this proposal being accepted.

[13]OECD (2008), "Government at a Glance" (p. 153).

data on contract amendments and on tracking procurement spending) in a large number of countries. If these data are difficult to access for public procurement, they are even more so for concession contracts. As for information about contract monitoring (*ex post*), it is virtually nonexistent for all PPPs. Yet, these data are necessary to develop scientific works allowing for a better knowledge of renegotiations, a complex yet unavoidable phenomenon of vital importance for the success of contractual relations.

Box 7: Object of Renegotiations and Probability of Renewal

Using a dataset of 151 concession contracts in the urban car park sector in France in the years 1965–2008 (of which 94 expired contracts), Beuve et al. (2013) conduct an analysis of the effect of renegotiations on the probability of the private operator being renewed (the probability of renewal is used as a proxy for good contract performance[14]).

Their findings indicate that:

- The occurrence of renegotiations does not influence the probability of renewal (*the fact that contracts have never been renegotiated or that they have been at least once does not affect the probability of renewal significantly*).
- The relation between the frequency of renegotiations and the probability of renewal is nonlinear (*the probability of renewal increases with the frequency of renegotiations in the first phase, before decreasing in the second phase*).
- Depending on their object, renegotiations may either be beneficial or detrimental to the performance of PPPs (*for instance, the probability of renewal increases when renegotiations are related to service quality and decreases when they are about the financial conditions of the contract*).
- The more quickly the contract is renegotiated after its award, the less likely it is of being renewed (*the probability of renewal decreases when the contract is renegotiated shortly after being awarded. This result is consistent with previous works on the effects of aggressive bidding*).

---

4 Conclusion

This review of empirical literature shows that while renegotiations are necessary because of the duration and complexity of PPP contracts, the stakeholders may "take advantage" of this situation to develop opportunistic strategies. The vital

---

[14]In the sector under study, the high level of competition makes it possible to consider renewal as an indicator of good contract performance. As an illustration, the renewal rate in this sector is close to 50%, against rates higher than 90% in the water and transport sectors, which are known to be less competitive.

challenge at stake here is therefore to implement contractual mechanisms, to develop public authorities' expertise in terms of public procurement, and to set up reliable institutional structures in order to favor "beneficial" adaptations while avoiding opportunistic renegotiations. The various elements tackled in this chapter show that solutions do exist, both contractual (operator selection, contractual clauses, information monitoring, and sharing procedures) and extracontractual (competition, reputation, expertise), to supervise the implementation phase of PPP contracts, thus favoring their adaptability to the economic, financial, and statutory environment. The new provisions associated with the European Directives on public procurement and concessions are evidence of a first step toward a new approach of renegotiations, granting more flexibility for contractual adaptations. For these directives to be effective and to improve public contract performance, they must however be combined with measures revolving around the three essential pillars that are transparency, competition, and expertise.

References

Alcazar, L., Abdala, M., & Shirley, M. (2002). The Buenos-Aires Water Concession. In *Thirsting for efficiency: The economics and politics of urban water system reform* (pp. 65–102). Elsevier Pub.

Amaral, M., Saussier, S., & Yvrande-Billon, A. (2009). Auction procedures and competition in public services: The case of urban public transport in France and London. *Utilities Policy, 17*, 166–175.

Athias, L., & Nunez, A. (2008). Winner's curse in toll road concessions. *Economics Letters, 101* (3), 172–174.

Athias, L., & Saussier, S. (2010). *Contractual flexibility or rigidity for public private partnerships? Theory and evidence from infrastructure concession contracts* (working paper Chaire EPPP).

Bajari, P., & Tadelis, S. (2001). Incentives versus transaction costs: A theory of procurement contracts. *RAND Journal of Economics, 32*(3), 387–407.

Bajari, P., MacMillan, R. S., & Tadelis, S. (2009). Auctions versus negotiations in procurement: An empirical analysis. *Journal of Law, Economics and Organization, 25*(2) 372–399.

Beuve, J., de Brux, J., & Saussier, S. (2013). Renégocier pour durer, une analyse empirique des contrats de concessions. *Revue d'économie industrielle, 141*(1), 117–148.

Beuve, J., Moszoro, M., & Saussier, S. (2015). *Political contestability and contract rigidity: An analysis of procurement contracts.* document de travail chaire EPPP.

Chong, E., Huet, F., & Saussier, S. (2006). Auctions, ex post competition and prices: The efficiency of public-private partnership. *Annals of Public and Cooperative Econnomics, 77* (4), 517–549.

Chong, E., Klien, M., & Moore, J. (2013). *Do politicians procure their way to Congress? An empirical analysis of public procurement and elections* (Working Paper Chaire EPPP).

Cour des Comptes. (2013). *Les relations entre l'Etat et les sociétés concessionnaires d'autoroutes.* Communication à la commission des finances de l'assemblée nationale.

Crocker, K. J., & Reynolds, K. J. (1993). The efficiency of incomplete contracts: An empirical analysis of Air Force engine procurement. *RAND Journal of Economics, 24*(1), 126–146.

De Brux, J. (2010). The dark and bright sides of renegotiation: An application to transport concession contracts. *Utilities Policy, 18*(2), 77–85.

Desrieux, C., Chong, E., & Saussier, S. (2013). Putting all one's eggs in one Basket: Relational contracts and the management of local public services. *Journal of Economic Behavior and Organizations, 89*, 167–186.

Domingues, S., & Sarmento, J. M. (2016). Critical renegotiation triggers of European transport concessions. *Transport Policy, 48(C)*, 82–91.

Engel, E., Fischer, R., & Galetovic, A. (2009). *Soft budgets and renegotiations in public-private partnerships* (Cowles Foundation Discussion Papers 1723). Cowles Foundation for Research in Economics, Yale University.

Engel, E., Fischer, R., & Galetovic, A. (2010). *The economics of infrastructure finance: Public-private partnerships versus public provision* (working document).

Engel, E., Fisher, R., & Galetovic, A. (2011). *Public-private partnerships to revamp u.s. infrastructure*. The Hamilton Project.

Estache, A., & Saussier, S. (2014). Public-private partnerships and efficiency: A short assessment. *CESifo DICE Report, 12*, 8–13.

Gil, R., & Marion, J. (2013). Self-enforcing agreements and relational contracting: Evidence from California highway procurement. *Journal of Law, Economics, and Organization, 29(2)*, 239–277.

Grossman, S., & Hart, O. (1986, August). The costs and benefits of ownership: A theory of vertical and lateral integration. *Journal of Political Economy, 94(4)*, 691–719. University of Chicago Press.

Guasch, J.-L. (2004). *Granting and renegotiating infrastructure concession: Doing it right*. Washington, DC: The World Bank.

Guasch, J.-L., Laffont, J.-J., & Straub, S. (2007). Concessions of infrastructure in Latin America: Government-led renegotiation. *Journal of Applied Econometrics, 22(7)*, 1267–1294.

Guasch, J.-L., Laffont, J.-J., & Straub, S. (2008). Renegotiation of concession contracts in Latin America: Evidence from the water and transport sectors. *International Journal of Industrial Organization, Elsevier, 26(2)*, 421–442.

Hart, O. (1995). *Firms, contracts and financial structure*. Oxford: Oxford University Press.

HM Treasury. (2003). *PFI: Meeting the investment challenge*. London: HM Treasury.

Iossa, E., Spagnolo, G., & Vellez, M. (2007). *Contract design in public-private partnerships*. Report for the World Bank.

ITF. (2017). *Public private partnerships for transport infrastructure: Renegotiation and economic outcomes*. Paris: OECD.

Kaufmann, D., Kraay, A., & Mastruzzi, M. (2004). Governance matters III: Governance indicators for 1996, 1998, 2000, 2002. *WBER, 18*, 253–287.

Kerf, M. (1998). *Concessions for infrastructures: A guide for their design and award* (World Bank Technical Paper no 399). Finance, Private Sector and Infrastructure Network.

Le Squeren, Z., & Moore, J. (2015). *The political cycle of public-private contract renegotiations: Evidence from the French Car Park Sector* (working document chaire EPPP).

Masten, S. E., & Saussier, S. (2000). Econometrics of contracts: An assessment of developments in the empirical literature of contracting. *Revue d'économie industrielle, 92*, 215–237.

McCubbins, M., & Schwartz, T. (1984). Congressional oversight overlooked: Police patrols versus fire alarms. *American Journal of Political Science, 28*, 16–79.

Ménard, C., Saussier, S., & Staropoli, C. (2003). L'impact des contraintes institutionnelles sur les choix contractuels des collectivités locales. *Annuaire des collectivités locales, 23*, 109–118.

Moszoro, M., & Spiller, P. (2012). *Third-party opportunism and the (in)efficiency of public contracts*. SSRN eLibrary.

National Audit Office. (2001). *Managing the relationship to secure a successful partnership in PFI projects*. Report by the Comptroller and Auditor General.

National Audit Office. (2003). *PFI: construction performance*. Report by the Comptroller and Auditor General.

OECD. (2008). *Les partenariats public-privé: partager les risques et optimiser les ressources*. OECD Publishing.

Oxley, J., & Silverman, B. (2008). Inter-firm alliances; A new institutional economics approach. In
    E. Brousseau & J.-M. Glachant (Eds.), *New institutional economics: A guidebook* (pp. 209–
    234). Cambridge: Cambridge University Press.
Prager, R. A. (1989). Franchise bidding for natural monopoly: The case of cable television in
    Massachusetts. *Journal of Regulatory Economics, 1*(2), 115–131.
Saussier, S. (2012, June). *An economic analysis of the closure of markets and other dysfunctions in
    the awarding of concession contracts.* European Parliament Note, Directorate General for
    Internal Policies, Policy Department A: Economics and Scientific Policy.
Saussier, S., & Farès, M. (2002). Coûts de transaction et contrats incomplets. *Revue Française
    d'Économie, 16*, 193–230.
Saussier, S., & Tirole, J. (2015, April). *Strenghtening the efficiency of public procurement.* Note
    for the French Council of Economic Analysis, no 22.
Spiller, P. T. (2008). *An institutional theory of public contracts: Regulatory implications.* Rapport
    technique, National Bureau of Economic Research, Inc.
Sueur, J.-P., & Portelli, H. (2014). *Les contrats de partenariats: des bombes à retardements.*
    Rapport d'information du Sénat no 733, juillet.
United States Government Accountability. (2009, March). *Defense acquisitions: Assessments of
    selected weapon programs.* Office Report to Congressional Committees.
Williamson, O. E. (1976). Franchise bidding for natural monopolies: In general and with respect to
    CATV. *Bell Journal of Economics, 7*(1), 73–104.
Williamson, O. E. (1985). *The economic institutions of capitalism.* New York, NY: The Free Press.
Zupan, M. A. (1989a). Cable franchise renewals: Do incumbent firms behave opportunistically?
    RAND Journal of Economics, 20(4), 473–482.
Zupan, M. A. (1989b). The efficacy of franchise bidding schemes in the case of cable television:
    Some systematic evidence. *Journal of Law and Economics, 32*(2), 401–456.

Comparative Performances of Delivery Options: Empirical Lessons

Miguel Amaral, Eshien Chong, and Stéphane Saussier

1 Introduction

The question of public service organization is among the themes that are regularly debated and are even, in some cases, the object of demonstrations and contests by users and citizens. Private management is often criticized for sacrificing the quality of an essential good or service in pursuit of profit. Are such concerns justified? What is the impact of public authorities' management methods (that is, their choices in terms of governance structure to provide public services) and contractual choices on the performance of public services? One only needs to consider the heated debates surrounding water management in Europe or the development of availability contracts, that is, public-budget pay PPPs to realize that the answer to that question constitutes a major issue of public policy, at the center of citizen concerns.

To further illustrate this point, let us go back to the particular case of water management in France. Indeed, this sector recently underwent some much-publicized re-municipalizations, with in particular the emblematic case of the city of Paris. These organizational changes are fueled by a number of academic studies and consumer association surveys, which regularly point out that users of water services managed under a concession contract pay a higher price than those whose

M. Amaral (✉)
ARAFER (Autorité de régulation des activités ferroviaires et routières), Paris, France
e-mail: miguelamaral75@gmail.com

E. Chong
Autorité de la concurrence & IAE Paris, Sorbonne Business School, Paris, France
e-mail: ceshien@gmail.com

S. Saussier
IAE Paris, Sorbonne Business School, Paris, France
e-mail: saussier@univ-paris1.fr

© Springer International Publishing AG 2018
S. Saussier, J. de Brux (eds.), *The Economics of Public-Private Partnerships*,
https://doi.org/10.1007/978-3-319-68050-7_7

water services are under direct public provision (CGDD, 2010; UFC, 2006; Ménard & Saussier, 2003). A survey published by the consumer association *UFC Que Choisir* in April 2010 thus estimated that the mean price deviation between the two delivery options was around 30% and based on this drew definitive conclusions about the relative efficiency of delivery options (that is, as it happens, about the superiority of public management over concession). A recent report from the French General Commission for Sustainable Development (Commissariat général au développement durable, CGDD, 2010) observed that between 2004 and 2008, "*a net flow of 300 municipalities, representing 120,000 inhabitants, equipped with* [the collective wastewater treatment service] *in 2004, have since then abandoned delegated or mixed management for public management.*" If this report mentions a clear difference in price between public management ($3.00€/m^3$) and delegated management ($3.57€/m^3$) in 2008, it nevertheless insists on the fact that "*private operators are more often faced with specific technical operating conditions relating to network density, origin of water, level of water purification treatment and wastewater treatment.*" This clearly illustrates how hazardous it can be to limit the evaluation of the relative performances of delivery options to a mere comparison of average end-user prices. If delivery options are not selected randomly, and if some of them are more frequently used in complex situations, the comparison of averages does not allow us to conclude that one structure is superior to another. Only a comparison realized *all other things being equal*, between municipalities with similar characteristics, would allow to point toward conclusive elements as to the relative performance of delivery options. However, the economic theory, as exposed in Chapter "An Economic Analysis of Public–Private Partnerships" of the first part of this book, suggests that no delivery option is more efficient than the others at all times and in all places. Each mode has its own characteristics, which renders it relatively more appropriate in certain specific situations. This makes it all the more difficult to draw an empirical comparison between delivery options, in which a number of variables should not be overlooked (competition level, size of the service, etc.), as these variables also have an influence on the efficiency of the methods in question.

From this point of view, econometric analyses are indispensable to provide robust answers to the question of the relative efficiency of delivery options, *all other things being equal*, even if the issue of efficiency measurements is a complex one that cannot be eluded. Can efficiency be limited to price? Certainly not. But most empirical studies, as we will see, simply focus on a single dimension of performance, such as price or costs, often eluding the more qualitative dimensions of public services, which admittedly are more difficult to quantify.

Can empirical studies provide insight into the question of the relative efficiency of public service delivery options? We believe so, and the object of this chapter is to make an assessment of these studies. A researcher who wants to shed light on the relative efficiency of delivery options for a given public service is faced with three essential questions: (1) Which measure of efficiency should be selected? (2) How can the choice of the delivery options be explained? (3) Aside from this choice, what are the other factors of efficiency?

First, this chapter proposes a review of empirical studies focusing on the efficiency of delivery options and draws a number of essential lessons from them. We will see that the economic literature on the topic does not settle the debate for good but points to different factors that are likely to contribute to the efficiency of the various delivery options. In particular, the role of competitive pressure (market structure, potential return under public management, etc.) stands out as a primordial element. In the second phase, we will go back to the *ex ante* choice made by delegating authorities in terms of delivery options. This issue, although essential, is frequently eluded by empirical studies. This decision to overlook public authorities' motivations in delegating a service or not, by considering such choices as exogenous and random, weakens most of the existing empirical findings, as there is every reason to think that the choice of the delivery option is not made randomly. The developments of the empirical literature summed up in this chapter confirm that statement, by showing that two types of determinants are at work in local authorities' choices: a desire to reduce production and transaction costs, on the one hand, and, on the other hand, nonmonetary factors such as political persuasion or the influence of interest groups. Investigating the reasons behind public decision-makers' choices is a major area of research for economists, as it is one of the ways to make for a more robust analysis of the comparative performances of governance modes.

2   Influence of the Delivery Option on Performance

The investigation of the relative performance of delivery options largely rests on the theoretical and empirical developments of economic science around the "make-or-buy" question and more particularly on the works of transaction cost economics (Williamson, 1975, 1976, 1985). A parallel can indeed be drawn between the decision by a firm to insource or to outsource an activity and the decision by a State or local authority to externalize the management of a public service or not. The underlying logic of these works is that the observed delivery options should result from a desire to reduce transaction and production costs. It is thus assumed that these choices are made based on considerations of economic efficiency. In other words, a local authority or a State decides to delegate a public service when it expects, by involving a private partner, to realize economies in terms of production costs (economies of scale, scope, and density), without these potential gains being canceled out by exceedingly high contracting costs (that is, when the introduction of competition between operators and the execution of contracts do not constitute major issues—see Chapters "The Relative Efficiency of Competitive Tendering" and "Renegotiating PPP Contracts: Opportunities and Pitfalls" of the second part of this book, specifying the conditions under which these costs may prove to be prohibitive). This theory suggests that the focal point of study should be the partnership, and more particularly the (transaction) costs associated with its setting up, rather than focusing of the involvement of the private sector to provide a public service for citizens.[1]

The application of this normative analytical framework to the study of the delivery option of public services offers useful lessons. Economists can thus provide the public decision-maker with precise recommendations regarding the practices that work and the organizational choices that yield efficient results on a socioeconomic level. By testing the validity of various theoretical assumptions, empirical studies participate in the development of a theoretical framework that is more robust and more consistent with the reality of public service. These studies use specific measures and methods to advance our knowledge of these difficult questions.

2.1   The Performance of Public Services: Which Measures and Which Methods?

The first problem one encounters when analyzing the efficiency of the management of public services, such as drinking water, urban public transport, or waste collection, is the question of which definition of service efficiency to select. In the case of public services, it is rather obvious that the sole criterion of profitability is not sufficient to assess performance. Indeed, the production and supply of these services, whether they are health services or cultural services, most often responds to several objectives that are difficult to reconcile with the sole search of profitability: service quality, accessibility, citizen welfare, sustainable development, etc. In addition, these services are also likely to be subjected to different forms of market "failures,"[2] thereby rendering insufficient the performance criteria usually applied to other "normal" industries.

In order to better apprehend public service performance, economists generally rely on the concept of social surplus, defined as the difference between the benefits of the service for society (welfare gains in monetary terms for end-users, positive external effects, etc.) and the actual cost of the service (production costs, external costs, subsidies, etc.). However, social surplus is a theoretical concept that is very

---

[1]Here, it should be reminded that the question of the private sector's involvement in the management of a public service is one that is generally approached in the wrong way. Indeed, no matter which delivery option, private companies participate in the management of public services and, therefore, even in the case of in-house provision, public–private partnerships are still concluded (in this case in the form of public contracts prior to service provision). Rather, the question revolves more fundamentally around the degree of involvement of the private partners in public service management.

[2]The economic analysis has highlighted the fact that it was possible for some characteristics associated with the production and supply of goods and services not to be compatible with an efficient running of the contracts (natural monopolies, externalities, and public goods mainly) and to require a public intervention that could take many forms (public production, regulation, etc.).

difficult to take into account in empirical studies. Indeed, it is difficult to measure, in monetary terms, the welfare provided to citizens and users by public services of quality.[3] To circumvent this issue, performance is then often assessed *via* productive efficiency or end-user price, which are components of the social benefit of a public service.

Other supplementary criteria may be used to evaluate public service performance. It is the case, for instance, of the level of investments, which play a crucial part in ensuring the continuity and quality of the service, or of satisfaction surveys.

No matter which indicator is selected, empirical studies aim at investigating (1) whether the delivery option truly determines performance and (2) to what extent. Econometrics is one of the essential tools that can help researchers make progress on these questions (see Box 1).

Box 1: The Econometric Tool to Compare Management Method Performances

One (too) simple way to evaluate the relative performance of delivery options is to use a statistic, such as an average, of the variable measuring performance. One can thus compare the average price of a service when it is organized as a concession and when it is under direct public management. Nevertheless, this method has one major disadvantage: it does not account for potential differences across available observations, which are likely to influence the observed performance. In other words, it is a mistake to limit oneself to the comparison of averages if nothing guarantees that the services provided when one delivery option is selected are comparable to those provided when a different delivery option is applied (same production scale, same difficulties, same quality levels, etc.). For instance, in the case of water distribution in France, it is now empirically established (Carpentier, Nauges, Reynaud, & Thomas, 2006; Chong, Huet, Saussier, & Steiner, 2006a) that municipalities that have chosen concession contracts are statistically different from those that have chosen direct public management (difference in size, treatment, density of population, etc.). These differences should therefore be accounted for, as they largely explain the average price disparities observed between municipalities, depending on whether public management or concession has been selected.

Thus, comparing performance averages is generally not sufficient to provide insight into the relative efficiency of delivery options and can even prove to be misleading. That is why economists often resort to econometric tools, so as to better account for differences across observations in a sample and to isolate the effect of the choice of delivery option on performance. In order to

(continued)

---

[3]However, there is a method known as contingent valuation that can be applied in order to determine user preferences and the influence of differentiated situations on their welfare [see for instance Haywood and Koning (2012) in the case of service quality in the Parisian subway].

Box 1 (continued)

do so, economists generally start by specifying an econometric model (often derived from theory), which can for instance take the following form:

$$Y_i = \omega\, O_i + \sum_k \beta_k X_{i,k} + \varepsilon_i$$

where Y_i is the performance measure for observation i (a given municipality), O_i is the management method selected by municipality i, and $X_{i,k}$ is a vector including k control variables accounting for the characteristics of the service of observation i. The components of $X_{i,k}$ correspond to variables such as the population of the municipality, the quality of service, production technology, etc., which can be thought to have an influence on the observed performance. ε_i is an error term, summarizing what the econometrician cannot observe or measure. ω and β_k are the coefficients associated with the variables in the model. These coefficients give us information about the influence of the associated variable on the explained performance, Y_i. They are thus the unknown parameters, which the econometrician is trying to evaluate. Then, the estimation of ω gives us information about the effect, *all other things being equal*, of the organizational or contractual method on performance, that is, about the effect, on average, of the organizational or contractual method on observed performance, controlling for the differences in the characteristics of the service provided.

In the following section, we focus on the comparative efficiency of in-house provision of a public service and a delivery option which involves an actor from the private sector.

2.2   Relative Efficiency of Delivery Options

Nowadays, there seems to be a consensus around the fact that, *in a competitive environment*, private firms are relatively more efficient than public bodies in sectors where markets are functioning properly (Megginson & Netter, 2001). This constitutes a strong argument in favor of private sector participation in the production of public services faced with market failures; this solution would make it possible both to avoid the complete privatization of the service—which is hardly possible because public services serve the general interest—and to benefit from the expertise and assets of the private sector in terms of productive efficiency. In other words, the various types of public–private partnerships would provide the advantages of both the private solution (strong incentives) and the public solution (production and price regulation), without the disadvantages of either the private solution (high prices in a monopoly situation) or the public solution (low incentives to produce efficiently). However, as noted previously, the consequences of private sector participation in the provision of public services continue to cause debate.

Let us first describe some empirical analyses which attempt to shed light on the relative efficiency of delivery options. Without trying to be exhaustive as regards the sectors under investigation, the section is limited to those sectors that have most often been analyzed so far (water, waste, transport, prison), and the findings of these studies will be highlighted. Rather than the delivery option itself, the regulatory and competitive contexts are determining factors to understand public service performance.

2.2.1 Potable Water Management

The water sector is emblematic of the difficulties in rationalizing the debate regarding which organizational method should be set up to provide a public service. Indeed, whether we consider discourses presenting water as a natural resource that should not be sold or used for profit-seeking—concealing the fact that what is being charged is the production, distribution, and purification services—or discourses announcing the privatization of the service—even though we are only dealing with a concession contract under which the whole infrastructure remains publicly owned—the debate on water management is often approached in the wrong way. This probably explains the recurrence of controversies on the topic, even though water on average only represents 0.8% of the average household income in France, far behind other public services for which private firms also intervene in the supply, without giving rise to such controversies.[4]

In France, the municipality is free to either call upon a private operator to provide water services or to provide the services internally (in-house provision). Concession contracts are very commonly used to carry out the service of potable water production and distribution (Fig. 1).

The empirical results derived from the French data are particularly interesting in that they reveal how an analysis limited to mere comparisons of averages can lead to erroneous conclusions. On average, if we focus on end-user prices, performance is lower when the potable water service is managed under a concession contract. More precisely, several studies using a representative data sample provided by the French Environment Institute (IFEN)[5] highlight the fact that, on average, consumers pay a higher price for water when the private sector intervenes in the supply of the service (Carpentier et al., 2006; Chong et al., 2006a, Chong, Saussier, & Silverman, 2015). The last study mentioned here estimates that in 2008, the average

---

[4]The success of the first citizens' initiative "Right2Water," which resulted in water being excluded from the new European directive on concessions (Directive 2014/23/UE), suggests that such considerations are not specific to France.

[5]This organism was dissolved in 2008 and replaced by the Service d'observation et des statistiques (SOeS), reporting to the Commissariat général du développement durable.

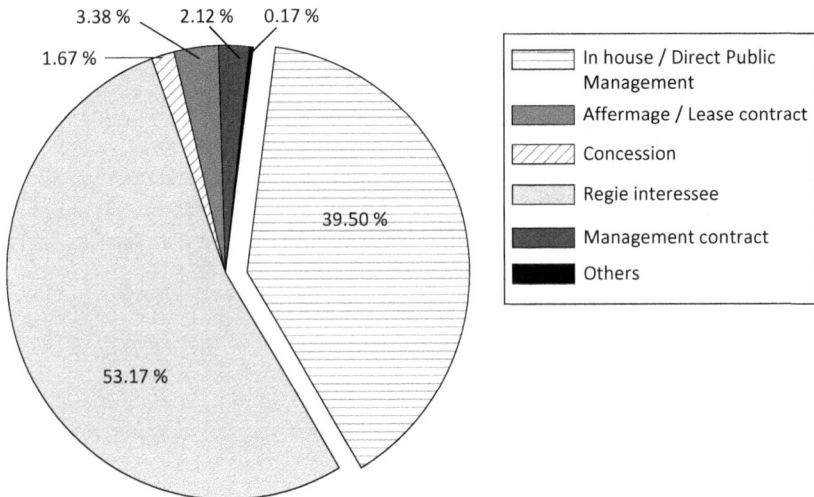

Fig. 1 Potable water delivery options and distribution in France. Source: Water survey of the French Environment Institute (*Institut français de l'environnement,* IFEN)/Observation and Statistics Department (*Service d'observation et des statistiques,* SOeS). Statistics computed by the authors based on a representative sample of 4674 French municipalities in 2008

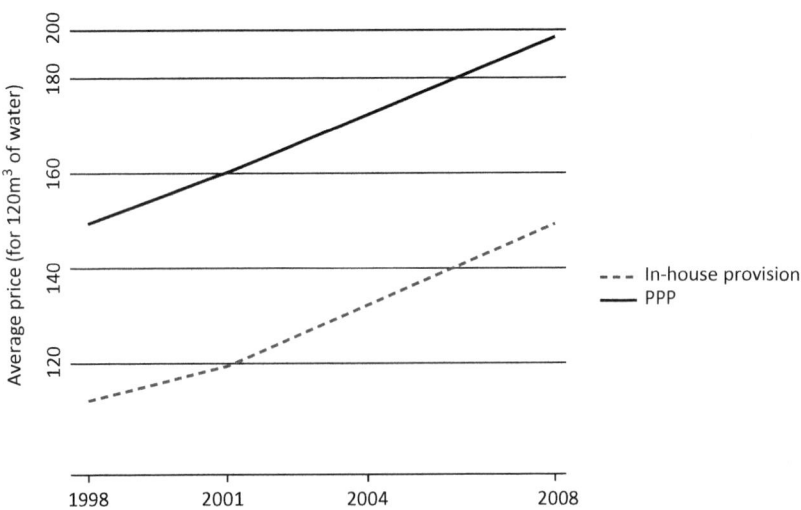

Fig. 2 Delivery option and price of water in France (Price excluding tax for 120 m^3). Source: Water survey of the French Environment Institute (IFEN)/Observation and Statistics Department (SOeS). Statistics computed by the authors based on a representative sample of 4674 French municipalities in 2008

price (non-deflated) paid by users for 120 m^3 of water was higher by about 30% when the water service was delegated to a private operator (the average bill was 150€) (Fig. 2).

However, when the various characteristics of municipalities are taken into account, in particular regarding the population served and the type of treatment required on raw water before it can be distributed, these gaps are reduced or even disappear. Carpentier et al. (2006) state that the only remaining price difference to the advantage of in-house provision is for small municipalities (under 10,000 inhabitants). Thus, in 1998, users supplied by a private operator in municipalities under 10,000 inhabitants paid 13.8% less on average than users living in municipalities of comparable size where the service was delivered in-house. These estimates are confirmed by a study by Chong et al. (2015) using more recent longitudinal data on the years 1998, 2001, 2004, and 2008. The authors, when they analyze the influence of the delivery option *all other things being equal*, taking into account the possible endogeneity of the preliminary choice of a structure (see Box 2), no longer find any price difference between municipalities operating with a concession and the ones which resort to in-house provision, for municipalities over 10,000 inhabitants. A price difference to the advantage of in-house provision remains for municipalities under 10,000 inhabitants, in the range of 8%. It is important to stress that such price gaps cannot be explained by differences in water quality. The study by Chong et al. (2015) also reveals an advantage of municipalities under a concession contract regarding the leak rate observed on the networks. This result is supported by a study conducted by Le Lannier and Porcher (2014), who find no significant price differences between in-house provision and externalization. Their study focuses on a different sample, concerning 164 services supplying over 15,000 inhabitants for the year 2009 (see Box 3).

Experience is particularly interesting in this country as France has a long tradition of resorting to private companies to handle water production and distribution services. Findings are thus less likely to reflect errors due to a lack of experience on the part of the public decision-maker, unlike data from countries where resorting to the private sector constitutes a new experience.

Box 2: The Issue of the Endogeneity of the Management Method
The approach described in Box 1 is only valid under certain assumptions: (1) the control variables all have the same effect on performance, regardless of the organizational method selected, and (2) the organizational method is selected randomly. The first point amounts to assuming, for instance, that public corporations and private operators use the same production technology to produce the service. This hypothesis can be tested and, if it is refuted, the econometric specification can be adapted to account for the differentiated effect of the control variables on the observed performance stemming from the organizational methods. The second point refers to the classical issue of endogeneity. This issue arises because, as detailed in Sect. 3, one may think that organizational choices are not made at random. This raises a problem if the researchers do not have the same set of information at their disposal as the

(continued)

Box 2 (continued)

public authority when making its decision. Some econometric techniques make it possible to correct this endogeneity problem. In particular, it is common to correct it by using a model that specifies not only the relationship between performance and organizational methods but also the choice of a given organizational method.

This results in a two-equation model: a first equation modeling the selection of the organizational method and a second one modeling performance, taking into account the preliminary choice of the organizational method. In order to obtain robust estimates with this method, it is necessary to use instrumental variables, i.e., variables that can explain the choice of a given organizational method, but that have no direct influence on performance. For instance, in empirical studies, it is often assumed that political variables, such as ideology, may lead public authorities to favor a particular organizational choice. These variables only have an influence on the observed performance (indirectly, by way of the chosen organizational method). They can therefore be used as instrumental variables. When using such variables, it becomes possible to correctly identify the impact of the organizational method on performance. It should be noted that the problem raised by the endogenous selection of organizational methods is in reality a problem of omitted-variable bias (Heckman, 1979). For an in-depth discussion of this problem, the reader can refer to Masten and Saussier (2002).

Experiences in the water sector in other European countries seem to lead to a similar conclusion. In Germany, for instance, where local public authorities are also free to choose between in-house provision and private sector participation to supply water services, Ruester and Zschille (2010) investigate a sample of 765 water services in 2003 and find that the retail price of potable water is, all other things being equal, higher on average under private management than under public management: 19 euros on average for 150 m^3 per year, once the various factors that have an influence on water prices are taken into account. Compared to the average observed price of water in the sample (279€ for a consumption of 150 m^3 per year), this amounts to an average additional cost of about 7% for consumers.

In Spain, like in France, municipalities enjoy a certain degree of freedom in organizing the supply of water services. They can manage the supply of these services internally; or delegate the service to a semi-public company, part of whose capital is held by the public sector; or choose delegation to purely private firms. Martínez-Espiñeira, García-Valiñas, and González-Gómez (2009) study 53 large municipalities (over 100,000 inhabitants) and find that the end-user price is higher when there is a form of private participation in the service (that is, in cases where the service is handled by a semi-public or private operator). This difference takes into account the specific characteristics of the services under study, as well as the fact that the organization method may be chosen endogenously. More recently, a study by Bel, Fageda, and Warner (2011), focusing on a sample of 162 municipalities in Andalusia, confirmed that the price of water is higher when the service is delegated to the private sector. This study also shows that the degree of competition is a factor contributing to price reductions in the water sector.

In the USA, water services are often provided by specialized companies known as "utilities," which can be either public or private. Public utilities hold the property rights for the distribution networks and are generally in charge of service production and operation. Private utilities, the capital of which is held by private investors, are most often subjected to a rate-of-return regulation (Crain & Zardkoohi, 1978). In that case, investors are guaranteed a return on their investments. A study by Bhattacharyya, Harris, Narayanan, and Raffiee (1995) uses cost data about 221 water utilities in 1992 and investigates the productive efficiency of utilities using stochastic frontier analysis. It is an empirical methodology which, based on empirical observations, aims to build a cost frontier (the lowest possible costs).[6] Thus, inefficiency is measured by observing the distance that separates the costs of a given firm from this frontier, which identifies the firms with the lowest costs, given the characteristics of the service to be produced. Bhattacharyya et al. (1995) find that public utilities are more efficient on average, except in the particular case of small-size contracts. In a more recent study using an exhaustive database of water systems in the USA from 1997 to 2003, Wallsten and Kosec (2008) focus on the compliance rate of water quality in relation to the standards in force. The result of this study indicates that the ownership type of the utilities does not seem to have any particular effect on this quality criterion.

In the end, in light of these studies, it is difficult to draw definitive conclusions as regards the relative efficiency of delivery options and governance modes in the water sector. Quite often, consumer prices seem higher under private management. However, the most accomplished studies, with the largest number of observations and the more details on service characteristics (Carpentier et al., 2006; Chong et al., 2006a, 2015), come to a more mitigated conclusion (no price difference between delivery options, at least in large cities). Moreover, in their representative samples, all existing studies fail to take into account other dimensions that are fundamental to appreciate the efficiency of water services, as for instance the quality of the service provided to users, through indicators such as the number of complaints, operator response time following these complaints, etc. Finally, they generally omit to conduct an in-depth analysis of the reasons that drive local authorities to delegate their water service.

---

[6]It should be noted that it is also possible to develop an efficiency frontier not in terms of costs but in terms of output (i.e., physical quantities produced thanks to the inputs).

**Box 3: Prices, Performance, and Management Methods of Water
Services in France—Le Lannier and Simon (2014)**
The study conducted by Le Lannier and Porcher (2014) identifies the critical
variable explaining the price gaps between services by relying on different
measures of prices and quality. The authors collected the Annual Reports on
prices and Quality (RPQS, *Rapports prix qualité service*) and the
Concessionnaires' Annual reports (RAD, *Rapports du délégataire*) for
320 services all including at least one municipality of over 15,000 inhabitants. 297 documents were obtained, of which 177 contained usable data. For
reasons of sample comparability, the final database includes 164 water services, of which 51 are public corporations with information about operating
revenues, the bill for 120 m^3, the revenue per m^3, the number of customers,
the volume of water billed, the length of the mains, and a lot of information
about the operating context (water treatment and origin, in particular). For
subsamples, the database contains information about regulatory quality indicators such as compliance with microbiological or physicochemical standards, linear leakage index, rate of return, level of debt of the specific water
service budget, etc.
   The study relies on two econometric methods. The first one uses the
ordinary least squares method to isolate the assumed impact of the delivery
option on consumer price. The second one uses a similar model, without
taking into account the delivery option, to calculate the price that should be
paid by the consumer depending on the operating context. A simple comparison of the price observed in reality and the price predicted based on the
operating context gives us an idea of the level of service overbilling or
underbilling. Finally, a parallel study was conducted using nonparametric
and stochastic methods to test the robustness of results.
   The average revenue and the price for 120 m^3 were estimated as follows:

$$P_i = \beta_1 \cdot (\text{customers/volumes})_i + \beta_2 \cdot (\text{length/volumes})_i + \Upsilon \cdot \text{MDG} + \tau \cdot X_{1i} + \varepsilon_{1i}$$

   where MDG is the delivery option and X_{1i} a set of variables representing
the complexity of service management. This model makes it possible to
isolate the potential impact of the delivery option. In order to create counter-
factual prices, the same model is estimated without the delivery option
variable:

$$P_i = \beta_1 \cdot (\text{customers/volumes})_i + \beta_2 \cdot (\text{length/volumes})_i + \tau \cdot X_{1i} + \varepsilon_{1i}$$

(continued)

Box 3 (continued)

This method makes it possible to predict the prices depending on network characteristics. A similar model is also used by the authors to estimate and explain the total revenue of the service depending on the delivery option. Several specifications are estimated, including log–log models in particular.

The results show that the total revenue, the average revenue, and the price for 120 m³ are indeed explained by the proposed model, largely *via* the selected physical outputs and service complexity. In contrast, the delivery option is not a discriminant variable. This suggests that the delivery option has no significant impact on the price of a bill for 120 m³ of water or on the average revenue. Under certain specifications, the delivery option has a significant impact but at the 10% level only. The variables with the most explanatory power are network density, the origin of water, and the complexity of treatment.

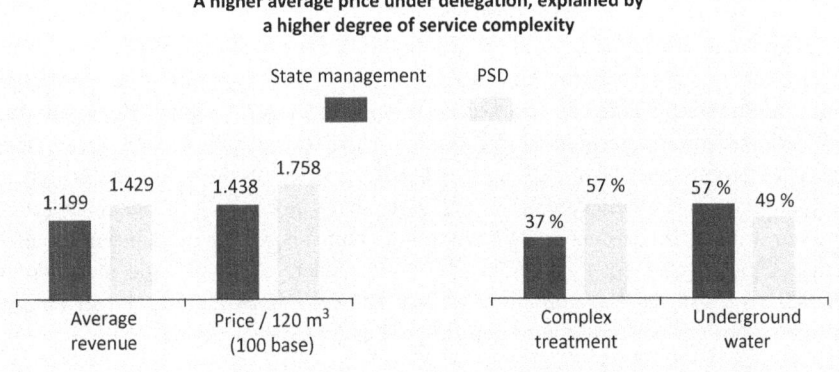

In developing countries, private sector participation in water supply raises different issues and stakes. Thus, according to the study of Galiani et al. (2005), the involvement of the private sector in water services in Argentina has led to an 8% reduction in the infant mortality rate in the areas in question. In addition, according to this study, the poorest areas are those that benefit most from this reduction in the mortality rate. For a more global perspective, Gassner, Popov, and Pushak (2009) conducted a study comparing the performance of 977 water services with private sector participation in 71 developing countries or countries in transition,[7] since the 1990s and until 2002. The authors highlight the fact that private sector participation in water services allowed for a better development of the service for residential

---

[7]The observations used in the study come in large part from Latin America and the Caribbean (43% of the total sample), from Central Asia and Central Europe (40%), and from East Asia and the Pacific (10%). Among these observations, 836 services are provided directly (in-house provision), while 141 services rely on private sector participation.

users, by increasing the rate of connection to the potable water distribution network and by improving productivity with a volume of water sold per employee higher by 18% in services managed under a concession contract. This suggests better access of users to potable water, which is a critical issue in developing countries. Finally, this study reveals that private sector participation also resulted in higher end-user prices, which can be justified by the higher quality of the service. Even so, it also raises the question of service accessibility for vulnerable populations. The scope of this study is limited, in that the authors were only able to control for a limited part of the high level of heterogeneity across observations. Nevertheless, the results of this study seem to be in keeping with more detailed case studies taking into account longer periods of time (such as Clarke, Ménard, & Zuluaga, 2000).

Despite these few studies, one should bear in mind that (1) PPPs in the water sector are not very usual in developing countries and (2) they are relatively concentrated geographically. It is therefore possible that, in these countries, services under private management are also the ones that can benefit most from this delivery option(picking strategy). Besides, the water sector has known a few resounding PPP failures in developing countries; for instance, the concession of Tucumán and Buenos Aires in Argentina in 1996 and 2006, or the concession in La Paz, Bolivia in 2005. Guasch (2004) also highlights the fact that, in this sector, PPP contracts concluded in Latin America are characterized by a rate of renegotiation that is far higher than the one observed in other sectors (see Chapter "Renegotiating PPP Contracts: Opportunities and Pitfalls" of the second part of this book). This seems to demonstrate how difficult it is to set up a PPP in the water sector, where infrastructure investments are heavy and assets have a very long life span compared to other sectors. In the context of developing countries, where most infrastructures remains to be built, these specificities of the industry, just like the institutional characteristics of these countries, can be determining in explaining the success or failure of private sector participation (Figs. 3 and 4).

2.2.2 Waste Treatment

The waste treatment sector is interesting in that, just like water management or transport services, it offers a variety of organizational structures and delivery options. It is also characterized by a large number of empirical studies, probably favored by an easier access to data in this sector compared to others.

The empirical literature shows that, in terms of waste collection, competition in the market between several firms is the most costly organizational solution (Dubin & Navarro, 1988). This can be explained by the existence of economies of density implying that production costs are minimized when a single firm handles the whole collection in a given geographical area, and it is therefore more efficient to establish geographical monopolies. The main challenge of the debate on organizational efficiency then consists in determining whether collection costs are lower when the monopoly is public or private.

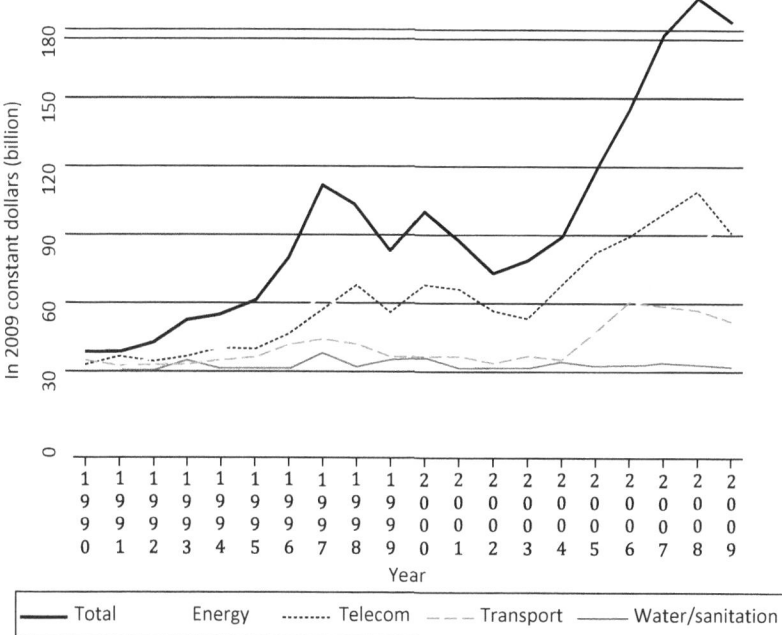

Fig. 3 Private participation in infrastructure in developing countries, by sector. Source: The World Bank and PPIAF, PPI project database

Out of the 23 articles we have listed (see Table 1), 10 consider private collection to be more advantageous, against 3 favoring public collection, while the last 10 studies give contradictory results or find the cost difference between the two delivery options to be nonsignificant.

If we limit ourselves to these simple figures, we may conclude that, overall, waste collection is almost always more efficient when contracted out to the private sector. Yet, this assertion should be qualified, insofar as the various studies are not characterized by the same quality level. The most recent studies resort to an assessment method that yields more robust results than the works published earlier; their findings are therefore less questionable. Out of the nine studies published over these past 10 years, only three conclude that private collection is more efficient.

It should also be noted that almost half of the published studies focus on the waste industry in the UK and the USA. Additionally, some of them use similar databases, expanded over time through the addition of new information. In any case, these two countries are overrepresented in the total set of published studies.

Finally, the sample size is also an important parameter to assess the quality of an empirical study. Works conducted on very small samples should be interpreted with more caution than those conducted on large samples.

Recently, Bel et al. (2010) published a statistical study (non-econometric) based on the samples of past studies, which suggests that, once the quality differences of

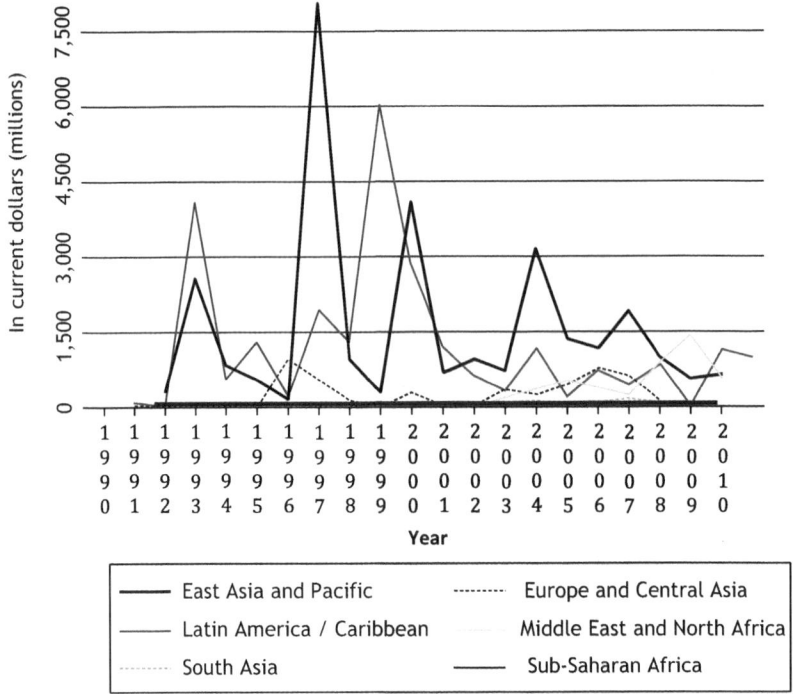

Fig. 4 Private participation in water distribution, by region. Source: The World Bank and PPIAF, PPI project database

the abovementioned publications are taken into account, public collection is not found to be less efficient than private collection.

Hirsch (1965) was the first to conduct an econometric study on waste collection. Using a database of 24 municipalities in the Saint Louis County in the USA, he found no difference in costs between the private or public modes. His cost function—the average cost for one ton of waste per municipality—takes into account the frequency of service, the quality of service (for instance, the type of equipment used for collection), the price of inputs, the type of technology used, the density of population served by one collection unit, the income per capita, the delivery option, and the financing arrangement of the service (budget of the local authority or usage-based pricing).

The same cost function was used in econometric simulations, with larger samples, using data on the States of Montana (Pier et al., 1974) and Missouri (Collins & Downes, 1977). Both articles come to the same conclusion as Hirsch (1965): there is no cost difference between public and private management.

Although a study on the State of Connecticut (Kemper & Quigley, 1976) and another one on a hundred Swiss local authorities (Pommerehne & Frey, 1977)

Table 1 Overview of empirical studies on waste collection and treatment

Author	Geographical area	Year	Obs.	Results
Hirsch (1965)	United States, Saint Louis City County	1960	24	No effect of the delivery option
Pier et al. (1974)	United States, Montana	1970	22	No effect of the delivery option
Kitchen (1976)	Canada	1970	48	Public collection is less efficient
Kemper and Quigley (1976)	United States, Connecticut	1972–1974	128	Private collection is less efficient (additional costs of 25–36%). Waste treatment is more efficient under a PPP (cost savings of 13–30% compared to public supply)
Collins and Downes (1977)	United States, Missouri	1970	53	Private collection is less efficient. No significant difference in costs between private supply (PPP) and public supply
Pommerehne and Frey (1977)	Switzerland	1970	103	Public collection is less efficient
Stevens (1978)	United States	1974	340	Private collection is more efficient in terms of costs and productivity. PPPs are more efficient for cities over 50,000 inhabitants (27–37%)
Tickner and McDavid (1986)	Canada	1981	132	Public collection is less efficient
Domberger et al. (1986)	England, Wales	1983–1985	305	No effect of the delivery option if contracts are awarded in a competitive manner. Less efficient otherwise
Dubin and Navarro (1988)	United States	1974	261	Public collection is more efficient
Szymanski and Wilkins (1993)	England, Wales	1984–1988	185–335	No effect of the delivery option
Szymanski (1996)	England, Wales	1984–1994	300	Prior to 1988: public collection is less efficient. After 1988: public collection is more efficient
Bello and Szymanski (1996)	England, Wales	1984–1993	132–528	Prior to 1988: public collection is less efficient. After 1988: public collection is more efficient
Reeves and Barrow (2000)	Ireland	1993–1995	48	Public collection is less efficient

(continued)

Table 1 (continued)

Author	Geographical area	Year	Obs.	Results
McDavid (2001)	Canada	1996–1997	327	Public collection is less efficient, but the performance gap diminishes over time
Callan and Thomas (2001)	United States, Massachusetts	1997	110	No effect of the delivery option
Dijkgraaf and Gradus (2011)	Netherlands	1996–1997	85	Public collection is as efficient (as delegated collection)
Ohlsson (2003)	Sweden	1989	115	Public collection is more efficient
Bel and Costas (2006)	Spain	2000	186	No effect of the delivery option
Dijkgraaf and Gradus (2007)	Netherlands	1998–2005	491	Public collection is more efficient in the absence of competition
Bel and Mur (2009)	Spain	2003	56	No effect of the delivery option
Bel et al. (2010)	United States, North Carolina	1997–2001– 2003	252	No effect of the delivery option
Beuve et al. (2013)	France	2007 and 2009	650	Private collection is more efficient

estimate private supply to be less expensive than public supply (by 13–30%), Stevens (1978) finds no difference at the national level between the costs for municipalities under 50,000 inhabitants but estimates that private monopolies are more efficient by 27–37% in cities over 50,000 inhabitants. This was due to the fact that private operators used more efficient technology, namely, trucks with larger containers, which allowed them to have lower payroll expenses.

The connection between delivery option efficiency and the size of the municipality is also analyzed by Dubin and Navarro (1988) on American municipalities. They show that some economies of scale are indeed realized with externalization, but only for municipalities that are sufficiently small. Beyond a certain size, in this case 20,000 inhabitants, the economies of scale allowed by externalization disappear. In the end, public supply is often less expensive than certain forms of PPPs.

More recent studies find no difference in costs between public and private management. In the USA, Callan and Thomas (2001) estimate two cost functions: one cost function for collection and one for waste recycling. The study concludes that there is no difference in efficiency between public and private collection. Based on 186 Spanish services, Bel and Costas (2006) realize estimates that do not reveal any difference in efficiency between public and private service provision. Bel and Mur (2009) use a different sample but come to the same conclusion. Likewise, Bae

(2010) uses a sample of 252 municipalities in North Carolina for the years 1997, 2001, and 2003. He does not find any significant cost differences between public supply and contracting out to private firms.

Other studies settle the argument in favor of public management or private management. Based on a sample of 115 Swedish local authorities, Ohlsson (2003) finds that public collection is more efficient than private collection. In contrast, McDavid (2001) conducts a statistical study based on 327 Canadian services and finds that local authorities delegating their waste collection to private operators incur lower costs than those remaining under direct public supply. This gap diminishes over time.

In conclusion, the oldest studies predominantly find private supply to be superior. The most recent studies, realized in the 2010s, do not find either one of the governance modes to be superior to the other, except for Beuve, Huet, Porcher, and Saussier (2013) (see Box 4).

Most importantly, the existing empirical works do not always distinguish between cost savings associated with a "competitive effect" and those associated with the delivery option. Indeed, in most countries, municipalities put their collection service up for tender by organizing an auction between several private firms. Thus, when private provision yields better results than public supply, it can be explained by the fact that awarding contracts through an auction generates a competitive pressure on private investors, to which public suppliers are not always subjected. For instance, this is the case in the French waste industry: public corporations are not forced to compete with private companies on a regular basis. Therefore, the difference in efficiency is not necessarily due to the status of the operator (public or private), and so to the fact that private managers have stronger intrinsic incentives to be efficient, but it can also derive from the competitive pressures.

Box 4: The Efficiency of Management Methods in French Waste Management (Beuve et al., 2013)

Several empirical works focusing on the waste collection sector were conducted in various countries (the Netherlands, the USA, Spain, Ireland, the UK, Canada, etc.). The main findings are summarized in this chapter and in Table 1. To our knowledge, no empirical study focuses on the case of France, except for one (Beuve et al., 2012).

In this study, the authors built a database including 650 waste collection services. *The unit of observation is thus the collection service. The year of observation is 2007 for some services and 2009 for others.* The services under study can be of very different natures (collection of glass, bulky waste, residual household waste, vegetable waste, . . .). These 650 services are organized within 62 different local authorities (municipalities or communities of municipalities), representing a served population of 14 million inhabitants.

(continued)

Box 4 (continued)

A first comparison of collection costs depending on the selected delivery option reveals an advantage in favor of private management.

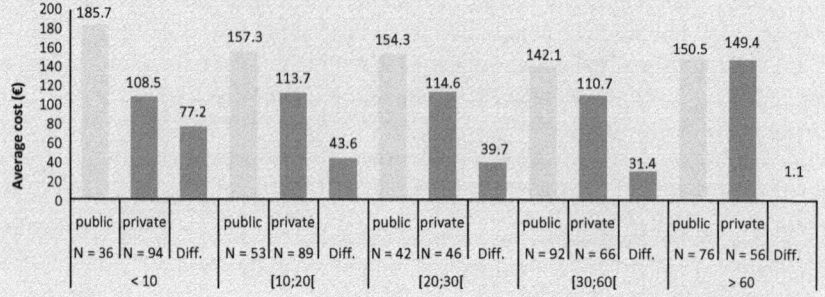

To go further, the authors estimate several relations.

The Choice of Management Method

$$Private_i = a_1 \cdot X_i + a_2 \cdot Z_i + \varepsilon_i$$

where *Private* is a discrete variable indicating the governance choice of the collection service i (1 if management is private–public service contracts; 0 if management is public–public corporation), X is a vector of explanatory variables corresponding to the considered service, and Z a vector of explanatory variables including information on the characteristics of the considered local authority.

An Analysis of the Average Collection Cost

$$AvCost_i = a_1 \cdot Private_i + a_2 \cdot X_i + \varepsilon_i$$

where *AvCost* is the collection cost per ton (excluding treatment), *Private* is the discrete variable indicating the governance choice of service i, and X is a vector of explanatory variables corresponding to this service i.

An Analysis of Efficiency Scores

$$Efficiency_i = a_1 \cdot \%Private_i + a_2 \cdot Z_i + \varepsilon_i$$

where *Efficiency* is the efficiency score of the considered local authority (calculated using the data envelopment analysis method), *%Private* is the percentage of collection services delegated to a private operator, and Z a

(continued)

Box 4 (continued)

vector of explanatory variables corresponding to the characteristics of the considered local authority.

Following an econometric analysis of these data, the results suggest that the choice of governance structure is driven by:

– Economic considerations: the probability of resorting to private management decreases with the size of the collection service, which means that the decision to make or buy is motivated first and foremost by a search for economies of scale.
– Political interests: the wealth level of inhabitants has a positive impact on the likelihood of resorting to private management.
– Budgetary considerations: the probability of delegating the management of collection services increases with the debt level of the local authority.

Regarding the performance of management methods, the results suggest that resorting to the private sector is more efficient than public supply in terms of the average cost of the collection service (the frequency of collection being equal, the average costs of private management are statistically lower than the average costs of public management). The cost difference between public collection and private collection decreases with the size of the service considered (in number of inhabitants served by the collection service). This result confirms the importance of economic considerations (a search for economies of scale) in the choice of management method. Finally, it emerges from the study that private operators are affected by the level of competitive pressure, in particular for large-size services (the average cost decreases with the number of operators managing at least one service in the collectivity).

2.2.3 Transport

In the transport industry, delegated management has known a few striking failures. For instance, we can think of the liquidation of Metronet in 2007, one of the two private firms that had been entrusted with the maintenance and renewal of the infrastructure and trains of the London underground. Despite these failures, the sector is undergoing a development of delegated management to private operators, thus providing researchers with a particularly fertile ground to investigate the comparative performances of private and public management.

Railway services, like the water industry, have undergone major organizational reforms in Europe: introduction of vertical separation in the monopolistic section of railway networks, sometimes followed by the privatization of public corporations and the introduction of competition, etc. The empirical literature has focused largely on the consequences of the vertical separation between infrastructure management and the operation of railway services (Friebel, Ivaldi, & Vibes,

2010; Yvrande-Billon & Ménard, 2005, etc.) and, as a corollary, it has also investigated the effects of the introduction of competition (Lalive & Schmutzler, 2008, 2011).

Cantos, Pastor, and Serrano (1999) analyze the effect of vertical separation, changes in the legal form of companies, the degree of price regulation, and the degree of government intervention in the sector on the total factor productivity of railway companies in 17 European countries, between 1970 and 1995. They observe an improvement in the total factor productivity following the introduction of vertical separation and the liberalization reforms introduced in this sector in the second half of the 1980s. For instance, British Railway, which is one of the companies that were rather inefficient at the beginning of the observation period, saw its total factor productivity improve toward the end of the observation period, especially following reforms in the sector (sector restructuring and ensuing privatization). The authors conclude that vertical separation appears to have had the strongest impact on railway efficiency. Friebel et al. (2010) adopt a similar perspective by investigating the effect of reforms in the railway sector on performance. Unlike Cantos et al. (1999), they use the variation over time of reforms in several European railway sectors to identify the effect of these reforms on performance. The authors consider 12 European countries during the years 1980–2003. Using a production frontier methodology, they find that the reforms introduced improved the productive efficiency of the sector. More precisely, the sector underwent an increase of 0.5% per year in technical efficiency due to deregulation. Even more interestingly, what emerges from this study is that the countries where reforms were implemented sequentially are also the ones where technical efficiency improved, as opposed to countries where multiple reforms were implemented simultaneously as a package. The authors explain this result by the fact that introducing reforms sequentially allows governments to find out about their desirability and thus to adapt further reforms before implementing them. Taken as a whole, these results once more underline the importance of the statutory framework to understand and explain the performance observed in a given economic sector.

Unlike industrialized countries, several developing countries have used externalization in the railway industry. Estache, González, and Trujillo (2002), among others, have investigated the effect of private sector concessions in the railway industry in Argentina and Brazil. The authors find that delegated management to private operators is associated with an improvement in service productivity. Moreover, this better relative performance does not seem to result from a reduction in the inputs used but from an increase in the production volume. In other words, their results suggest that delegated management does not necessarily entail a drop in the level of employment and that resorting to the private sector can be beneficial in developing countries, even if these findings cannot be generalized, given how few empirical studies have been realized on the topic in this sector.

Urban public transport is a sector in which public authorities very often resort to PPPs. Even so, existing studies on this industry focus for the most part on the effect of contractual form on service performance (see for instance Gautier and Yvrande-Billon, 2013). One of the few studies comparing the relative performance of delegated management and public management (in-house provision) uses French data (Roy & Yvrande-Billon, 2007). In France, urban public transport services can be managed directly by a public corporation or delegated to a semi-public company (in France, semi-public companies are defined as firms for which public entities detain at least 51% of the shares) or to a private operator. The delegation to a private operator is most frequent (69% of networks), followed by the delegation to a semi-public company (21%) and by direct public management (10%).[8] The study conducted by Roy and Yvrande-Billon (2007) is based on a sample of 135 urban public transport networks in France between 1995 and 2002. The authors show that services under direct public management or managed through a semi-public company are relatively weaker in terms of productive efficiency than those that are delegated to a private operator. Surprisingly, the authors also show that networks where the service is delegated to a semi-public company are the least efficient ones. According to them, this result could be explained by the fact that this "half-way" governance structure could favor the development of opportunistic behaviors on the part of both parties (the public authority and the private operator), leading to inefficient decisions in terms of productive resources allocation.

2.2.4 Prisons

In a pioneering article on the role of the private sector in public services, Hart, Shleifer, and Vishny (1997) highlighted a possible arbitration between public and private management. While private management entails an increase in the level of incentives to produce efficiently by reducing costs, it also results, in many cases (those where quality is non-contractible and consumers are captive), in a drop in service quality due to the attempt to minimize production costs. That is why the authors consider that private sector participation can be desirable in certain kinds of prisons, in particular those dedicated to juvenile offenders who have not committed serious offenses, as the deterioration of quality, which in the USA takes the form of a higher frequency of jailbreaks, only has little impact. Is reality consistent with this theoretical forecast? Are prisons under a public–private partnership managed more efficiently, at the cost of a drop in service quality?

A first answer can be found in the report published by the French Court of Auditors on July 19th 2010 (Cour des Comptes, 2010). This report states that private sector participation has been possible in France since 1989 and that there are currently 46 institutions in which the private sector is involved. In most cases, the private sector is only in charge of building the infrastructure and of services such as collective catering and cleaning; the public party remains responsible for all other activities, including guard services. The assessment established by the Court of Auditors on the private management of food services in French penal institutions

---

[8]Source: Roy and Yvrande-Billon (2007). This distribution is based on observations for the year 2002.

is critical, in particular because of the high prices observed. In addition, the Court observes that the cost of vocational training is higher in prisons under delegated management.[9]

In the USA, private sector participation in this service is relatively ancient as it goes back to 1983 in Tennessee. After that, it gradually spread to other States (Cabral & Saussier, 2011). As in the other sectors, this development of private sector participation in prisons gave rise to studies investigating the comparative performances of public and private management. Thus, a study by Bayer and Pozen (2005) focuses on penal institutions for young offenders in Florida. This study is particularly interesting in that it compares three organizational forms: public management, delegation to a private for-profit firm, and delegation to a nonprofit operator. According to this study, the participation of a private for-profit company entails lower costs than the other two organizational methods. Other studies show a similar result in Brazilian prisons (Cabral & Saussier, 2011). However, Bayer and Pozen (2005) find that the recidivism rate is higher among individuals incarcerated in facilities managed by a for-profit company. They show that although delegating to a private for-profit operator is beneficial in the short run in terms of production costs, this advantage is far less evident in the long run on a socioeconomic level.

Private sector participation in prison services has also developed in Brazil. In this country, the private sector can be in charge of the internal security of prisons, their health services, and legal assistance. Like in the USA, guard services necessarily remain under the responsibility of the public entity. According to Cabral, Lazzarini, and Furquim de Azevedo (2010), prison facilities involving the private sector not only incur lower costs compared to public prisons with comparable characteristics but also entail a lower average number of jailbreaks and deaths. In addition, inmates seem to benefit from better medical care. These results clearly speak in favor of this organizational method, since the cost-quality arbitration is evidently absent in the Brazilian case, contrary to the findings of Bayer and Pozen (2005). It should nevertheless be noted that this study does not take into account the recidivism rate, even though it constitutes an essential performance criteria for this type of public service.

This review of the existing literature suggests that private sector participation fosters better performance in terms of productions costs. Cabral et al. (2010) also observe that delegated management can generate an improvement in the inmates' quality of life. Yet, as underlined in this section, the studies highlight that recidivism is more significant under delegated management. It is then quite possible that the social cost associated with recidivism cancels out the short-term advantages of delegated management in terms of cost and quality. Therefore, it is essential to take a closer look to the comparative performances of governance structures taking into account this criterion. In conclusion, it should be stressed that, as claimed by Cabral and Saussier (2011), the type of contract and institutional characteristics quite

---

[9]It should nevertheless be noted that the report by the Cour des comptes does not take into account all penal institutions.

certainly play a central role in the relative performances of the various organizational methods for this service.

In the end, depending on the sector considered, the data collected and the efficiency criterion selected, empirical studies do not allow to draw definitive conclusions regarding the superiority of one delivery option over another. The works mentioned above do not always distinguish between cost savings associated with a "competitive effect" and those associated with the delivery option. Indeed, in most countries, municipalities open their services up to competition by organizing an auction between several private firms. Thus, when private provision yields better performance results than public supply, it can be explained by the fact that awarding contracts through an auction generates a competitive pressure on private suppliers, to which public suppliers are not always subjected. Therefore, the difference in efficiency is not necessarily due to the status of the operator (public or private) and thus to the fact that private managers have stronger intrinsic incentives to be efficient, but it can also derive from the fact that only private suppliers are subjected to competitive pressures. This leads us to ponder the role of competitive pressures but also of other factors that may potentially influence the performance of public services.

3 Other Factors Influencing the Relative Efficiency of Delivery Options

3.1 The Role of Competitive Pressure

Competition is an essential aspect that can explain cost reductions, but whose effects on service quality as a whole are still uncertain. Several studies, mostly relating to the waste industry, try to measure the effect of competition.

Domberger, Meadowcroft, and Thompson (1986) investigate 305 English and Welsh municipalities between 1983 and 1985 and found no difference in efficiency between private collection and public collection when the service has been opened up to competition beforehand. The study falls into a particular context since in Great Britain, prior to 1988, the opening up to competition of waste services was not compulsory. Most local authorities used public collection, but some of them deliberately delegated their service through a competitive procedure, either to public companies or to private companies.

The article of Domberger et al. (1986) was the first to make a distinction between two effects on service performance: the competition effect and the effect of "operator status." Within this framework, the governance structure is less significant to explain performance differences than the intensity of competition for the market, or the existence of competition between different operators within the market itself.

Using a markedly different dataset, Szymanski and Wilkins (1993) find no significant difference in efficiency between private and public collection. Overall, even if 71% of municipalities retained public collection after the service was opened up to competition, their collection costs do not differ significantly from those of municipalities where the service was entrusted to a private firm, which confirms the findings of Domberger et al. (1986).

Using a larger sample, with 300 observations from 1984 to 1994, Szymanski (1996) studies the effect of compulsory competitive tendering, established in 1988 for all collection services, on the performance of these services. This study thus proposes to analyze the cost differences between public and private supply before and after 1988, in order to test whether the performance differences between services can be explained by the status of the supplier (public or private) or by the competitive pressure exerted on operators, whether public or private. The results suggest that before the introduction of compulsory competitive tendering, public collection was more costly than PPPs awarded by local authorities on a voluntary basis. After 1988, the introduction of competition immediately led to a 10% fall in costs for public supply and a 20% fall for PPPs. However, although at first the opening up to competition was immediately followed by cost reductions, these gains then faded gradually as time passed. This result thus suggests that competition and the status of the company play a part in the efficiency of services.

These findings are confirmed by McDavid (2001), who, based on a sample of Canadian services, estimates private collection to be less costly because private operators are exposed to stronger competitive pressure. In local authorities where collection is divided up between public and private operators, overall costs are lower than the national average, which means that competition can give public managers an incentive to modify their work organization and to make more decisions aiming for productivity gains and cost saving.

Based on a sample from the Netherlands, Dijkgraaf and Gradus (2011) find that the status of the operator has no impact, but that competitive pressure has an influence on actors' incentives to reduce their costs. Using a larger sample, Dijkgraaf and Gradus (2007) confirm the importance of competitive pressure on cost reduction but grant more importance to the governance mode depending on the degree of competition for the market. Thus, in low-competition areas, public collection is more advantageous than private collection. However, when competition is strong or moderate, private collection leads to 18% lower costs.

The effect of competition on the efficiency of private management can take various channels. At the time of the call for tenders, it can generate more competitive tenders, thus contributing to a higher efficiency of the private solution as long as price is the selected performance criterion. Thus, Amaral et al. (2013) analyzed the effect of the number of bidders on the price obtained by public authorities during calls for tenders relating to bus passenger transport in the city of London. After studying over 800 calls for tenders, they find that when there are a higher number of bidders, whether actual or expected, the organizing authority tends to receive lower bids, which reduces the cost of service for users. They conclude that in terms of reform, one of the priorities should be the organization of procedures aiming to guarantee real competition during calls for tenders. Competition can also have an influence at the stage of contract renewal. Thus, in their study, Chong, Huet, and Saussier (2006b) investigate the relationship between the price of water in municipalities using a concession or lease contract and the end of the contract. They highlight an effect of competition, both between operators and between governance modes (potential re-internalization of the service), which gets stronger as the end of the contract approaches and when neighboring municipalities are managed by competitors. This last result also appears in the study of Plunket, Huet, and Saussier (2008).

In conclusion, competition always has a positive impact on performance in terms of operator costs, whereas the status of the operator is not always determining to explain performances.

3.2   The Role of the Types of Outsourced Delivery Options

These past few years, empirical studies have developed to shed light on the relative performances of delivery options in the supply of public services. However, the question is made more complex by the fact that each structure actually involves various relationships that can be quite heterogeneous. In particular, concessions contracts are not at all identical regarding the contractual clauses governing them: duration, operator remuneration, renegotiation clause, and flexibility *versus* rigidity of the agreement. Thus, in a study on highway concessions, Athias and Saussier (2007) are able to highlight the existence of over 14 different operator remuneration clauses in the contracts they analyze. According to the authors, these clauses reflect different levels of rigidity or flexibility introduced in contracts, which ultimately influence the contractors' ability to adapt the contractual relationship in an efficient manner (See Chapter "Renegotiating PPP Contracts: Opportunities and Pitfalls," Part 2, of the book for a discussion on the impact of flexibility/rigidity on the possibility to adapt contractual terms to contingencies revealed *ex post*).

Numerous empirical works have analyzed the influence of contractual choices on the performances of private or semi-public operators. The tested hypotheses are based on the developments of contract theory, according to which cost-plus contracts and fixed-price price-cap contracts differ in their adaptive and incentive properties (Bajari & Tadelis, 2001; Laffont & Tirole, 1993). Thus, fixed-price contracts are supposed to give stronger incentives as, unlike in cost-plus arrangements, the contractor's remuneration depends on operating results.

In the case of urban public transport, the result according to which operators under fixed-price contracts are more efficient seems quite robust. Indeed, most empirical studies on the topic support this hypothesis. Using stochastic frontier analysis, Gagnepain and Ivaldi (2002a) assess the cost-effectiveness of 59 urban public transport networks in France in 1993. Their findings confirm the hypothesis according to which the cost-effectiveness of the operators under fixed-price contracts is significantly better than that of operators under cost-plus contracts. In addition, Gagnepain and Ivaldi (2002a) show that, on a socioeconomic level, resorting to cost-plus contracts is not efficient in this sector, given the cost of public funds. Additionally, investigating the cost-effectiveness of 44 Italian urban public transport networks in the years 1993–1999, Piacenza (2006) and Margari, Erbetta, Petraglia, and Piacenza (2007) obtain similar results, and Roy and Yvrande-Billon (2007) come to the same conclusion, using a database of 135 French networks in the years 1995–2002. This last study (Roy & Yvrande-Billon, 2007) draws its strength from the use of an econometric technique that allows to simultaneously evaluate productive inefficiency and its explanatory factors. In this respect, the results obtained are more rigorous.

Empirical studies aiming to understand the effects of the contractual form on performance have also focused on the water sector. The study conducted by Aubert and Reynaud (2005) is one example. The authors examine the case of water services in Wisconsin in the USA and find that operators under a cost-plus contract enjoy better cost effectiveness than those regulated by a fixed-price contract. According to the authors, this paradoxical result is largely explained by the fact that the regulator carries out very regular audits of the operators' activity in order to reduce information asymmetry. This allows the regulator to force operators to be efficient, even though these contracts have low incentives. This is quite a strong result, which points to the importance of information in regulation. However, given the limits of their data, the authors do not have any information on auditing costs and therefore cannot compare the global costs of the various types of regulation. This article helps to show that the monitoring, control, and expertise of delegating authorities constitute decisive factors for contract efficiency.

Besides, it should be noted that the study conducted by Aubert and Reynaud (2005) does not take into account the necessary *ex post* adaptations characterizing any long-term contract (see Chapter "Renegotiating PPP Contracts: Opportunities and Pitfalls," Part 2). As it happens, cost-plus contracts allow for better *ex post* coordination and adaptation compared to fixed-price contracts (Bajari & Tadelis, 2001). Indeed, the strong incentives provided by a fixed-price contract tend to lead contracting parties to negotiate more aggressively and to block contract modifications. The issue of optimal contract flexibility is complementary with the question of remuneration clauses and should not be overlooked (Athias & Saussier, 2007; Bajari et al., 2014; Masten & Saussier, 2000; Saussier, 2000).

3.3   The Choice of Delivery Option

An important weakness shared by all the works mentioned above lies in the fact that they very often consider organizational choices to be exogenous. This is a strong hypothesis which, if it is not disproved, can introduce a bias in the performance analysis and help explain the heterogeneity of the results previously underlined.

At first glance, empirical studies reveal a certain stability in the choice of the governance structure, which seems to indicate that there is a form of inertia in the

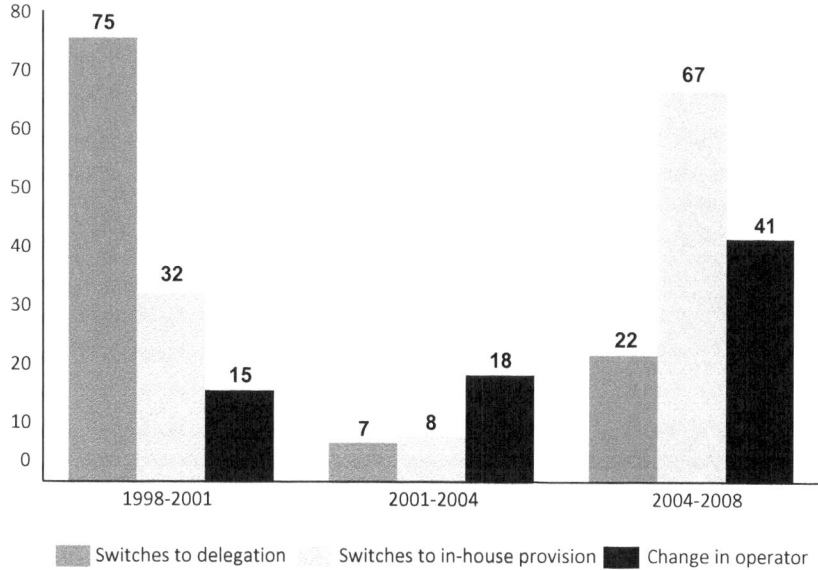

Fig. 5 Changes in delivery option in the French water sector. Source: Calculations made by the authors based on the IFEN-SoeS water surveys 1998–2001–2004–2008 focusing on over 5000 local authorities

choices made by public decision-makers. For instance, Zupan (1989) finds that in the USA, in 99.8% of cases, the incumbent operator had its franchise agreement renewed in the sector of cable TV. However, the data available to economists on the topic also reveal frequent changes in governance. The case of water in France is an interesting example in this regard. First, the data available unambiguously indicate that changes in delivery option do occur in the sector, since out of the 5000 local authorities investigated by Chong et al. (2015), 228 municipalities switched delivery option between 1998 and 2008. Second, an interesting shift in trend can be observed: shifts back to in-house provision are far more numerous in the years 2004–2008, whereas they were a minority between 1998 and 2001 (see Fig. 5).

This result, which is also valid for other sectors such as urban transport,[10] confers legitimacy on the study of determinants of the delivery option. As a general rule, economists tend to focus on the following question: are the decisions made by contracting authorities driven by economic considerations or by constraints such as political persuasion or pressure from interest groups?

Examining these questions is essential, as it aims to disprove the strong hypothesis according to which organizational choices are exogenous, and thus to improve

---

[10]Several urban public transport networks have gone for in-house provision since 2010. It is the case, for instance, of the French cities of Cannes, Clermont-Ferrand, Dax, Forbach, Maubeuge, Nice, Saumur, or Saint-Brieuc.

the robustness of the analysis of each delivery option performance, and ensuing public policy recommendations.

The determinants of externalizing the delivery of local public services have been the object of numerous empirical studies, which can be divided into two categories. A first set of works puts forward criteria of economic efficiency (production and transaction cost reduction) to explain public authorities' decisions (Sect. 3.1). Another set of works puts aside these criteria to emphasize the effect of determinants pertaining more to political economics, such as the pressure exerted by interest groups or the political persuasion of public decision-makers (Sect. 3.2).

3.3.1 Economic Factors

In line with the works of Coase (1937) and Williamson (1975, 1985), it is possible to maintain that one determinant of the arbitration between make or buy lies in a desire to reduce the production and transaction costs associated with each of them. This first line of explanation, resting upon the developments of transaction cost economics, takes on special significance in countries and for public authorities that are faced with strong budgetary constraints.

From this perspective, several works have tried to evaluate the extent to which local authorities take into account the consequences of their choices in terms of production costs. On this point, a first argument in favor of delegated management has to do with the economies of scale and scope that private firms can potentially realize, unlike public corporations which are generally constrained to operate in defined (and limited) geographical areas. Indeed, private operators can operate a large number of services on several territories, whereas the activity of public corporations most often remains limited to the scope of the public authority to which they report. Thus, the study conducted by David and Chiang (2009) on emergency medical services in the USA reveals that local authorities have a stronger tendency to delegate a service in situations where the private operator is able to realize such economies of scale, in particular because it is already operating the service for neighboring authorities. Moreover, private firms to which this service is delegated are often members of major groups engaged in several activities, allowing them to realize economies of scope. If the local authorities have already delegated other public services, they may prefer to delegate the service to benefit from the ensuing reductions in production costs (Fraquelli et al., 2004 or Levin & Tadelis, 2010).

Economies of scale and scope are not the only sources of production cost reductions from which a local authority seeks to benefit by delegating a service. The advantage of outsourcing in terms of production costs can also originate in the difference in competition intensity in relation to in-house provision. Indeed, private operators are selected through a tendering procedure and are consequently subjected to a competitive goad, which is not the case for public corporations. This argument should, however, be used with caution, as many theoretical and empirical studies have shown that the positive effect of the *ex ante* level of competition only held when very specific conditions were verified (Amaral, Yvrande, & Saussier, 2012; Hong & Shum, 2002). Nevertheless, empirical works show that this effect seems to be taken into account by public authorities. For instance, Levin and Tadelis (2010), Ménard and Saussier (2000), or Amaral and Yvrande (2012) find that large-size public authorities have a stronger tendency to outsource services, which the authors interpret as a desire to benefit from the competitive effect resulting from their attractiveness and this even if they are large enough to benefit from economies of scale under in-house provision.

Production costs are only one component of the costs that should be taken into account in the arbitration between public in-house management and delegated management of a service. Given the advantage provided by private firms in terms of production costs, the question of the choice between two delivery options would not be raised if delegating authorities were able to develop and award complete contractual arrangements at no cost. But this hypothesis is not in keeping with the reality of outsourced contracts and particularly PPPs, due to their complexity and the uncertainty surrounding the evolution of some parameters that are essential to their financial equilibrium (e.g., the evolution of demand in the long term). In other words, delegating service provision necessarily gives rise to transaction costs that are relatively higher than under public management, and these should be taken into account. They are, in particular, the costs associated with organizing calls for tenders and with monitoring and managing contractual arrangements.

The empirical works investigating the effect of the expected level of transaction costs on the likelihood of delegating the service are relatively rare because of the difficulty to collect relevant data. Nevertheless, the few empirical studies tackling this issue confirm the hypothesis according to which contractual difficulties[11] associated with concession contracts constitute a key determinant. As an example, the study conducted by Ferris and Graddy (1994) on health services in the USA reveals that local authorities take into account not only the production costs but also the transaction costs associated with each of the two methods. Investigating the delivery option selected by 63 American cities for a set of public services, Nelson (1997) comes to the same conclusion. More recently, the article by Levin and Tadelis (2010) uses a database on the organizational choices of over 1000 cities in the USA for 64 local public services and also shows that if delegating authorities expect serious contractual difficulties, they will be less likely to externalize service provision. The level of anticipated contractual difficulties derives, in part, from the level of environmental uncertainty the agents are facing. For instance, an important degree of uncertainty around the evolution of demand generates a higher probability of having to revise the contract. In this case, it is possible to maintain that local authorities will be inclined to choose in-house provision of the service to avoid transaction costs associated with the potential renegotiation of the contract. In the

---

[11]They are, for instance, difficulties associated with drawing up the contract (certain specifications, such as those of the urban public transport contract for the city of Lyon, are over 10,000 pages long), monitoring it, and, where necessary, renegotiating it.

case of urban public transport in France, Amaral and Yvrande (2012) have thus shown that the complexity of the service and the uncertainty surrounding demand increased the probability of the service being managed internally.

All these works underline the economic rationality presiding over the choice of the delivery option by authorities. However, although it is reasonable to claim that, in the case of private firms operating in a purely competitive environment, the arbitration between the two options rests solely on criteria of economic efficiency, such criteria can prove insufficient to explain the choices made in the case of local public service industries. Indeed, it is very likely that political issues as well as institutional constraints (Boycko, Shleifer, & Vishny, 1996; Savas, 2000) also come into play in this particular case.

3.3.2 Nonmonetary Determinants of the Choice of Delivery Option

Part of the literature relating to the organizational choices of local public authorities does not focus on considerations of economic efficiency but highlights the importance of nonmonetary constraints such as political persuasion or the influence exerted by interest groups. This approach rests upon the hypothesis that general interest is not the sole objective pursued by decision-makers, who as a consequence are highly sensitive to external pressures such as citizen discontent. With this in mind, the decision to delegate a service or not will depend on the level of relative pressure exerted by various interest groups. This results in choices that do not necessarily respond to an objective of economic efficiency maximization.

Citizen Pressure
Local decision-makers may derive a political advantage from public management in case of social tensions in their urban area. The organizational choice for public services can be one of the public policy levers used to influence the level of wages and the employment rate. Naturally, the effect of the delivery option on unemployment or wage levels may be weak. Nevertheless, the public authority can derive a political advantage from the signal it sends to voters when announcing that it chooses public management in answer to voters' concerns regarding unemployment or wages.

What are the results emerging from empirical works on this question? Estache, Guasch, Iimi, and Trujillo (2008) highlight the fact that socioeconomic characteristics such as the unemployment rate have significant influence on the organizational choices of contracting authorities.

Influencing the employment level proves to be simpler under in-house provision as, under delegated management, the authority's co-contractor retains a degree of autonomy in this regard, especially as it is generally expected to maximize work productivity by dismissing unnecessary employees. For similar reasons, the rate of unionization among employees of public corporations has a negative impact on the probability of delegating the service. Indeed, unions demonstrate a more pronounced preference for in-house delivery option (Warner & Hebdon, 2001).

Along the same lines, Amaral and Yvrande (2012) find that the level of income inequality among the population lowers the likelihood of the service being delegated.

Other works also highlight the fact that, in cities where the level of local taxation is high, the ensuing citizen discontent may lead local decision-makers to resort to a private operator to provide the service, even though in-house provision would be more efficient. Thus, in a study focusing on waste collection in the Netherlands, Dijkgraaf, Gradus, and Melenberg (2003) show that a high level of local taxation has a positive impact on the likelihood of externalization.

Pressure from Industrial Groups

Industrial groups may also constitute a powerful interest group in favor of outsourcing the delivery of public services. For example, recent works in spatial economics (Chong et al., 2006a; Plunket et al., 2008) on the water sector in France reveal that local authorities' choices are very clearly influenced by those of neighboring local authorities. In other words, it suggests that the geographical distribution of delivery options is not random; outsourced management is more likely to be selected if the neighboring local authorities also outsource the service. This effect may derive from the pressure exerted by industrial interest groups operating in neighboring municipalities, but also from the fact that by choosing the same delivery option as nearby authorities, the authority can benefit from shared skills and expertise regarding the organization of calls for tenders, contract monitoring, or public corporation management (Gence-Creux, 2001).

Political and Institutional Characteristics

Finally, political characteristics may also constitute a determinant of the choice of management method. One generally expects right-wing local authorities to have a more pronounced preference for private firm intervention in public service management and, consequently, to be more inclined to outsource public services delivery. This assumption is confirmed by Dubin and Navarro (1988) in the case of household waste treatment in the USA, but the economic literature is far from unanimous on this point. Indeed, it seems that at the local level, decisions are more pragmatic than ideological.

Although they do not test the effect of ideological orientation on decisions made by public decision-makers, Levin and Tadelis (2010) nevertheless find that political considerations can hold a certain explanatory power. Indeed, their study shows that American cities where a manager is appointed to manage public services are more likely to delegate services than when the mayor elected by the city's inhabitants manages them directly. The explanation they provide is that elected mayors are far less susceptible to economic determinants and prefer to manage the service internally in order to derive political advantages from it. In a recent study, Beuve and Le Squeren (2016) find that cities that have been governed by numerous left-wing mayors in the past are more likely to provide their public services in-house. This study therefore suggests that make-or-buy choices are influenced by ideology (that is, the political affiliation of mayors). The authors further show that once a public service has been externalized, re-integration is challenging because of the length of delegation contracts and because of the loss of competencies externalization implies. Beuve and Le Squeren (2016) conclude that political variables should be measured over long periods of time and that empirical studies, which fail to do so, are less likely to find an impact of those variables on the organizational choices.

Finally, studies have shown that an institutional dimension such as the legal status of the local authority could also, through the degree of autonomy it confers on public decision-makers (Lopez de Silanes, Shleifer, & Vishny, 1997), have an impact on the choice of the delivery option.

4   Conclusion

Despite the amount and quality of existing studies, we still lack perspective to appreciate the long-term effects of the various delivery options on performance. In addition, we also often lack reliable and detailed information on service quality, which prevents researchers from taking into account this dimension of public services, even though it is an essential one. For instance, we can think of the studies on the management of prison services which, for the most part, do not take into account the recidivism rate, for want of exploitable data. Moreover, except for a few studies (Clarke et al., 2001 or Gagnepain & Ivaldi, 2002b), the evaluation of performance in terms of social welfare remains relatively rare in the existing literature. Some methodological difficulties, as well as a lack of relevant data, are the reasons why most studies use performance indicators that are only proxies for the social surplus derived from service operation. Now, not being able to assess performance from the angle of social welfare makes it difficult to draw definitive conclusions regarding the relative performance of delivery options or contractual arrangements.

Although some studies conclude that contracting out is the most efficient solution, the improvement it entails may only be temporary, and, in certain cases, the relative performances of public and private management may converge in the longer term. The first article to mention this erosion of gains is the one by Szymanski (1996), which shows that cost reductions associated with the introduction of competition gradually fade over time.

Using a larger database and following the same method (see below), Bello and Szymanski (1996) show that putting services up for tender leads to a cost reduction of 34% after the first year compared to the costs observed prior to outsourcing. After the second year, gains still amount to 31% and after the third year to 27%. So there is indeed an erosion of gains over time. Moreover, when contracts are assigned to public bodies, overall costs are 11% higher on average than when they are awarded to private firms. Gains associated with the introduction of competition are thus significantly lower when the contract is awarded to a public entity. This result is consistent with the idea that competitive pressure and operator status have an impact on incentives to reduce costs.

The authors then compare collection costs for the year before competition is introduced ($t - 1$) with collection costs for the year following the introduction of competition ($t + 1$), for identical services. They find that a cost reduction in the range of 22% follows the auctioning off of the service. These findings suggest that the cost difference between public and private operators tends to remain stable over time, at about 15%. These conclusions confirm the findings of Bello and Szymanski (1996).

Finally, more recent studies support the hypothesis of a gradual erosion over time of gains resulting from the introduction of competition and of a convergence of cost levels between private and public operators. Using data on Spanish services, Bel and Costas (2006) find no significant difference in costs between formerly privately outsourced services and public supply. However, municipalities that concluded their first contract after 1990 have significantly lower costs than local authorities using public collection and authorities where outsourcing is older, which suggests that the efficiency gains derived from the introduction of competition disappear over time. Dijkgraaf and Gradus (2007) obtain similar results using data relating to the Netherlands between 1998 and 2005.

Overall, empirical studies point toward an erosion of the gains derived from the introduction of competition, generally after the third year, and conclude that the respective costs of services outsourced long ago and public supply tend to converge.

These various limitations constitute as many areas of further research for economists.

References

Amaral, M., Saussier, S., & Yvrande-Billon, A. (2013). (Potential) Number of bidders and winning bids: Evidence from the London bus tendering model. *Journal of Transport, Economics and Policy, 47*(1), 17–34.

Amaral, M., & Yvrande-Billon, A. (2012). *Make or buy urban public transport services: A rational choice?* (Working paper Sorbonne Business School).

Athias, L., & Saussier, S. (2007). Un partenariat public-privé rigide ou flexible ? Théorie et applications aux concessions routieres. *Revue Economique, 58*(3), 565–576.

Aubert, C., & Reynaud, A. (2005). The impact of regulation on cost efficiency: An empirical analysis on Wisconsin Water Utilities. *Journal of Productivity Analysis, 23*, 383–409.

Bae, S. (2010). Public versus private delivery of municipal solid waste services: The case of North Carolina. *Contemporary Economic Policy, 28*(3), 414–428.

Bajari, P., Houghton, S., & Tadelis, S. (2014). Bidding for Incomplete Contracts: An Empirical Analysis of Adaptation Costs. *American Economic Review, 104*(4), 1288–1319.

Bayer, P., & Pozen, D. E. (2005). The effectiveness of juvenile correctional facilities: Public versus private management. *Journal of Law and Economics, 48*(2), 549–589.

Bel, G., & Costas, A. (2006). Do public sector reforms get rusty? Local privatization in Spain. *The Journal of Policy Reform, 29*(1), 1–24.

Bel, G., & Mur, M. (2009). Intermunicipal cooperation, privatization and waste management costs: Evidence from rural municipalities. *Waste Management, 29*, 2272–2778.

Bel, G., Fageda, X., & Warner, M. E. (2010). Is private production of public services cheaper than public production? A meta-regression analysis of solid waste and water services. *Journal of Policy Analysis and Management, 29*(3), 553–577.

Bel, G., González-Gómez, F., & Picazo-Tadeo, A. J. (2011). *Does competition affect prices in the urban water industry? Evidence from Spain.* document de travail.

Bello, H., & Szymanski, S. (1996). Compulsory competitive tendering for public services in the UK: The case of refuse collection. *Journal of Business Finance & Accounting, 23*(5-6), 881–903.

Beuve, J., & Le Squeren, Z. (2016). *When does ideology matter? An empirical investigation of French municipalities' make-or-buy choices* (Chair EPPP working paper).

Beuve, J., Huet, F., Porcher, S., & Saussier, S. (2012). *Les performances des modes de gestion alternatifs des services publics: Le cas de la collecte des déchets en France.* Report for the Agence de l'Environnement et de la Maîtrise de l'Energie (ADEME).

Beuve, J., Huet, F. Porcher, S., & Saussier, S. (2013). *Les performances des modes de gestion alternatifs des services publics: le cas de la collecte des dechets en France* (143 p). Rapport ADEME.

Bhattacharyya, A., Harris, T. R., Narayanan, R., & Raffiee, K. (1995). Specification and estimation of the effect of ownership on the economic efficiency of the water utilities. *Regional Science and Urban Economics, 25*(6), 759–784.

Boycko, M., Shleifer, A., & Vishny, R. W. (1996). A theory of privatization. *Economic Journal, 106*(435), 309–319.

Cabral, S., & Saussier, S. (2011). *Organizing prisons through public-private partnerships: A cross-country investigation.* document de travail.

Cabral, S., Lazzarini, S. G., & Furquim de Azevedo, P. (2010). Private operation with public supervision: Evidence of hybrid modes of governance in prisons. *Public Choice, 145*, 281–293.

Callan, S. J., & Thomas, J. M. (2001). Economies of scale and scope: A cost analysis of municipal solid waste services. *Land Economics, 77*(3), 548–560.

Cantos, P., Pastor, J.-M., & Serrano, L. (1999). Productivity, efficiency and technical change in the European railways: A non-parametric approach. *Transportation, 26*, 337–357.

Carpentier, A., Nauges, C., Reynaud, A., & Thomas, A. (2006). Effets de la délégation sur le prix de l'eau potable en France: Une analyse à partir de la littérature sur les effets de traitement. *Économie & Prévision, 174*(3), 1–19.

CGDD. (2010). *Services d'eau et d'assainissement: une inflexion des tendances?* Unpublished manuscript.

Chong, E., Huet, F., Saussier, S., & Steiner, F. (2006a). Public-private partnerships and prices: Evidences from water distribution in France. *Review of Industrial Organization, 29*(1), 149–169.

Chong, E., Huet, F., & Saussier, S. (2006b). Auctions, ex post competition and prices: The efficiency of Public-Private Partnerships. *Annals of Public and Cooperative Economics, 77* (4), 517–549.

Chong, E., Saussier, S., & Silverman, B. (2015). Water under the bridge: Cith size, bargaining power, price and franchise renewals in the provision of water. *Journal of Law, Economics and Organization, 31*(1), 3–39.

Clarke, G., Ménard, C., & Zuluaga, A. M. (2000). *The welfare effects of private sector participation in Guinea's water supply* (World Bank Policy Research Paper no 2361).

Clarke, G., Ménard, C., & Zuluaga, A. M. (2001). *The welfare effects of private sector participation in Guinea's water supply.* World Bank Policy Research Paper no. 2361.

Coase, R. H. (1937). The nature of the firm. *Economica, 4*(16), 386–405.

Collins, J. N., & Downes, B. T. (1977). The effect of size on provision of public services: The case of solid waste collection in smaller cities. *Urban Affairs Quarterly, 12*(3), 333–347.

Cour des comptes. (2010). *Le service public pénitentiaire: prévenir la récidive, gérer la vie carcé rale.* Rapport public thématique.

Crain, W. M., & Zardkoohi, A. (1978). A test of the property-rights theory of the firm: Water utilities in the United States. *Journal of Law and Economics, 21*(2), 398–408.

David, G., & Chiang, A. J. (2009). The determinants of public versus private provision of emergency medical services. *International Journal of Industrial Organization, 27*(2), 312–319.

Dijkgraaf, E., & Gradus, R. (2007). Fair competition in the refuse collection market? *Applied Economics Letters, 14*(10), 701–704.

Dijkgraaf, E., & Gradus, R. (2011). *Efficiency effects of privatising refuse collection: Be careful and alternatives present* (Discussion Papers no 11-156/3). Tinbergen Institute.

Dijkgraaf, E., Gradus, R., & Melenberg, B. (2003). Contracting out refuse collection. *Empirical Economics, 28*(3), 553–570.

Domberger, S., Meadowcroft, S. A., & Thompson, D. J. (1986). Competitive tendering and efficiency: The case of refuse collection. *Fiscal Studies, 7*(4), 69–87.

Dubin, J. A., & Navarro, P. (1988). How markets for impure public goods organize: The case of household refuse collection. *Journal of Law, Economics and Organization, 4*(2), 217–241.

Estache, A., González, M., & Trujillo, L. (2002). What does 'privatization' do for efficiency? Evidence from Argentina's and Brazil's railways. *World Development, 30*(11), 1885–1897.

Estache, A., Guasch, J.-L., Iimi, A., & Trujillo, L. (2008). Multidimensionality and renegotiation: Evidence from transport-sector PPP transactions in Latin America. *Review of Industrial Organization, 35*(1), 41–71.

Ferris, J., & Graddy, E. (1994). Organizational choices for public service supply. *Journal of Law, Economics, and Organization, 10*(1), 126–141.

Fraquelli, G., Piacenza, M., & Vannoni, D. (2004). Scope and scale economies in multiutilities: Evidence from gas, water and electricity combinations. *Applied Economics, 36*(18), 2045–2057.

Friebel, G., Ivaldi, M., & Vibes, C. (2010). Railway (de)regulation: A European efficiency comparison. *Economica, 77*(305), 77–91.

Gagnepain, P., & Ivaldi, M. (2002a). Stochastic frontiers and asymmetric information models. *Journal of Productivity Analysis, 18*(2), 145–159.

Gagnepain, P., & Ivaldi, M. (2002b). Incentive regulatory policies: The case of public transit systems in France. *RAND Journal of Economics, 33*(4), 605–629.

Galiani, S., Gertler, P., & Schargrodsky, E. (2005). Water for life: The impact of the privatization of water services on child mortality. *Journal of Political Economy, 113*(1), 83–120.

Gassner, K., Popov, A., & Pushak, N. (2009). Does private sector participation improve performance in electricity and water distribution? *Trends and Policy Options, 6*. The World Bank, PPIAF.

Gautier, A., & Yvrande-Billon, A. (2013). Contract renewal as an incentive device. An application to the French urban public transport sector. *Review of Economics and Institutions, 4*(1), 1–29.

Gence-Creux, C. (2001). Élections et favoritisme dans l'attribution des marchés de services publics locaux. *Revue économique, 52*(3), 753–763.

Guasch, J.-L. (2004). *Granting and renegotiating infrastructure concession: Doing It right*. Washington, DC: The World Bank.

Hart, O., Shleifer, A., & Vishny, R. W. (1997). The proper scope of government: Theory and an application to prisons. *Quarterly Journal of Economics, 112*(4), 1127–1161.

Haywood, L., & Koning, M. (2012). Avoir les coudes serrés dans le métro parisien: évaluation contingente du confort des déplacements. *Revue d'Economie Industrielle, ½*, 111–144.

Heckman, J. J. (1979). Sample selection bias as a specification error. *Econometrica, 47*(1), 153–162.

Hirsch, W. Z. (1965). Cost functions of an urban government service: Refuse collection. *Review of Economics and Statistics, 47*(1), 87–92.

Hong, H., & Shum, M. (2002). Increasing competition and the winner's curse: Evidence from procurement. *Review of Econnomic Studies, 69*(4), 871–898.

Kemper, P., & Quigley, J. (1976). *The economics of refuse collection*. Cambridge, MA: Ballinger.

Kitchen, H. M. (1976). A statistical estimation of an operating cost function for municipal refuse collection. *Public Finance Review, 4*(1), 56–76.

Laffont, J.-J., & Tirole, J. (1993). *A theory of incentives in procurement and regulation.* Cambridge: MIT Press.

Lalive, R., & Schmutzler, A. (2008). Exploring the effects of competition for railway markets. *International Journal of Industrial Organization, 26*(2), 443–458.

Lalive, R., & Schmutzler, A. (2011). *Auctions vs Negotiations in public procurement: Which works better?* CEPR Discussion Papers. http://ideas.repec.org/p/cpr/ceprdp/8538.html.

Le Lannier, A., & Porcher, S. (2014). Efficiency in the public and private French water utilities: Prospects for benchmarking. *Applied Economics, 46*(5), 556–572.

Levin, J., & Tadelis, S. (2010). Contracting for government services: Theory and evidence from US cities. *Journal of Industrial Economics, 58*(3), 507–541.

Lopez de Silanes, F., Shleifer, A., & Vishny, R. W. (1997). Privatization in the United States. *RAND Journal of Economics, 3*(8), 447–471.

Margari, B., Erbetta, F., Petraglia, C., & Piacenza, M. (2007). Regulatory and environmental effects on public transit efficiency: A mixed DEA-SFA approach. *Journal of Regulatory Economics, 32*(2), 131–151.

Martínez-Espiñeira, R., García-Valiñas, M. A., & González-Gómez, F. (2009). Does private management of water supply services really increase prices? An empirical analysis in Spain. *Urban Studies, 46*(4), 923–945.

Masten, S. E., & Saussier, S. (2000). Econometrics of contracts: An assessment of developments in the empirical litterature of contracting. *Revue d'Economie Industrielle, 92*, 215–237.

Masten, S. E., & Saussier, S. (2002). Econometrics of contracts: An assessment of developments in the empirical literature on contracting. In E. Brousseau & J.-M. Glachant (dir.) *The economics of contracts* (pp. 273–293).

McDavid, J. (2001). Solid-waste contracting-out, competition, and bidding practices among Canadian local governments. *Canadian Public Administration, 44*(1), 1–25.

Megginson, W. L., & Netter, J. M. (2001). From state to market: A survey of empirical studies on privatization. *Journal of Economic Literature, XXXIX*(2), 321–389.

Ménard, C., & Saussier, S. (2000). Contractual choice and performance: The case of water supply in France. *Revue d'Economie Industrielle, 92*, 385–404.

Ménard, C., & Saussier, S. (2003). La délégation de service public, un mode organisationnel efficace ? Le cas de la distribution d'eau en France. *Revue d'économie publique, 12*(1), 99–129.

Nelson, M. A. (1997). Municipal government approaches to service delivery: An analysis from a transaction cost perspective. *Economic Inquiry, 35*(1), 82–96.

Ohlsson, H. (2003). Ownership and production costs: Choosing between public production and contracting-out in the case of Swedish refuse collection. *Fiscal Studies, 24*(4), 451–476.

Piacenza, M. (2006). Regulatory contracts and cost efficiency: Stochastic frontier evidence from the Italian local public transport. *Journal of Productivity Analysis, 25*, 257–277.

Pier, W. J., et al. (1974). An empirical comparison of government and private production efficiency. *National Tax Journal, 27*(4), 653–656.

Plunket, A., Huet, F., & Saussier, S. (2008). La dimension spatiale dans le choix des collectivités de déléguer leurs services publics: le cas de la distribution d'eau en France. *Revue d'économie industrielle, 123*, 45–65.

Pommerehne, W. W., & Frey, B. (1977). Public versus private production efficiency in Switzerland: A theoretical and empirical comparison. *Urban Affairs Annual Review, 12*, 221–241.

Reeves, E., & Barrow, M. (2000). The impact of contracting out on costs of refuse collection Services: The case of Ireland. *Economic and Social Review, 31*(2), 129–150.

Roy, W., & Yvrande-Billon, A. (2007). Ownership, contractual practices and technical efficiency: The case of urban public transport in France. *Journal of Transport Economics and Policy, 41*, 257–282.

Ruester, S., & Zschille, M. (2010). The impact of governance structure on firm performance: An application to the German water distribution sector. *Utilities Policy, 18*(3), 154–162.

Saussier, S. (2000). Transaction costs and contractual incompleteness: The case of Electricite de France. *Journal of Economic Behavior and Organization, 42*(2), 189–206.

Savas, E. S. (2000). *Privatization and public-private partnerships.* New York: Chatham House.

Stevens, B. J. (1978). Scale, market structure, and the cost of refuse collection. *Review of Economics and Statistics, 60*(3), 438–448.

Szymanski, S. (1996). The impact of compulsory competitive tendering on refuse collection services. *Fiscal Studies, 17*(3), 1–19.

Szymanski, S., & Wilkins, S. (1993). Cheap rubbish? Competitive tendering and contracting out in refuse collection. *Fiscal Studies, 14*(3), 1-19109-130.

Tickner, G., & McDavid, J. C. (1986). Effects of scale and market structure on the costs of residential solid waste collection in Canadian cities. *Public Finance Quarterly, 14*(4), 371–393.

Union Fédérale des Consommateurs (UFC). (2006). *Eau: Scandale sur facture.* Que Choisir n°434.

Wallsten, S., & Kosec, K. (2008). The effects of ownership and benchmark competition: An empirical analysis of U.S. water systems. *International Journal of Industrial Organization, 26* (1), 186–205.

Warner, M., & Hebdon, R. (2001). Local government restructuring: Privatization and its alternatives. *Journal of Policy Analysis and Management, 20*(2), 315–336.

Williamson, O. E. (1975). *Markets and hierarchies, analysis and antitrust implications: A study in the economics of internal organization.* New York, NY, USA: Free Press.

Williamson, O. E. (1976). Franchise bidding for natural monopolies: In general and with respect to CATV. *Bell Journal of Economics, 7*(1), 73–104.

Williamson, O. E. (1985). *The economic institutions of capitalism.* New York, NY: The Free Press.

Yvrande-Billon, A., & Ménard, C. (2005). Institutional constraints and organizational changes: The case of the British rail reform. *Journal of Economic Behavior & Organization, 56*(4), 675–699.

Zupan, M. A. (1989). Cable frenchise renewals: Do incumbent firms behave opportunistically? *RAND Journal of Economics, 20*(4), 473–482.

Horizontal and Vertical Agreements in PPPs

John Moore and Carine Staropoli

1 Introduction

The award procedures specific to public–private contracts (including traditional public procurement, concession, and availability contracts) are conducive to various types of horizontal and vertical agreements.

At the European level, out of the five decisions of the European Commission that led to the most severe sanctions against cartels, two were related to practices that had, at least partly, taken place during public calls for tenders. In France, as far as horizontal agreements are concerned, over the past 20 years, the French Competition Authority (*Autorité de la concurrence*) has sanctioned over 750 different companies for such practices in various sectors (construction of works, public and medical transport, hospital supply, etc.). Between 2006 and 2011, penalties for collusive practices in PPPs represented half of all sanctions imposed by the Competition Authority against agreements.

Vertical agreement practices are no exception to this. In 2004, the World Bank estimated that the total amount of bribes associated with corruption in PPPs represented about 200 billion dollars, or around 3.5% of the value of global public procurement.

These various types of agreements in PPPs are a persistent problem for public decision-makers. And yet, efforts have been made by most governments in the fight against such practices. All international organizations such as the United Nations and multilateral development banks recommend their member Countries

J. Moore
ARAFER—Autorité de régulation des activités ferroviaires, Paris, France
e-mail: john.moore@arafer.fr

C. Staropoli (✉)
Paris School of Economics (Université Paris 1), Paris, France
e-mail: carine.staropoli@univ-paris1.fr

© Springer International Publishing AG 2018
S. Saussier, J. de Brux (eds.), *The Economics of Public-Private Partnerships*,
https://doi.org/10.1007/978-3-319-68050-7_8

organizing tendering procedures to award public contracts and in particular PPP contracts. It is even sometimes a condition for their financial participation in the projects.

In France, Law n°93-122 of 29 January 1993, known as the "Sapin Law," introduced a set of rules for the award of concession contracts, which until then had not been subjected to compulsory tendering procedures. In particular, this law aimed to enhance transparency and fight favoritism and corruption, for instance by creating a commission made up of elected representatives whose role is to select candidates and analyze their tenders. In 2008, France finally ratified the Council of Europe's civil law and criminal law conventions on corruption, signed in 1999 to bring about an intensification of the fight against corruption, in particular by reinforcing cooperation between national authorities. The same year, the Competition Authority, in charge of detecting and sanctioning horizontal agreements, was also granted additional resources, in particular in terms of investigation.

What do we know about the organization and impact of these various kinds of agreements? Can economic theory contribute to the definition of mechanisms allowing for the prevention and detection of these behaviors on the one hand and for the determination of a level of sanctions based on the damage inflicted to the economy on the other hand? Are theoretical recommendations compatible with legislation? In this chapter, we will describe both theoretical and empirical economic works to answer these questions. After introducing the organization of such agreements and the damage they inflict on the economy, the first section will outline the methods developed by economists to detect them, which constitute the main way to fight these practices *ex post*. Examples of sanctions imposed by the relevant authorities will be described. A second section will then present the mechanisms identified in the economic literature for the prevention of collusion, favoritism, and corruption. We will focus on the choice of the award procedure and on the way in which companies internalize the rules for which we highlight the conditions of efficiency.

2   Vertical and Horizontal Agreements: Overview, Detection, and Sanction

Economists distinguish between two ways of fighting agreement practices in PPPs. The first one consists in setting up, *ex ante*, an institutional framework that deters actors from resorting to collusion, favoritism, or corruption. For instance, regulators may choose to favor certain award procedures identified as little conducive to collusive agreements. A second way of fighting these different types of agreements consists in intervening *ex post*, that is, after the practice has begun. In this first section, we will investigate this second way of fighting agreements by distinguishing each type of practice. In each case, we will start by reminding the organization of the practice and the damage it inflicts on the economy. We will then focus on the techniques developed by economists to detect such practices *ex post*, when they exist. Finally, we will discuss the sanctions imposed by the relevant authorities.

2.1   Horizontal Agreements in PPPs

2.1.1   Creation and Organization

Agreements may be tacit or explicit and are concluded between several companies with the aim of reducing competition for the market. This reduction in competition aims to stabilize or increase the profits generated by the firms participating in the agreement, compared to a situation of competition. One then talks about "supra-competitive profits" yielded by the agreements. Porter and Zona (1993) identify several factors favoring the creation of such agreements. Among other things, a small number of homogeneous firms must be repeatedly in competition for the award of public contracts. Barriers to entry (for instance in terms of necessary technology or financial resources) must be strong enough to prevent new companies from deciding to participate in these auctions, which would jeopardize the collusive strategy. Contacts between executives, whether insignificant or justified in theory, also favor the creation of an agreement. These contacts may for instance be established during professional union meetings, which may otherwise be legitimate. Finally, the regularity and predictability of calls for tenders allow firms to get better organized in the medium or long term.

Once the agreement is set up, the supra-competitive profit thus generated is shared between members. Various schemes allow for such profit allocation. The first one consists in direct monetary transfers between firms: the designated winner of the contract remunerates other cartel members through side payments. In that case, the firm chosen by cartel members to win the contract will have to be selected, for instance by holding a pre-auction within the cartel to choose the most efficient firm, that is, the one that is likely to generate the most substantial supra-competitive profit (Graham & Marshall, 1987; Lyk-Jensen, 1996; McAfee & McMillan, 1992). Although economists sometimes judge this type of distribution to be the most efficient one, they consider, however, that such monetary transfers between firms are easily detectable by competition authorities (McAfee & McMillan, 1992). The same system of pre-auction may be used when the companies decide to share out collusive profits through subcontracting. In that case, the firm appointed by the cartel to win the tender will pay the other members by allocating them the execution of part of the contract. Finally, "bid rotation" is another profit distribution system that is frequently studied in the economic literature. It consists in each firm of the agreement taking turns to submit the tender that is supposed to win the contract (Aoyagi, 2003; Ishii, 2009). Given the scale and relative stability of public entities' needs, companies anticipate that there will be a sufficient number of future contracts on the scale of an area or a sector for collusive profits to be evenly shared out among cartel members. However, McAfee and McMillan (1992) show that this distribution strategy will always be less efficient than monetary transfers between members. Regardless of the chosen scheme, cartel members that have not been selected to submit the winning tender will then be required to withdraw from the award procedure or to simulate competition by submitting deliberately higher tenders. These practices are known respectively as "bid suppression" and "cover bidding." Box 1 provides practical illustrations of bid-rotation and cover-bidding schemes.

Box 1: When Cartels Show Imagination
Bid Rotation and Moon Phases
     The case of the Electrical Conspiracy in the USA is a good illustration of the inventiveness that can be deployed by members of a cartel. During the 1950s, 29 suppliers entered into an agreement to respond to public calls for tenders regarding the supply of electrical generators and equipment. These companies used a bid-rotation scheme based on the phases of the moon. Each firm was associated with a moon phase. Thus, during calls for tenders, moon phases were used to determine which firm should submit the tender that was to win the contract. The other companies submitted cover bids (Asker, 2010; McAfee & McMillan, 1992; Smith, 1961).
Automatic Calculation of Cover Bids
     The "moon phase" cartel was uncovered by the public buyer, who was surprised to receive several tenders with identical amounts (the cover bids) for each contract. One company thought it had found a way to prevent these cover bids from being too easily detectable (while limiting their preparation costs). After being dismissed, an IT engineer working for a major French group in the construction industry revealed that he was the creator of the Drapo program ("*Détermination aléatoire du prix de l'offre*," Random determination of the tender price). This software had been used by the company in question to automatically calculate the value of cover bids to be submitted by members of a cartel. The cartel behind the "case of the Drapo program" was the object of a decision by the Competition Authority, which sentenced the firm in question to the maximum sanction of 5% of its turnover, i.e., 3.4 million euros.

2.1.2   How Much Does a Collusive Agreement Cost?

Empirical works assessing the damage inflicted on the economy by horizontal agreements in PPPs come to very different conclusions, even when they focus on equivalent practices. Although part of these differences may be attributed to the specificity of each agreement, they otherwise arise from a difficulty in measuring damages (Combe, Connor, Jenny, Buccirossi, & Spagnolo, 2006). Indeed, in order to come up with a precise estimate of the additional costs incurred by the presence of an agreement, we have to be able to determine how much the participation of each cartel member cost for each public contract on which the cartel operated. We would then need to apply a "reasonable" margin and to compare the amount thus obtained with the value of the winning tender of each contract. However, even if we look past the difficulty of estimating these amounts for each contract, results obtained this way would only constitute rough approximations of reality and would potentially skew the damage calculations. In order to remedy this problem, economists favor two approaches (Combe, 2006). These two approaches are introduced below.

Yardstick methods consist in comparing the prices of a given contract with prices applied for an identical contract in an environment free of anticompetitive practices (that is, in a different area, country, or market), which is referred to as the benchmark. These methods imply an evaluation "all other things being equal," which means that the entire terms of implementation of the compared contracts must be similar. Froeb, Koyak, and Werden (1993) use a yardstick method to measure the damages caused by a cartel operating on public contracts for the supply of frozen fish to the American Department of Defense between 1981 and 1989, when the agreement came under formal investigation. Purchases were made in the form of first-price sealed-bid auctions. The agreement had been organized based on a bid-rotation scheme in which a firm was supposed to win the contract while the others submitted cover bids. The authors use the market price of fish as benchmark. Using data from 1984 to 1989, the results of their estimates reveal additional costs associated with the agreement ranging from 23.1 to 30.4%, depending on the period considered. Applying the same method, Lee (1999) studies a tacit agreement relating to public contracts for the supply of milk to schools between 1980 and 1992 in Dallas-Fort Worth. He compares the prices in this contract with those applied in San Antonio for the same type of contracts but with no detected agreement. Contract repetition allowed the actors in Dallas-Fort Worth to agree upon a tacit reallocation of contracts to incumbent firms, using cover bids to simulate competition. The author finds an average price difference of 18% between the two cities, which he attributes to the agreement.

Before-and-after methods compare the prices paid by the contracting authority when the practice was active with prices applied in the pre- or post-cartel periods. These methods are faced with the challenge of determining the precise duration of the infringement. Indeed, it is difficult to know the precise date when the agreement was set up and to detect whether or not prices continued to be influenced by it even after its detection. Indeed, Harrington (2004, 2005) identifies three reasons explaining the fact that prices do not drop dramatically immediately after an agreement is detected. First of all, even if the formal agreement between the firms is weakened by its detection, a residual tacit collusion may sometimes remain between its former members. Moreover, pre-cartel periods are often characterized by unusually intense competition, which makes it particularly profitable for the firms to enter into an agreement. Finally, members of the detected collusive agreement may also continue to skew their prices upward, in an attempt to artificially minimize the competition authorities' calculations of damages to the economy. Lee and Hahn (2002) use the before-and-after method to measure the damages caused by cartels operating in construction contracts of over ten million dollars in South Korea between 1995 and 1998. The authors show that cartel members divided up contracts among themselves based on the construction location. To measure the damages associated with cartel activity, they compare the prices applied by firms over that period with those applied over the next period. They estimate that these practices caused 4.13 billion dollars of damages, i.e., 15.5% of the global value of these contracts. In decision 11-D-02, the French Competition Authority tries to estimate the damages inflicted on the economy by an agreement between 14 firms that operated in public contracts for the restoration of historical monuments in three French regions. Depending on the region, this agreement lasted for 4 or 5 years and divided up "over 90% of contracts." Analyzing prices applied in this sector, the Competition Authority shows that these dropped by over 20% following the breaking up of the cartel.

2.1.3 Autopsy of a Cartel

Agreements have a limited life span. Economists consider the average duration of an agreement to be between 5 and 8 years (Combe & Monnier, 2012). However, some agreements may operate over longer periods. It was the case, for instance, of the cartel of TV and cathode ray tube producers, whose collusive practices stretched over two decades. The 2012 decision sanctioning this case resulted in the highest sanction ever imposed on a cartel by the European Commission. The dissolution of an agreement can occur for two reasons. First of all, the cartel can self-dissolve due to the deviation of some of its members, internal disagreements, or the entry of new competitors in the market, which Levenstein and Suslow refer to as "natural death." In that case, cartel stability is to "blame" (Motta, 2004). The agreement can also be dissolved following its detection by a competition authority. As far as natural deaths are concerned, there are two potential sources of cartel instability: internal stability, which has to do with the deviation of cartel members, and external stability, which has to do with losses suffered by the cartel due to the presence of external tenderers.

Internal stability is jeopardized by the possibility of a member of the cartel to deviate from the agreement. Internal stability problems arise when one of the cartel members deliberately decides not to follow the instructions dictated by the cartel coordinator, for instance by submitting a lower tender than the cartel member designated to win the contract, or by reporting the cartel to a competition authority. This type of behavior is the result of an arbitration by the would-be deviant firm between immediate gains (profits generated by submitting a lower tender or immunity from sanctions in the event of a denunciation to a competition authority) and future losses (opportunity cost of no longer belonging to the cartel and potential retaliation from other cartel members). In order to prevent deviations, some collusive agreements plan retaliatory measures in advance in case a firm deviates. For these threats of retaliation to be deterrent, they have to be credible, i.e., inexpensive to implement for cartel members and, conversely, very costly for the deviant firm. One extreme type of retaliation (in that it is very costly to implement) studied in the literature is the "price war." It consists, for the cartel, in punishing the deviant firm by applying very aggressive prices during the calls for tenders following the deviation, thus reducing its expected profits. Ishii (2009) studies data from contracts for the paving of the city of Ibaraki in Japan, on which a cartel operated between 2002 and 2006. The author shows that a firm that might have deviated from the collusive agreement was the target of a "price war" that lasted for 5 months, after which it took back its position within the cartel.

External stability refers to the possibility that a firm from outside the cartel will submit a tender that is more competitive than the cartel's tender and thus win the contract. The loss of a contract constitutes a loss of revenue for the cartel and may therefore lead to its dissolution, as its members are no longer rewarded for the risks they are taking. A collusive agreement is therefore all the more unstable as this type of incident is frequent or likely to occur. Moore (2012) studies the effect of the number of external tenderers on the likelihood of the cartel winning public contracts. The author uses data from calls for tenders in which a case of collusion was sanctioned by the French Competition Authority between 1991 and 2010. He finds that an increase in external competition does not affect the probability of cartels winning calls for tenders. Indeed, the intensity of external competition is anticipated by cartel members, who adapt their tenders based on this parameter. An increase in external competition then results in lowering the value of tenders submitted by cartels (thus reducing the supra-competitive profit) but does not affect the number of public contracts won. Box 2 describes a collusive agreement in which none of the four members managed to win a public contract.

Box 2: When Cartels Make Mistakes...
While some cartels are remarkable for the complexity and efficiency of their collusive schemes, others are notorious for their infelicities. Decision 01-D-17 of the *Autorité de la Concurrence* (French Competition Authority) mentions an agreement between four companies that operated on three public contracts for the electrification of the area around Le Havre. External tenderers won two out of the three contracts. During the third call for tenders, a firm from the cartel was in a position of lowest tenderer but got disqualified: on the document of one of the firms submitting a cover bid was a post-it with the name of the lowest tenderer as well as the value of the cover bid. The four firms won neither one of the three electrification contracts and the forgotten post-it provided material evidence that allowed the *Autorité de la concurrence* to sanction these firms by sentencing them to pay a global fine of over a million and a half euros.

The lack of reliable data on cases of collusion in public contracts drove economists to develop more or less elaborate detection techniques, some of which were designed for direct application by contracting authorities or competition authorities. We will now introduce a few representative examples of these techniques.

Porter and Zona (1993) analyze data on public calls for tenders for the construction of highways by the *New* York State Department of Transportation, between April 1979 and March 1985. Suspicions of collusions surrounded the award of these contracts. A firm was sanctioned and four others were suspected of complicity. The authors suspect that cover bids were used to simulate competition between these five firms. To confirm their suspicions, they use tests comparing the alleged cover bids with the entire set of competitive tenders. They find a statistically significant difference between the two kinds of tenders, which they attribute to the fact that cover bids are not supposed to win the contract and that, as a consequence, they are not competitive tenders designed for winning the contract, quite the opposite. Bajari and Ye (2003) use data from public auctions for the seal coating of highways between 1994 and 1994 in the States of Minnesota, North Dakota, and South Dakota. They estimate the distance between the firm's headquarters and the location of the project, the firm's number of ongoing projects, and they use the administration's estimate as a proxy for the costs of completing the project. They show that, for a tender to be competitive, it has to be based solely on these three factors. In contrast, a tender submitted by a cartel member will not depend solely on these factors. The authors show that all companies from their sample meet the criteria for competitive tenders except for two, which were recently sanctioned for collusive practices.

A number of arguments show that in the presence of collusion, prices are less volatile. For instance, it is more costly for cartels to adjust their prices to certain sudden changes in external factors, especially in terms of organization, than for competitive firms which by definition are acting alone. Starting from this idea, Abrantes-Mertez, Froeb, Geweke, and Taylor (2006) developed a collusion screen test based on the variance of prices paid by the public buyer. The idea is that strong price variance should be associated with periods of competition, while low variance should indicate collusive periods. They study data from a conspiracy in public contracts for the supply of frozen seafood to the American Department of Defense in the 1980s. When the conspiracy collapsed, prices dropped by 16% on average and their variance increased by over 250%. Padhi and Mohapatra (2011) attempt to set up a simple collusion detection method that could be implemented by contracting authorities during bid opening. Unlike the first techniques introduced in this chapter, the method they develop does not rely on econometrics but on a series of seven rudimentary statistical tests applied to all tenders submitted by companies, normalized by the public authority's reserve price. The authors use data from public auctions for road construction projects in India in 2003–2007. Using cluster analysis, among other things, they divide their sample of tenders into two clusters and show that the cluster with the higher mean, median, and variance value corresponds to collusive bidding. Other detection methods are based, for instance, on the number of zeros in the bid price (Ishii, 2013), or on unsuccessful calls for tenders (Kawai & Nakabayashi, 2014).

Box 3: Are Cartels as Astute as We Think?

Given all the elements mentioned above, a conspiracy must at once get organized to generate a supra-competitive profit and find an efficient way to share it out among its members all the while ensuring its own stability (i.e., finding means of retaliation in case of deviation from the agreement, preventing other firms from entering the market) and avoiding detection. All these considerations suggest complicated organizational methods. But it would seem that in practice, conspiracies are less complex than we might think. Arai, Ishibashi, and Ishii-Ishibashi (2011) use data from cartel cases that were sanctioned by the Japan Fair Trade Commission (2010), the Japanese competition agency. They find that, in most cases of collusion, the implemented schemes are simple ones. In particular, in 20% of cases, the cartel organizer does not concern itself with the fairness of contract allocation among its members. However, as the data they use comes exclusively from sanctioned cases, it is likely that these simple organizational methods are easier to detect, which would explain their predominance in this study.

Some empirical studies manage to come up with a precise estimate of the probability of a cartel being detected. Bryant and Eckard (1991) consider that this likelihood lies within a range of 13–17%. This estimate gives us an idea of how difficult it is for the various competition authorities to detect conspiracies. Indeed, detecting cartels is a delicate task, one that requires considerable resources, especially as it entails substantial costs of market surveillance and investigation. The creation of leniency procedures (Box 4) by competition authorities responds to these problems by giving firms that belonged or still belong to a cartel an incentive to denunciate the cartel in question. Such a denunciation, as well as the provision of concrete evidence of the existence of a collusive agreement, is rewarded by a reduction in sanction that can go as far as full immunity. Although these procedures aim to increase the detection ability of competition authorities while limiting its cost, they also aim to undermine existing cartels and to prevent their formation by casting doubt about the possibility of a denunciation by a cartel member.

Box 4: A Little Leniency, But Not Without Compensation!

The leniency procedure was introduced in the USA as early as 1978, but it only achieved real success after its modification in 1993, which made exemptions from sanctions more automatic for informers and thus increased the firms' incentives to reveal their possible collusive agreements (Stephan, 2009). The European Commission set up a similar procedure in 1996. It was then revised in 2002 and 2006. Hammond stresses the fact that, since 1993, the leniency procedure has been the most efficient investigative tool

(continued)

Box 4 (continued)

used by the Department of Justice (DoJ), the American competition authority. However, empirical studies provide more contrasting results. Stephan (2009) lists all cartel cases processed by the European Commission between 2000 and April 2007 and shows that, in over 70% of cases, detection resulted from the use of a leniency program. However, he notes that the majority of leniency cases registered by the Commission followed on from a cartel failure or an investigation by the DoJ for similar practices.

Empirical studies focusing on the leniency procedures launched by the DoJ and European Commission were published, respectively, by Miller (2009) and Brenner (2009). The results they obtain show a wide gap between the two authorities. Miller (2009) studies all cartel cases sanctioned by the DoJ between 1985 and 2005, representing a total of 342 different cartels. He shows that the number of processed cases increased significantly immediately after the introduction of the leniency procedure of 1993 and then fell after this date. He justifies these two trends by an increase in the power of detection for the first phase, and by the deterrent effect generated by the introduction of the leniency procedure after 1993. Brenner (2009) investigates the effects of the leniency procedure introduced in 1996 by the European Commission. He underlines the positive effect of the program on cartel detection and investigation duration. However, he finds no significant deterrent effect as regards the formation and stability of cartels. Brenner attributes the differences in efficiency between the two leniency programs to the fact that, in the USA, firm participation in a cartel falls within the scope of criminal law and may result in jail sentences for the managers in charge. Leniency may then result in an exemption from such sentences for the managers of denunciatory firms. An increase in the DoJ's power of detection through the leniency program thus increases the probability of managers facing a jail sentence, which explains the greater efficiency of the American program in terms of cartel formation and stability.

2.1.4 Sanctioning Cartels

In this section, we will focus on sanctions imposed on cartels. We will begin by outlining the sanctioning policy for cases of collusive agreements in PPPs, relying on a notice published by the French Competition Authority. We will then introduce the debates surrounding the level of sanctions. The empirical works that are presented in this section make no distinction between agreements operating in public–private contracts and agreements in "classical" sectors.

On May 16, 2011, the French Competition Authority published a notice relating to the method applied to determine financial penalties in cases of collusive agreements. It states that penalties are calculated for each company and based on four criteria: the seriousness of the facts, the extent of the harm done to the economy, the situation, especially financial, of the sanctioned firm, and the possible reiteration. The Authority singles out anticompetitive practices in PPPs, which do not pertain to "a complex and continuous infringement" and specifies that, unlike for anticompetitive agreements in "classical" sectors, penalties will not be calculated based on the value of each firm's sales, as this is not an appropriate indicator of the involvement of each firm in the case of cartels operating in PPPs. In particular, the submission of cover bids and possible bid suppressions would not be accounted for by a calculation based on the value of the firms' sales. The value of the financial penalties will then be calculated by applying a coefficient—"which will be set in view of the seriousness of the facts and of the importance of the harm done to the economy"—to the total turnover of the firm or of the group to which it belongs. If the penalty thus calculated exceeds the maximum threshold of 10% of the firm's turnover, it will be lowered to this threshold.

Box 5: Sanctioning Anticompetitive Behaviors: A "Double Penalty"?

Aside from financial penalties, a ruling by a competition authority may also have other effects on sanctioned firms (effects on the reputation or value of the firm, for instance). Langus, Motta, and Aguzzoni (2013) analyzed the effect of events resulting from a sanctioning decision from the European Commission on the value of the publicly listed companies involved. They selected all decisions pronounced between 1979 and 2005 for all types of sanctioned practices (abuse of a dominant position, cartels, etc.). They find that reports of a surprise inspection (indicating the beginning of an investigation) and the announcement of an infringement decision both lead to a significant drop in the offending firm's share prices, by 1.9% and 3.6%, respectively. In contrast, the annulment of a decision by judgment leads to a significant increase in share prices, between 1 and 1.9%.

The authors conclude their study by showing that the amount of the imposed penalty only accounts for one-quarter to one-third of the drops in share prices observed in case of sanctions. In fact, the majority of the loss in the firm's value is due to the cessation of illegal activities. In the case of a cartel, for instance, an authority's decision will in all likelihood put an end to the practice, which means that its members will lose their supra-competitive profit.

The level of sanctions currently imposed by the various competition authorities has sparked numerous debates. Some economists consider these sanctions to be higher than the optimal penalty (Allain, Boyer, & Ponssard, 2011; Ehmer & Rosati, 2009; Veljanovski, 2011), while others find the level of fines to be far lower than this threshold (Combe & Monnier, 2009; Connor & Lande, 2004; Lee, 2008). These disagreements are due mostly to broad variations both in the measure of damages and in the evaluation of the likelihood of cartel detection. Indeed, economists think in terms of anticipated sanction, that is, the amount of the fine which an as yet undetected cartel can expect to receive, multiplied by the probability of this cartel actually being detected.

Despite these discrepancies, economists have been in agreement about the expected effect of an optimal sanction since Becker's works (1968). A sanction is said to be optimal when the anticipated sanction for a given anticompetitive agreement is at least equivalent to the collusive gains realized by this agreement. In that case, the sanction will have two effects: it will both punish the detected cartels and deter companies from forming new cartels, since the hope to profit from a cartel will then be negative or nonexistent. To this end, and given the low likelihood of a cartel being detected, the imposed fines must be higher than the estimated damages inflicted on the economy. Veljanovski (2011) studies the European Commission's sanctioning decisions in cases of anticompetitive agreements since the clarification of its method for determining the amount of fines in 2006. Comparing these decisions with those pronounced between 1999 and 2006, the author demonstrates an increase in the value of fines. Calculating a ratio between the imposed sanction and the total value of sales made by the cartel, and based on conservative estimates of damage measures and of the likelihood of cartel detection, Veljanovski finds that sanctions imposed by the Commission are in fact quite close to the optimal sanction. Studying data on a cartel operating in public contracts for the supply of milk to schools in the State of Texas in the 1980s, Lee (1999) finds different results. This cartel was sanctioned by the DoJ, the American competition authority. Using all available data, the author shows that the damage estimate used by the DoJ to calculate the cartel's sanction underestimated the actual amount. In this case, the imposed sanction was consequently below the optimal amount. Box 6 is based on the work of Combe et al. (2006) and introduces various methods aiming to increase the level of sanctions in order to deter collusive behaviors.

Box 6: How Can Effective Sanctions Be Brought Closer to the Optimal Sanction?

The financial sanctions imposed on firms by the various authorities are capped at a certain percentage of their turnover. Some economists recommend increasing the level of sanctions or supplementing them by allowing for or facilitating the possibility of civil action, the objective of which would be for consumers or consumer associations to claim compensation from firms that participated in a cartel. However, sanctions must be punitive but should not systematically drive companies to bankruptcy. Indeed, if fines are too high, they risk jeopardizing an already problematic level of competition. To reach higher levels of sanction, one must then rely on other elements than financial penalties.

(continued)

Box 6 (continued)

A first possibility would be to increase the number of detected cartels. If more cartels are detected and sanctioned, it will reduce the firms' incentives to form or participate in collusive schemes. This is one of the reasons why the leniency procedure was introduced or simplified by competition authorities. Detection can also be improved by increasing the financial resources allocated to these authorities. Competitive watch could then be organized in markets that are particularly conducive to collusion. However, although an increase in authorities' financial resources would indeed result in improving detection, the scope of such an improvement would likely be limited.

A second possibility would be to supplement financial penalties with criminal sanctions against the managers in charge of collusive firms. The main advantage of criminal sanctions is that they do not come up against the firms' inability to pay. Moreover, this type of sanction may lead to jail sentences, which have a particularly strong deterrent effect on individuals. However, Combe et al. (2006) observe that the application of such a solution in Europe clashes with the fact that *"the effective use of criminal prosecution can only be justified in the eyes of public opinion if cartel practices are the object of strong moral condemnation, which is not yet the case in Europe."*

The following graphs illustrate the differences between the European and American sanctioning policies. In particular, the absence of jail sentences in Europe is coupled with high fine amounts. American authorities, in contrast, seem to favor jail sentences.

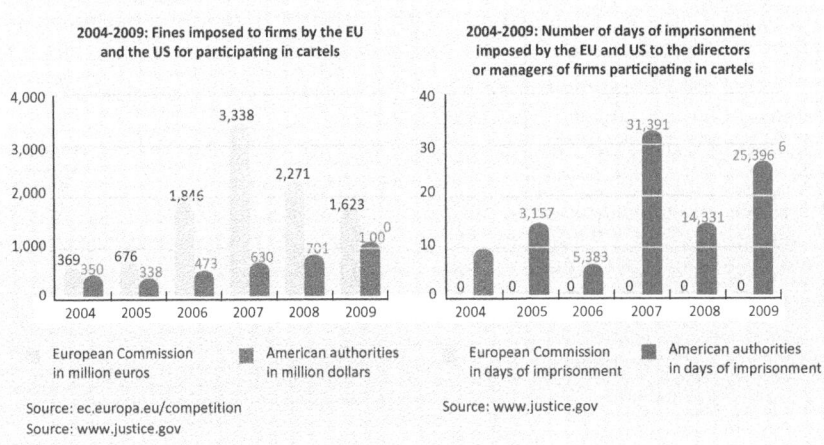

2004-2009: Fines imposed to firms by the EU and the US for participating in cartels

European Commission in million euros	American authorities in million dollars

Source: ec.europa.eu/competition
Source: www.justice.gov

2004-2009: Number of days of imprisonment imposed by the EU and US to the directors or managers of firms participating in cartels

European Commission in days of imprisonment	American authorities in days of imprisonment

Source: www.justice.gov

2.2 Vertical Agreements in PPPs

In this section, we will distinguish between two offenses associated with public–private contracts involving the public party. *Favoritism* refers to the granting of an unjustified advantage to a tenderer by any contracting authority, in violation of the guarantees of freedom and equality of candidates in public procurement. As for *corruption*, it corresponds to the granting of an unjustified advantage to a tenderer by a public authority in return for any kind of compensation. We will further distinguish between *passive corruption*, for the contracting authority, and *active corruption*, for the tenderer.

2.2.1 From "Legal Favoritism"...

Some favoritism practices are authorized under the various laws in force relating to PPPs. These practices are mostly motivated by the social or economic objectives of regulators. In several legal frameworks, it is for instance possible to give preferential treatment to companies whose staff includes a majority of people with disabilities. The current crisis is driving policy-makers to adopt stances that blur the boundary between discriminatory practices and proactive policies even further. Public procurement can be used as a tool to pursue other objectives than the mere satisfaction of public needs, such as for instance environmental, social, or industrial objectives.

As concession and availability contracts are global contracts which may be difficult to access for small and medium-sized enterprises, the public entity may include, among the award criteria, a percentage of the contract to be allocated to Small and Medium-sized Enterprises (SMEs) by the selected candidate. Such practices could be referred to as "legal favoritism"–.

In the USA, the Small Business Act lays down some rules aiming to support the access of SMEs to public contracts. Such favoritism can take the form of "bonuses" applied to tenders submitted by SMEs or of a percentage of contracts reserved exclusively for SMEs. Marion (2007) analyzes data from public road construction contracts in California. During some of the tendering procedures, the public authority applies a preferential scheme whereby SMEs receive a 5% bid preference. The author shows that the buyer's costs increase by almost 4% when the preferential scheme is applied. These additional costs are attributed to the reduced participation of large firms in such auctions because of the preferential treatment applied. Still in the USA, Athey, Levin, and Seira (2011) investigate cases where a percentage of contracts is reserved solely for SMEs, using data on public auctions for the allocation of forest parcels. 14% of parcels are reserved for competition between small and medium-sized enterprises only. The authors show that the public auction revenue decreases by 17% when parcels are reserved for SMEs. They conclude that revenues could have been higher if the contracting authority had used a "bonus" system on tenders, as in the case of Californian roads.

2.2.2 ...to the Offense of Favoritism

Aside from the few special cases that can be likened to "legal favoritism", any breach of transparency or of the principle of equal treatment and access of candidates to public contracts can be punished according to the Art. 14 of the Criminal Law. Several behaviors can be described as favoritism. In particular, they mention granting an informational advantage to a company that is likely to be favored by it, deliberately underestimating a contract in order to declare a call for tenders unsuccessful and to negotiate with one company and giving preferential treatment to a local firm.

Two empirical studies mention determinants of the likelihood of favoritism from municipalities. Coviello and Gagliarducci (2010) investigate all public contracts awarded by Italian municipalities between 2000 and 2005. The authors attempt to determine the effect of the time spent as mayor of a city on the probability of resorting to favoritism. They observe that various indicators of the quality of public contract award deteriorate with the mayor's longevity. In particular, the number of bids received per call for tenders diminishes and prices paid by the public party increase. Moreover, the likelihood of a local firm winning a municipality's public contract increases with the time the mayor has spent in power. The authors show that favoritism is the most likely explanation for these deteriorations in public procurement. The mayor's political persuasion is also thought to have an impact on the practice of favoritism. Hyytinen, Lundberg, and Toivanen (2008) analyze all cleaning contracts awarded by Swedish municipalities between 1990 and 1998. The authors find that, despite how easy it is to contract out this type of project, municipalities mostly use best-value award procedures without prior publication of the criteria used to select the winner. These procedures are deemed discretionary. The authors show that, in the majority of calls for tenders, the contracts are not awarded to the firms that submitted the lowest tender, which leads, in these cases, to an additional cost of about 43% compared to the lowest tender. Left-wing municipalities are more price sensitive but also more likely to select a local firm. Like Coviello and Gagliarducci (2010), the authors conclude that this kind of favoritism has a negative impact on public expenditure.

2.2.3 Corruption...

Unlike favoritism, which does not imply compensation from firms (because the practice satisfies the interests of the legislator—social and economic objectives, like the preference for SMEs—, or of the public contractor—preference for local firms in order to stimulate local economy, for instance), corruption in public–private contracts implies an exchange of favors. Typically, public contracts may be awarded to firms in exchange for bribes.

Corruption may also take on several forms (Lengwiler & Wolfstetter, 2006). It can occur before the call for tenders. The public contractor may disclose confidential information regarding the projects in return for compensation. One example of this type of corruption is mentioned in the OECD report of 2007. Public employees and a local elected representative in charge of awarding public contracts revealed confidential information to various firms of the construction industry in return for money and benefits in kind. The disclosed information had to do with confidential studies conducted by the public party for each project and included, in particular, the range of acceptable prices for these projects. The firms then used this information to divide up the contracts among themselves. To avoid detection, money transfers were done through similar techniques as the ones used for money laundering, and benefits in kind included such things as renovations (for free or at cost price) in the home of the local representative, as well as the financing of one of his campaign spots.

Corruption can also occur during the call for tenders, especially by way of a request to modify the bidder's tender in return for compensation (Burguet & Perry, 2007; Menezes & Monteiro, 2006). This type of corruption was used in school construction contracts for the city of New York studied by Ingraham (2005), where the corrupted firms' prices were modified by employees in charge of bid opening in return for compensation from the firms. We refer the reader to Box 7, where this case and the detection method developed by the author are outlined.

Finally, corruption can also occur after the contract awarding phase. Indeed, the practice can focus on the level and form of risk sharing between the public and private sectors (Iossa & Martimort, 2011), as well as on the level of quality expected by the public entity (Celentani & Ganuza, 2001; Lengwiler & Wolfstetter, 2006). Soreide (2002) shows that this last form of corruption is more difficult to fight, as it is more complex both to detect and to prove.

Box 7: The First Corruption Detection Test

The first econometric test designed to detect corruption was developed by Ingraham (2005). He used data from auctions for school constructions in the New York City School Construction Authority, where two employees were sentenced in 1994 for accepting bribes from firms. One of the employees met with the firm that agreed to compensate him and, at bid opening, would keep this firm's envelope for last. After announcing all tenders aloud, the employee then opened this last envelope and announced a false price directly below the one offered by the lowest tenderer. The firm was thus guaranteed to win the contract at the highest possible price. First, the author shows that when the corruptive scheme was active, the gap between the winning tender and the second tender was significantly smaller than that same gap for all other contracting authorities. Additionally, the author uses data from 1990 to 1997 to analyze the prices applied before and after the media coverage of the case. He shows that two other employees probably resorted to the same type of scheme over the same period, but that they stopped their practices following the first suspicions of corruption.

2.2.4 . . .and Its Complementarity with Collusion

A growing number of indexes connect collusion with corruption (Lambert-Mogiliansky, 2011). In such a case, contracts are awarded successively to each firm in the cartel in return for compensation paid to the contracting authority. Theoretical works especially underline the contribution of corruption to stabilize collusive agreements in an uncertain environment (Compte, Lambert-Mogiliansky, & Verdier, 2005; Kosenok & Lambert-Mogiliansky, 2009; Lambert-Mogiliansky & Sonin, 2006).

What Lambert-Mogiliansky (2011) calls *strategic complementarities* between collusion and corruption is at the heart of the so-called "case of the public procurement contracts for Île-de-France (Paris region) high schools," made famous by the publication, in September 2000, of a posthumous tape in which a member of the right-wing political party "RPR" testifies about his role in the covert financing of this political party. This case combining collusion and corruption was the object of decision 07-D-15 of the French Competition Authority. This decision sanctioned twelve companies of the construction sector for sharing out 88 public contracts for the renovation of high schools in the Île-de-France region between 1989 and 1996, for a total amount of 1.5 billion euros. The RPR's treasurer summarizes this mechanism combining collusion and corruption as follows: "(. . .) *I understood that there was an agreement for high school contracts in the Île-de-France region: the firms came to an agreement among themselves and had to commit to paying a percentage to the RPR and the Republican Party to win the contracts (. . .).*" The decision also explains the role of a company that, in its capacity as consulting engineers firm, "*contributed to the execution of the agreement by shortlisting the companies approached about winning the contracts, for each wave of public works contracts.*" The sanctions imposed by the Competition Authority as well as criminal sanctions imposed in the case of the Ile-de-France high school public contracts are presented in Box 8.

Box 8: Sanctions in the Case of the Ile-de-France High Schools
This box outlines the sentences and sanctions imposed in this case. We make a distinction between the criminal sentences pronounced against individuals and the sanctions imposed on companies by the French Competition Authority.
Criminal Sanctions:
  On October 26, 2005, the 11th chamber of the Paris criminal court delivered sentences against 32 of the 47 defendants in the case of the Ile-de-France high schools. Suspended jail sentences were received by all actors, coupled with financial sanctions ranging from 5000 to 100,000 euros. Only one of the convicted elected representatives received a 1-year mandatory jail term, combined with a 2-year suspended sentence. On appeal, these sentences

(continued)

Box 8 (continued)

were made more severe for two of the three treasurers of the political parties, and the elected representative's mandatory jail sentence was confirmed.
Sanctions Imposed by the Autorité de la Concurrence:
   In its decision of 2007, the Competition Authority sanctioned the twelve companies of the construction industry belonging to this cartel. It reports that the companies divided up 88 contracts among themselves for a total value of 1.5 billion euros. The *"particularly serious damage to the economy justifies exemplary penalties"*; indeed, each company was inflicted a penalty representing the maximum threshold of 5% of its turnover. In total, the penalties amounted to 47.3 million euros, with amounts per company ranging from 7600 euros to over 20 million euros.

There is still a lack of empirical works on the issue of vertical agreements in general: only a few articles list or detail precise cases. Indeed, such practices are especially difficult for authorities to detect and therefore rarely uncovered. Moreover, using the results of questionnaires sent to Norwegian firms, Soreide (2008) shows that the beaten competitors of corrupt firms do not report such corruptive practices, mostly because they fear repercussions on their future opportunities. Thus, authorities cannot rely on the help of companies that are victims of corruption to detect it. Naturally, the absence of data does not help compare economic theory with the reality of practices.

In this section, we have reviewed the forms of the various types of agreements in PPPs, as well as the different ways of fighting these practices *ex post*. But in order to be efficient, an antitrust and anticorruption policy must also deter agents from resorting to such practices. The next section introduces these means of prevention.

3   The Prevention of Horizontal and Vertical Agreements

For public authorities, fighting vertical and horizontal agreements implies, insofar as possible, acting ahead by creating adverse conditions for corruption, in particular during the process of contract award and contractor selection. Motta (2004) thus considers that *"it is preferable to try and create an environment that deters corruption initially rather than attempt to prove illegal behaviors* ex post."

The various measures a public authority may use to prevent corruption beforehand and block horizontal and vertical agreements in PPPs, and more particularly in public procurement contracts, are largely defined by the legislative and statutory framework and mostly rely on contract award procedures and candidate selection processes that are supposed to ensure transparency and integrity. Like all public–

private contracts, traditional public procurement contracts may be affected by horizontal and vertical agreement practices during the award procedure due to their object and the amounts at stake, as well as to their frequency and relative predictability (Caillaud, 2001; OECD, 2008). That is why the literature essentially focuses on traditional public procurement contracts, and more particularly on the call for tenders, which is the most widely used procedure to award these contracts— even if other procedures do exist. In the literature of auction theory (Klemperer, 2004; Milgrom, 2004) and mechanism design (Myerson, 1981), the call for tenders is likened to an auction and the other procedures to negotiations.

Box 9: Auctions and Mechanism Design in Theory… and in Practice
An auction is a competitive mechanism that is used to discover the "fair market price." It is a set of rules determining the conditions of the competitive confrontation of supply and demand for a good or service in a market. Public entities very often use auctions to purchase a good or a service, sell assets, or finance sovereign debt in the financial markets. The award of a concession, of a public works, service, or supply contract (public contract), or of a license in mobile telephony can also be achieved through an auction. Auctions are characterized by several aspects:

– The specificities of the object or objects in case of multiple goods (such as Treasury bills), in particular the common or private nature of the value of the good
– The way in which bids are submitted (the bid submission procedure)
– The way in which the winner is chosen (the award procedure)
– The payment rule

In practice, there are standard auction designs, commonly used and with well-known properties. But more often than not, these auctions cannot be used for complex objects and in a specific context; for instance, it is the case of auctions that had to be designed for a particular purpose (UMTS auctions for the award of mobile licenses, electronic auctions in wholesale markets, auctions for the award of airport slots, etc.). In theory, studies analyze auction properties based on the formalization limitations associated with the hypotheses, in particular in terms of available information. The theory of mechanism design (Hurwicz, 1972; Myerson, 1981) rests upon game theory (Bayesian games) to find the optimal mechanism to get the players to disclose private information by applying the revelation principle. Among the fundamental findings of studies in mechanism design theory, the revenue equivalence theorem established by Vickrey (1961) shows that a number of standard auction designs will result in the seller receiving the same level of revenue and that this is the maximum revenue it can hope to receive. This theorem rests upon particularly strong hypotheses that reduce its scope of application.

(continued)

Box 9 (continued)

Vickrey's auction model (1961) was then further developed by Clarke (1971) and Groves (1973) to tackle issues of public goods for which the cost of a project—a bridge, for instance—is borne by the collectivity. They propose an auction mechanism that can solve the "tragedy of the commons." These works have since then spread to information economics (Myerson, 1981), but above all, they have given rise to a particularly abundant literature in auction theory. However, as highlighted by Klemperer (2002), the actors involved in developing auctions in practice must move beyond models, which are too restrictive, to take into account reality, and especially vertical and horizontal agreements: *"What really matters in auction design* [implied: 'in practice'] *are the same issues that any industry regulator would recognize as key concerns: discouraging collusive, entry-deterring and predatory behavior. In short, good auction design is mostly good elementary economics."*

Krishna (2009) shows that, in the 1980s, 75% of collusion cases handled by the American Antitrust had to do with the manipulation of auction procedures. The Japan Fair Trade Commission (2010) observed that half of the competition cases it handled gave rise to sanctions relating to collusive behaviors during award procedures for public contracts. As for the OECD (2008), it considers that "a significant part of cartel operations involve the rigging of calls for tenders or of public contracts." (Porter and Zona, 1999).

The choice of the most suitable procedure, given the particularities of the public contract at stake, is thus the starting point for any effort aiming to ensure the efficiency of public contract award.

The theoretical and empirical literature on auctions helps identify the conditions of efficiency of the various procedures—often with a comparative approach—and proposes tools to assist public authorities in making decisions in terms of collusion and corruption prevention. The study of auctions is one of the most visible applications of game theory. Most theoretical models on auctions assume that bidders make their decisions independently (it is the case for private value auctions and common value auctions), i.e., that they do not act in a concerted manner. That is why noncooperative game theory, which focuses on strategic behavior, is used as a priority. As soon as the players cease to be strategically independent, it is necessary to rely on cooperative game theory and to study the formation of coalitions of bidders, their stability, and the way in which they divide up their profits.

These models analyze the circumstances under which collusion is maintainable (in particular the size of the cartel and the identity of the coordinator), the gains that can be derived from such behaviors, as well as the way in which cartel members divide up the benefits among themselves. Among these favorable circumstances, the nature of the good or service at stake (private value or common value, in particular) and the format of the auction are the main elements favoring collusion.

Theoretical studies overlook a number of aspects associated with the institutional environment and governance structures regulating public–private contracts, despite the fact that these may be assumed to have a strong influence on collusion. For example, it is difficult to develop a model accounting for the conditions of organization of the award procedure, the expertise and integrity of the public actor, the credibility of the institutions in charge of regulation, or the enforcement power of the contract. Yet these various aspects have a substantial influence on the conditions of PPP efficiency, insofar as they generate costs (costs associated with procedure organization and resorting to external consulting firms, renegotiation costs, participation costs for bidders).

Wilson (1987) highlights another difficulty associated with the implementation of theoretical models. The mechanisms that are meant to deter collusion in these models rest upon a very strong hypothesis, namely that the organizer of the auction knows the distribution function based on which bidders estimate their payable price, which is not the case in practice. The organizer must also know which bidder belongs to which cartel, which is particularly difficult to determine. Finally, Wilson (1987) suggests finding "detail-free auctions," that is, auctions that do not require this type of information.

The theoretical predictions only gave rise to few empirical tests, especially because of the lack of data available to compare the predictions with hard facts, which limits the scope of the theoretical results. However, empirical works focusing on specific procedures organized in particular markets have allowed for the identification of collusive behaviors and the analysis of their consequences. The sector of highway construction, traditionally characterized by powerful cartels, has given rise to several studies highlighting collusive strategies based on the manipulation of auction procedures (McMillan, 1991; Porter & Zona, 1993). Other empirical studies have focused on more unusual activities and fields, such as the supply of milk to schools (Pesendorfer, 2000), timber-cutting contracts (Athey, Levin, and Seira, 2011; Paarsch, 1992), or auctions organized for the award of Official Development Aids (ODA) in Japan (Iimi, 2004).

Relying partly on these works and on expertise and feedbacks, institutions such as the OECD and organizations like Transparency International, as well as national governments (the French Directorate of legal affairs [*Direction des affaires juridiques*] at the Ministry of the Economy in France), have established best practices guides to prevent collusion and detect it if necessary (OECD, 2008, 2010). Their recommendations focus on actions revolving around three dimensions: (Sect. 3.1) competitive intensity, (Sect. 3.2) the most suitable degree of transparency, and (Sect. 3.3) institutional and organizational mechanisms.

3.1 Increasing Competitive Intensity

There is theoretical evidence that when competitive intensity is stronger, the benefits to be derived from an opening up to competition tend to be higher, provided that the auction design is appropriate (Gupta, 2002). However, this does not mean that a high number of participants in an auction are enough to guarantee competitive efficiency, precisely because of the possibility of collusion or corruption. Empirically, numerous studies focusing on many different sectors confirm this result: investigating the case of auctions for Official Development Aids in Japan, Iimi (2004) shows that a 1% increase in the number of bidders leads to a 0.2% fall in the equilibrium price. In the case of auctions for highway construction in the USA, Gupta (2002) shows that increasing the number of participants up to eight bidders allows for a significant drop in prices. Beyond eight bidders, the intensification of competition no longer has any effect on prices. Working on auctions for cut timber, Paarsch (1992) confirms the negative effect on prices of an increase in the number of bidders. Finally, Amaral, Saussier, and Yvrande-Billon (2013) investigate the effect of the number of effective and potential bidders on prices paid by the London municipality for the operation of its bus lines. The authors show that, as the number of effective and potential bidders decreases, the costs borne by the municipality increase.

Therefore, the objective of public authorities should be to do everything in their power to increase the number of potential bidders during award procedures, so as to prevent a situation where the same actors systematically find themselves in competition, as this favors the creation and sustainability of cartels. To this end, they must encourage new actors (foreign companies, SMEs, new companies) to respond to their calls for tenders by limiting the barriers to entry, as the presence of such new actors is likely to destabilize a cartel between companies traditionally present in the market. Several measures can be used to limit barriers to entry and encourage companies to participate (especially SMEs and new companies): the submission costs borne by bidders must be reduced (or assumed by the public authority in the form of compensation), which is an argument in favor of procedure dematerialization; the conditions of participation (size, structure, and nature of the company, location, financial guarantees) must not be too restrictive, which is an argument in favor of open calls for tenders.

And yet, some public authorities choose to resort to prequalification procedures (as part of restricted calls for tenders, negotiated procedures, or competitive dialogue procedures), which automatically reduce the number of bidders. The argument generally put forward to justify the use of this type of procedure is that open auctions are less efficient in the case of goods or services that are technically complex or difficult to contract out (Bajari & Tadelis, 2001; Bajari, McMillan, & Tadelis, 2009). As regards the use of restricted auction procedures, empirical results are contradictory. Coviello et al. (2013) find that the use of restricted auctions has a neutral effect in terms of *ex ante* efficiency (number of bidders, proposed price), but that they reduce efficiency *ex post* (in particular through a lengthening of project delivery times). Conversely, Chever, Saussier, and Yvrande-Billon (2012) find that resorting to restricted auction procedures enables the buyer to receive more competitive bids, without any detrimental effect on quality.

In addition to whether or not the procedure is open, the choice of auction design is determining to stimulate bidder participation and reduce the risk of collusion. Indeed, the conditions of bid opening are crucial for the success of this type of auction. With this in mind, first-price sealed-bid calls for tenders render the selection far more competitive than open calls for tenders, in the form of ascending- or descending-bid auctions. They foster the participation of new or small companies, whose likelihood of winning increases if the firm that is theoretically the lowest tenderer seeks to obtain a price that is higher than its best bid, that is, the one it would have submitted during a call for tenders open to competition (OECD, 2008). In addition, the efficiency of this type of auction is reinforced if no information is disclosed about the received bids (which reduces transparency even more).

The use of qualitative criteria during the tendering procedure also has an influence on the intensity and efficiency of competition, not only for the project at stake but also for future projects (OECD, 2010). If the process takes place in a satisfactory manner based on criteria that are viewed as transparent and impartial, it can constitute a positive signal for nonselected firms to participate in the next calls for tenders, thus ensuring strong competitive intensity in the long term. Moreover, if they are chosen well, these criteria can even promote technological innovation and efficiency (through cost reduction) and thus strengthen competition. These arguments speak in favor of the use of qualitative criteria. But many studies have shown that the risk of capture is particularly high in auctions using qualitative criteria (Caillaud, 2001). Indeed, the decision to resort to qualitative criteria and to assign them significant weight allows the public agent or expert in charge of the procedure to influence the award outcome to their own convenience, which creates an obvious risk of favoritism (Laffont & Tirole, 1991), or even corruption (Burguet & Che, 2004; Celentani & Ganuza, 2001). Hyytinen et al. (2008) observe that between 1990 and 1998, Swedish municipalities chose not to make their award criteria explicit during the award of public contracts for cleaning services. The authors show that municipalities may have exploited this lack of transparency to favor certain firms. Left-wing mayors, for instance, awarded more contracts to local firms than right-wing mayors. To test the effect of auction design and the use of qualitative criteria on the level of corruption, Tran (2008) uses the internal records of an Asian firm that resorted to bribery. Until 2001, auctions were not mandatory in the country. Starting from 2001, the country generalized the use of best-value auctions first, and then, from 2004, of best-price auctions. The author shows that the use of best-value auctions did not reduce the level of corruption. It was only in 2004, when it became mandatory to use best-price auctions, that the level of corruption fell significantly. The author attributes this result to the fact that best-price auctions reduce the buyers' discretionary power in choosing a supplier.

We could even consider an extreme situation where companies would agree upon an attempt at generalized capture to influence the public authority's decision.

By using potentially manipulable qualitative criteria, the public authority can indeed make it easier for cartel members to share out their gains by influencing the designation of the winner and protect the cartel by excluding a sincere and competitive tenderer through the weighting of criteria to its disadvantage. A particularly ill-intentioned public officer may even contribute to the sustainability of the cartel by rating harshly any firm that deviates from the collusive pact. As we can see, the necessarily discretionary nature of the choice of criteria, which may be strengthened by a lack of transparency regarding these criteria, may prove to be particularly dangerous for the efficiency of the procedure, sometimes resulting in collusion, favoritism, and corruption. To avoid such behaviors, the public officer or the expert in charge of the procedure, as well as the methods for monitoring their actions, should be chosen with particular care, in order to limit their discretionary power and to prevent any breach. Additionally, the criteria should be described and weighted correctly. The announcement of the criteria and their respective weight should occur at the right time, that is, early enough before the public tendering procedure is closed to avoid complaints and suspicions of favoritism, but not too early, so as not to facilitate coordination. The public authority must therefore arbitrate between a will to enhance transparency and fight favoritism on the one hand and the prevention of collusion between bidders on the other hand.

Another important parameter to increase competition is the value of the contract. Contradictory considerations can be found on this topic. If we accept the fact that collusion develops more easily when bidders meet frequently during repeated calls for tenders, the logical extension of this is that it is preferable to reduce the number of calls for tenders. This leads to grouping contracts together in time and space by setting up contracts with higher value, that is, avoiding contracts that are too segmented or allotted (multiple-object auctions). Thus, if calls for tenders are sufficiently spaced out [in the case of calls for tenders for a concession or an availability contract, this amounts to extending contract duration so as to space out renewals (Saussier & Yvrande-Billon, 2007)], each company will have less reason to fear retaliation in the event of a deviation from the collusive pact. And yet, the French legal framework recommends resorting to allotment whenever possible, considering that it increases market opportunities for firms and therefore intensifies competition. The literature does not allow us to settle the debate between these two trends, as the result varies depending on the auction type. Indeed, auctions can be more or less vulnerable to collusion. In repeated auctions involving multiple homogeneous objects, an ascending-bid scheme is highly vulnerable to the risk of collusive agreement, as it makes any deviation from the agreement easily detectable and gives other cartel members the opportunity to reintroduce competition in order to oust the "traitor" (Robinson, 1985). Gupta (2001) studies collusion in a situation where companies are involved in multiple contracts (they are repeatedly in contact over time or in different markets). In these markets, the public buyer uses a best-price sealed-bid auction. The author seeks to confirm the hypothesis according to which the more participants are in competition in multiple markets, the higher the risk of collusion will be, based on an empirical study investigating 1937 traditional public procurement contracts for highway construction in Florida between 1981 and 1986. He shows that, indeed, frequent interactions in these markets have a positive impact on prices. This result confirms the theoretical predictions: when more information is available during calls for tenders and bid opening, it is easier for cartel members to monitor each other.

Here, we can also mention the innovative solution authorized by the French Competition Authority (decision n° 10-DCC-198 of 30 December 2010, published on 24 January 2011), namely, the creation of a competition stimulation fund in the French sector of urban public transport (see Chapter "The Evolution of Financing Conditions PPP Contracts: Still a Private Financing Model?" Part 1 of this book).

To conclude, the efficiency of the various measures that may be used to stimulate competition while limiting risks of collusion lies in the design of the procedure but also in the conditions of its implementation, which depend on the type of market, the sector, and the public authority's discretionary power. It is impossible to establish simple rules that are valid all other things being equal.

3.2   Choosing the Appropriate Level of Transparency: "Too Much Transparency Kills Transparency"

In terms of purchase, the public sector is subjected to strong transparency requirements intended to prevent any abuse of power from public officers in charge of public funds. That is why the laws regulating award procedures establish legal requirements in terms of advertising, from the notice of a competitive public tender to the publication of results. Arguments in terms of public procurement efficiency are also regularly put forward. Ohashi (2009) shows that enhanced transparency in the award procedure for public works contract in Japanese municipalities led to an 8% reduction in public procurement costs. But in the case of public contracts, full transparency in the public contract award procedure and the result of the call for tenders may also favor collusion LaCasse (1995). One theoretical result that is now well established is that the excessive disclosure of information to bidders should be avoided and communication between bidders even more so (Klemperer, 2002; Krishna, 2009).

The choice of auction design is also crucial on this point, as it determines the amount and type of information that should be disclosed to bidders, as well as the conditions of its disclosure. Simultaneous open calls for tenders, which by definition are more transparent than sealed-bid calls for tenders, favor the circulation of information during the procedure as regards the identity of bidders and the terms and conditions of each bid submission. At the same time, it also allows competitors to detect any deviation from the arrangements made as part of an agreement, to punish the firms that fail to observe them, and to improve coordination for the next calls for tenders (Robinson, 1985). Preserving bidder anonymity during a tendering procedure—either by using a sealed-bid auction, by only mentioning an identification number, or by authorizing submissions by other means than physical presence on a given date and in a given place—thus makes it possible to prevent coordination within a cartel. Kovacic, Marshall, Marx, and Raiff (2006) and Marshall and Marx (2007) show that, in the case of shill bids, which allow tenderers to submit bids under fake names (completely neutral assumed names), it is more difficult for cartels to monitor their members' practices. Thus, with respect to anonymity, contrary to what we saw when increasing competitive intensity is at issue, it is preferable to favor a sealed-bid tendering procedure rather than a simultaneous open call for tenders, which facilitates detection within cartels. But the repetition and multiplication of auctions, even with sealed bids, and the predictability of public demand also entail risks of collusion. The solution is then to diversify purchase practices, insofar as possible (in terms of amounts, durations, frequencies, allotments), which reduces market predictability and makes it more difficult to share out contracts *ex ante* within the cartel. Pesendorfer (2000) studies the terms of agreements between milk producers in contracts for the supply of schools in Texas and Florida. He shows that one of the factors favoring agreements is the fact that the market is divided into multiple "small" supply contracts—multiple units—thus allowing for a precise sharing of benefits within the cartel. When allotment is used, transparency is enhanced by the disclosure of information about the winners' identity and the bids submitted for each unit, which favors the detection of cartel members' behavior and therefore the sustainability of the agreement.

Transparency is the indispensable condition for procedure efficiency if the objective is to fight corruption and favoritism. However, the conditions of transparency must not favor collusion by circulating information ahead of the procedure, which can then be manipulated once a candidate is selected. Paradoxically, cases where the search for transparency leads to the disclosure of too much information considered useful for cartel coordination are numerous. Thus, the theoretical and empirical literature ponders how opportune it is to reveal the cost estimates established by the public buyer, the identity of the bidders, the details of technical specifications for the project, the reserve price... The amount and nature of the information available to bidders determine the category of auction that is used (private value auction, interdependent value auction [common or not]) and therefore, ultimately, the bidders' strategy (Klemperer, 2002; Khrishna, 2010). De Silva et al. (2008, 2009) analyze the evolution of tenders submitted by candidates in procedures for the award of highway construction contracts in the State of Oklahoma following the decision, implemented in April 2000, to disclose the cost estimates established by the public entity. The objective was to reduce the uncertainty surrounding common cost components. On the one hand, this policy of information disclosure led all candidates to the calls for tenders to submit more aggressive bids (De Silva et al., 2008). On the other hand, De Silva et al. (2009) show that the asymmetry between the level of bids submitted by incumbent operators and new entrants decreased following the disclosure of information by the public entity. This study shows that, in this instance, the improvement of transparency through the disclosure of information on cost estimates (which is strongly correlated with the public entity's reserve price) improved competition.

The question of the reserve price (the maximum price accepted by the public entity, beyond which the contract is not awarded) is particularly sensitive on this subject: if it exists, should it necessarily be disclosed? How high should it be? Following the pioneering study of Riley and Samuelson (1981), which showed that, in a standard auction, it is optimal to set and disclose a reserve price, Graham and Marshall (1987) were the first to theoretically justify the use of a public reserve price in cases where there is a risk of collusion. The reserve price must be sufficiently low to deter collusion, insofar as, by limiting illicit gains, it does not leave the cartel any leeway. If it allows the cartel to retain some gains, it will limit the play of competition, even in the presence of bidders that are external to the agreement, as all bidders will be tempted to adhere to this price. However, a low reserve price may also discourage potential candidates from submitting a bid. Another solution consists in not making the reserve price public, while announcing that it exists and recording it in the file or registering it with a public authority, so that it remains credible *ex post* (Caillaud, 2001).

Calculating the reserve price and disclosing it also presents some drawbacks. The public buyer may not be able to calculate this reserve price (for lack of expertise, competence, and financial resources). It may also be unable to commit to it when there is a strong risk that no eligible tender will be submitted or that there will be one but that it will be renegotiated *ex post* (for instance, if the buyer was too optimistic). Kovacic et al. (2006) study the case of multidimensional auctions and show that in this instance, the optimal response is not a simple reserve price. Instead, the public entity should announce a reservation utility, which is the minimum level of utility that the firm's bid provides the public entity with. Typically, the authors show that the reservation utility is nonlinear in price and quality.

Box 10: An Example of Successful Reform in the Fight Against Collusion

Some reforms use several levers to fight against horizontal or vertical agreement practices. In May 2002, the Japan Fair Trade Commission (JFTC), the Japanese competition authority, launched an investigation into allegations of collusion in the award of a municipality's civil engineering public contracts. In early 2003, the JFTC required that the municipality take action to put an end to collusive agreements. The mayor decided to organize its reforms along three lines. First, it authorized bids from firms based outside the city. It also decided to disclose the contract cost estimates to all candidates before the calls for tenders. Finally, it introduced an electronic bidding system to avoid all contact between companies. Tanno and Hirai (2012) investigate all calls for tenders relating to engineering public contracts in this city between 2000 and 2006. They show that this triple reform increased the level of competition and lowered the costs paid by the city. They conclude that the arrival of new entrants thanks to this reform weakened the cartel that was operating in this market.

Another way of preventing collusion consists in imposing transparency regarding the conditions of execution of the contract. In particular, the public entity may require that bidders reveal, from the start, any intention they might have of contracting out, as subcontracting may be a way to share out benefits among the firms that took part in concerted bid submission.

Finally, full transparency has its limitations. Too much transparency with the aim of fighting corruption and favoritism cancels out the expected positive effect of transparency, since it may favor the formation of a cartel and above all its sustainability Klitgaard (1991).

3.3   Importance of the Institutional and Statutory Framework

Defining the right tools and the right procedures is not enough to prevent anticompetitive behaviors; one must also have the ability, the credibility, the expertise, and the resources to do so, which Bain (2009) refers to as the "institutional infrastructure." It is thus necessary to have quality institutions and to be able to limit the public authority's discretionary power (in order to reduce the obvious risks of corruption and favoritism), while leaving it enough flexibility to choose the appropriate tools and procedures depending on the circumstances. If its discretionary power is too strong, it will lead to a distortion in firms' behavior and to the possibility of regulator capture (Laffont & Tirole, 1991, 1993; Stigler, 1971; Tirole, 1986). There is an extensive literature on regulator capture, starting with the works of the Chicago School (Becker, 1983; Peltzman, 1971; Stigler, 1971), which focus on the firms' demands for regulation and allow for a better understanding of the channels of capture, both in the political market and between interest groups—the lobbies—, as well as of the social cost of such behaviors. Recent empirical works highlight the political and institutional factors that strengthen the risks of opportunism from the public entity, the private operator, and all third parties that are interested in the contract in one way or another. Thus, Gence-Creux (2001) underlines the specific situation of a public entity (the mayor of a municipality for instance) who not only pursues a private objective of reelection but who, due to the principles of free administration and *intuitu personae*, also enjoys discretionary power. In this situation, Gence-Creux (2001) shows that this public entity will be tempted to delegate several public services to a single operator, which may lead it to show favoritism by choosing an operator that is sometimes less efficient. To limit this type of behavior, one of the solutions recommended in the economic literature is to make public actors more accountable by increasing the scrutiny to which they are subjected, for instance through the use of audits. As far as this solution is concerned, an experiment conducted in Indonesia shows that an increase in the number of audited traditional procurement contract award procedures reduces the occurrence of corruption. Olken (2007) conducted this experiment in Indonesia, a country with a high level of corruption, especially in public procurement. The author uses two methods to encourage the attendance of a larger number of citizens to the public meetings during which public entities explain how they used funds for projects. He shows that a 40% increase in the average participation in these meetings had the effect of reducing the amounts extorted by project managers by about 30%. The author concludes that increasing the accountability of public authorities could have a real impact on the level of corruption. These conclusions converge with those of Di Tella and Schargrodsky (2003) who, focusing on the case of hospital-related public expenditure in Argentina in the middle of the 1990s, show that the frequency of audits led to a reduction in the level of corruption. Nevertheless, Spiller (2010, 2011) reminds us that the specificity of public contracts lies in the fact that they deal with public funds, which, as a result, places them *de facto* under the scrutiny of all contract stakeholders, namely, the third parties (citizen-voters, firms with potential access to the contracts, political opponents, associations...). Spiller (2011) focuses on the role of third parties in the political market, that is, on political opponents in whose interest it is to demonstrate that the practices of the authorities in place in terms of public funds management are harmful, or even reprehensible. In particular, he implies that a political opponent may show opportunism insofar as the accusations it will formulate will not necessarily be supported by facts: a simple rumor may be enough to discredit a policymaker. For fear of being suspected of favoritism or corruption by a political opponent, a public decision-maker in place may be led to make a choice that is inefficient from an economic point of view, but which reduces the likelihood of suspicion. Chong, Staropoli, and Yvrande-Billon (2012) explain that the choice between a negotiated procedure and an auction is affected by this phenomenon. They use a dataset of public works contracts in France in 2007 and show that, among the determinants of the choice of procedure, the political variables used to approximate the electoral competition to which the public decision-maker is subjected (measured by the concentration of the political market and the influence of the political opponent) have a significant impact on the choice of contract award procedure, whereas considerations of economic efficiency are not as influential. This study is a good illustration of the limitations of increased accountability and of the monitoring of public actors in the fight against practices of favoritism and corruption: to appear transparent and avoid being discredited, public actors may be led to make suboptimal choices.

4   Conclusion

As we have seen, when it comes to the award of public–private contracts, full transparency, a principle which is supposed to guarantee competition, is not necessarily efficient, quite the opposite. Negotiated procedures, competitive dialogue, or the adaptation of the traditional procedures to take into account the advances of regulations (dynamic acquisition systems, adapted procedures) all aim precisely to grant the necessary flexibility and to supervise information disclosure. Apart from their innovative nature, they require important expertise on a legal, financial, and technical level, which public entities do not necessarily have. As a result, the authorities in charge of introducing competition for the market need to develop their skills and expertise in the award of contracts [see Moszoro and Krzyzanowska (2011) for a study on the conditions of PPP award efficiency in the case of the municipality of Warsaw].

In addition to nonspecialized skills and expertise (about procedures, regulations, and technical and financial aspects), it is necessary for the public entity to have sufficient expertise and human and financial resources in terms of competition to identify circumstances that are favorable to agreements and to implement the necessary tools to prevent them. To this end, it must be able to assess the risks specific to the different markets. The experience and training of the individuals in charge of public procurement are a key element, which is why the OECD recommended the development of training programs for employees and the strengthening of relationships between public buyers, competition authorities, and independent legal consulting firms and technical experts (OECD, 2010). The independent nature of these consulting firms cannot be decreed, and one should be cautious when resorting to financial, legal, or technical experts. All precautions must be taken in order to minimize the risks of conflict of interests arising between these firms and the bidders but also any transfer of information that would favor collusion in current and future contracts (Marshall and Marx, 2007).

More generally, the OECD recommends rationalizing the collection and treatment of data relating to competitive tendering procedures, with the aim of improving the detection of suspicious patterns, especially in sectors that are most conducive to collusion (repeated contracts, low competitive intensity). Pesendorfer (2000) suggests that if the entities in charge of purchasing milk for the schools of various Boards of Education in Texas and Florida were to coordinate, it would enable them to pool their knowledge and experience in order to reduce collusion and to improve cartel detection.

The institutional and statutory framework is essential for the credibility and efficiency of prevention policies against collusion, corruption, and favoritism. It involves establishing legal rules to restrict the discretionary power of public decision-makers, while granting the latter sufficient leeway. It also implies the implementation of a proactive policy by public authorities to give public decision-makers the human and financial resources necessary to act in full knowledge of the cause and to fight on equal terms against cartels' attempts at destabilization.

Encouraging compliance with competitive rules during the award of contracts is a necessary condition but not a sufficient one to eliminate the difficulties encountered in the execution of public–private contracts. As we have seen in Chapters "Renegotiating PPP Contracts: Opportunities and Pitfalls" and "Comparative Performances of Management Methods: Empirical Lessons" Part 2, incentive schemes must be set up throughout contract duration in order to ensure that the commitments made *ex ante* are honored *ex post*. In anticipation of contract renewal, actors may be tempted to act in an opportunistic manner.

Notes

1. In this chapter, we will talk about horizontal agreements when referring to collusion between tenderers and about vertical agreements when tackling the issues of corruption and favoritism.
2. See the French Competition Authority's activity reports.
3. Sources: Daniel Kaufmann's report "Six Questions on the Cost of Corruption," available on the website of the World Bank and "*Silence sur la corruption*" ("Silence on corruption") by E. Auriol, published in *L'Expansion*, no 717 of March 2007.
4. Ruling 06-D-07, available on the website of the French Competition Authority.
5. See Fehl and Güth (1987) for a theoretical study of these two types of collusive agreement stability.
6. See Robinson (1985) and von Ungern-Sternberg (1988) for theoretical studies of the internal stability of cartels.
7. See Ayres (1987) for a theoretical study of the various possible sanctions in cartels.
8. This study predates the introduction of leniency programs. However, studies subsequent to their introduction give similar results. Thus, the OECD report (2003) considers that "*no more than one cartel out of six or seven* [between 14 and 17%, editor's note] *is detected and prosecuted.*"
9. In this box, we do not differentiate between cartels operating in "classical" markets and cartels in PPPs.
10. Journal Officiel C 207, 18.07.1996, p. 4–6.
11. Scott D. Hammond is one of the directors of the anti-cartel division of the DoJ. His 2004 speech is available here: http://www.justice.gov/atr/public/speeches/206611.htm
12. Notice of 16 May 2011 on the method relating to the setting of financial penalties, available on the website of the Autorité de la concurrence.
13. According to the notice, the seriousness of the facts depends on the seriousness of the infringement at stake (anticompetitive agreements between firms generally being considered as particularly serious infringements), the nature of the sector and the number of persons liable to be affected, as well as the objective characteristics of the infringement (in particular, in the case of cartels, the degree of formalization, and refinement of the collusive agreement will be taken into account).
14. As the authors rendered anonymous all corruption cases presented in this report, it is impossible for us to specify the country of origin and the date of the practices.
15. This technique is commonly known as the "magical number."
16. Sources: Decision 07-D-15 from the French Competition Authority, as well as the press release of 9 May 2007 relating to the Île-de-France high schools. Available on the website of the Authority: www.autoritedelaconcurrence.fr.

Sources: *"Les peines des autres acteurs du scandale politico-financier,"* published in *Le Monde* of 28 October 2005 and "Marchés Publics d'IDF peines durcies pour Roussin et Cassetta," published on 27 February 2007 on the website Nouvelobs.com.

17. Press release of 9 May 2007 relating to *Secondary schools in the Île-de-France region*, available on the website of the Competition Authority.

18. Collusion may also arise during the regulation process, once a concession contract has been awarded through a procedure of competition for the market. In Chapter "Regulatory Instruments for Public–Private Partnerships" Part 1, we saw how companies regulated through benchmarking can establish—either explicitly (Chong & Huet, 2006; Laffont & Martimort, 2000; Pouyet, 2002; Tangerås, 2002) or tacitly (Potters, Rockenbach, Sadrieh, & van Damme, 2004)— an agreement aiming to skew the benchmark in order to limit the constraints weighing down on them. This necessarily damages the efficiency of yardstick competition.

19. The statutory texts regulating public–private relationships have evolved over these past few years and have recently evolved further in Europe, in particular under the influence of the European Directives.

20. On average, traditional public procurement contracts represent over 15% of the GDP of OECD countries. They represent an even larger share of the GDP of countries that are not members of the OECD. Moreover, they often relate to goods and services that play a significant economic and social role, such as transport infrastructure, hospitals and health services, as well as education.

21. For an introduction of the various procedures, see Chapter "The Relative Efficiency of Competitive Tendering" of the second part of this book.

22. When the State or public entity is the only buyer, as is the case in public contracts, and introduces competition between potential suppliers, one talks about a seller's auction. The objective is then to obtain the lowest possible price for a given service.

23. When the State or public entity is a seller and the other agents are potential buyers, one talks about a buyer's auction, and the objective for the seller introducing competition between buyers is of course to sell at the highest possible price.

24. In private value auctions, bidders only know the value of the items up for auction in their own case. In common value auctions, the value of the items up for auction is unknown to bidders as it depends on exogenous parameters, but it is identical across bidders *ex post*. Interdependent value auctions are common value auctions for which, most of the time, each bidder only has a signal of other bidders' value (and therefore of the common value) (for instance for an oil well up for auction, agents have the same technical information but may interpret them differently, in particular if they can infer different profit outlooks from such information).

25. The winner can be selected based on one or several criteria. When there is only one criterion, it is price. Other qualitative criteria may be added, for instance in

public contracts: quality, SME participation, social or environmental clauses, elements relating to deadlines, etc.

26. A sealed-bid auction may be "first-price" or "second-price"; in the first case, the winner pays (or respectively receives in a seller's auction) the price written in its bid. In the second case, the winner pays (or receives in a seller's auction) the second-highest bid price in descending order (or respectively in ascending order). Second-price auctions exist in theory (and have strong efficiency properties; see Vickrey, 1961), but they are rarely used in practice.

27. It is the case of oral auctions such as ascending-bid auctions (English auctions), with or without reserve price and with or without a fixed amount by which the next bid must exceed the current highest one, and descending-price auctions (Dutch auctions). Written auctions, which are commonly used in public contracts where they are known as calls for tenders, are auctions in which potential suppliers (or buyers) submit their tender in writing, in a sealed envelope, within a given period of time. When this period of time expires, all envelopes are opened; the winner is the one that has submitted the best tender, that is, the one offering the highest price in the case of a buyer's auction and the one offering the lowest price in the case of a seller's auction.

28. *"What really matters in auction design* [implied: 'in practice'] *are the same issues that any industry regulator would recognize as key concerns: discouraging collusive, entry-deterring and predatory behaviors. In short, good auction design is mostly good elementary economics."* (Klemperer, 2002, p. 170)

29. There is a famous counterexample presented by Cramton and Schwartz (2000) in the case of simultaneous multiple object auctions for the Hertzian spectrum in the USA. They show that competitors were able to send messages to members of a cartel, telling them on which objects to bid and which ones to avoid, for instance by using code bids (that is, bids in which the figures of the hundreds, tens, and ones constituted a code or a user name for the firm).

30. The data involve information about all PPPs for highway construction awarded by the Oklahoma Department of Transportation between January 1997 and August 2003.

31. *"Different elements of institutional infrastructure have to be in place for PPPs to succeed: strong watchdogs and regulators, a robust system of audit, support, good advisors, a banking system that is prepared and a public sector that has bought-into the concept and is working to become a smarter procurer."* (Bain, 2009, p. 18)

References

Abrantes-Mertez, R., Froeb, L., Geweke, J., & Taylor, C. (2006). A variance screen for collusion. *International Journal of Industrial Organization, 24*(3), 467–486.

Allain, M.-L., Boyer, M., & Ponssard, J.-P. (2011). The determination of optimal fines in cartel cases: Theory and practice. *Concurrences, 4*, 32–40.

Amaral, M., Saussier, S., & Yvrande-Billon, A. (2013). Expected number of bidders and winning bids: Evidence from the London Bus Tendering Model. *Journal of Transport Economics and Policy, 47*(1), 17–34.

Aoyagi, M. (2003). Bid rotation and collusion in repeated auctions. *Journal of Economic Theory, 112*(1), 79–105.

Arai, K., Ishibashi, I., & Ishii-Ishibashi, R. (2011). Research and analysis on bid rigging mechanisms. *Japan and the World Economy, 23*(1), 1–5.

Asker, J. (2010). A study of the internal organization of a cartel. *American Economic Review, 100* (3), 724–762.

Athey, S., Levin, J., & Seira, E. (2011). Comparing open and sealed bid auctions: Evidence from timber auctions. *The Quarterly Journal of Economics, 126*(1), 207–257.

Ayres, I. (1987). How cartels punish: A structural theory of self-enforcing collusion. *Columbia Law Review, 87*(2), 295–325.

Bain, R. (2009). *Review of lessons from completed PPP projects financed by the EIB*. Luxembourg: European Investment Bank.

Bajari, P., & Tadelis, S. (2001). Incentives versus transaction costs: A theory of procurement contracts. *The RAND Journal of Economics, 32*(3), 387.

Bajari, P., & Ye, L. (2003). Deciding between corruption and collusion. *Review of Economics and Statistics, 81*, 971–989.

Bajari, P., MacMillan, R., & Tadelis, S. (2009). Auctions versus negotiations in procurement: An empirical analysis. *Journal of Law, Economics and Organization, 25*(2), 372–399.

Becker, G. (1968). Crime and punishment: An economic approach. *Journal of Political Economy, 76*(2), 169–217.

Becker, G. (1983). A theory of competition among pressure groups for political influence. *The Quarterly Journal of Economics, 98*, 371–400.

Brenner, S. (2009). An empirical study of the European corporate leniency programme. *International Journal of Industrial Organization, 27*(6), 639–645.

Bryant, P., & Eckard, E. (1991). Price fixing: The probability of getting caught. *Review of Economics and Statistics, 73*(3), 531–536.

Burguet, R., & Che, Y.-K. (2004). Competitive procurement with corruption. *The RAND Journal of Economics, 35*, 50–68.

Burguet, R., & Perry, M. (2007). Bribery and favoritism by auctioneers in sealed-bid auctions. *The B.E. Journal of Theoretical Economics, 7*(1).

Caillaud, B. (2001). *Ententes et capture dans l'attribution des marchés publics*. Enchères et gestion publique – Rapport du CAE.

Celentani, M., & Ganuza, J.-J. (2001). *Corruption and competition in procurement*. Universitat Pompeu Fabra, document de travail no 464.

Chever, L., Saussier, S., & Yvrande-Billon, A. (2012). *The law of small numbers: Investigating the benefits of restricted auctions for public procurement* (chaire EPPP, working paper).

Chong, E., & Huet, F. (2006). Enchères, concurrence par comparaison et collusion. *Revue é conomique, 57*(3), 583–592.

Chong, E., Staropoli, C., & Yvrande-Billon, A. (2012). *Auctions versus negotiations in public procurement: The implication of political scrutiny* (chaire EPPP, working paper).

Clarke, E. (1971). Multipart pricing of public goods. *Public Choice, 11*, 17–33.

Combe, E. (2006). Quelles sanctions contre les cartels? Une perspective économique. *Revue Internationale de droit économique, 1*(1), 11–46.

Combe, E., & Monnier, C. (2009). Les amendes contre les cartels: la Commission européenne en fait-elle trop ? *Concurrences, 4*, 41–50.

Combe, E., & Monnier, C. (2012). Les cartels en Europe: une analyse empirique. *Revue française d'économie, 27*(2).

Combe, E., Connor, J., Jenny, F., Buccirossi, P., & Spagnolo, G. (2006). L'efficacité des sanctions contre les cartels: une perspective économique. *Concurrences, 4*, 9–30.

Compte, O., Lambert-Mogiliansky, A., & Verdier, T. (2005). Corruption and competition in procurement auctions. *The RAND Journal of Economics, 36*(1), 1–15.

Connor, J., & Lande, R. (2004). *How high do cartels raise prices? Implication for reform of sentencing guidelines* (working paper no 01-04). American Antitrust Institute.

Coviello, D., & Gagliarducci, S. (2010). *Tenure in office and public procurement* (CEIS Research Paper 179).

Coviello, D., Guglielmo, A., & Spagnolo G. (2013). Forthcoming in *"Management Science"* [Coviello, D., Guglielmo, A., & Spagnolo, G. (2017). The effect of discretion on procurement performance. *Management Science* (forthcoming)].

Cramton, P., & Schwartz, J. (2000). Collusive bidding: Lessons from the FCC spectrum auctions. *Journal of Regulatory Economics, 17*, 229–252.

De Silva, D. G., Dunne, T., Kankanamge, A., & Kosmopoulou, G. (2008). The impact of public information on bidding in highway procurement auctions. *European Economic Review, 52*(1), 150–181 (32 p).

De Silva, D., Kosmopoulou, G., & Lamarche, C. (2009). The effect of information on the bidding and survival of entrants in procurement auctions. *Journal of Public Economics, 93*(1–2), 56–72.

Di Tella, R., & Schargrodsky, E. (2003). The role of wages and auditing during a crackdown on corruption in the city of Buenos Aires. *Journal of Law and Economics, 46*(1).

Ehmer, E., & Rosati, F. (2009). Science, myth and fines: Do cartels typically raise prices by 25%? *Concurrences – Law and Economics, 4*, 1–8.

Fehl, U., & Güth, W. (1987). Internal and external stability of bidder cartels in auctions and public tenders: A comparison of pricing rules. *International Journal of Industrial Organization, 5*(3), 303–313.

Froeb, L., Koyak, R., & Werden, G. (1993). What is the effect of bid-rigging on prices? *Economics Letters, 42*(4), 419–423.

Gence-Creux, C. (2001). Élections et favoritisme dans l'attribution des marchés de services publics locaux. *Revue économique, 52*(3), 753–763.

Graham, D., & Marshall, R. (1987). Collusive bidder behavior at single-object secondprice and English auctions. *The Journal of Political Economy, 95*(6), 1217–1239.

Groves, T. (1973). Incentives in teams. *Econometrica, 41*(4), 617.

Gupta, S. (2001). The effect of bid rigging on prices: A study of the highway construction industry. *Review of Industrial Organization, 19*(4), 453–467.

Gupta, S. (2002). Competition and collusion in a government procurement auction market. *Atlantic Economic Journal, 30*(1), 13–25.

Harrington, J. (2004). Post cartel pricing during litigation. *Journal of Industrial Economics, 52*, 517–533.

Harrington, J. (2005). Optimal cartel pricing in the presence of an antitrust authority. *International Economic Review, 46*, 145–169.

Hurwicz, L. (1972). On informationally decentralized systems. In C. B. McGuire & R. Radner (Eds.), *Decision and organization*. Amsterdam: North Holland.

Hyytinen, A., Lundberg, S., & Toivanen, O. (2008). *Politics and procurement: Evidence from cleaning contracts* (Discussion Paper no 233).

Iimi, A. (2004). (Anti-)competitive effect of joint bidding: Evidence from ODA procurement auctions. *Journal of Japanese and International Economy, 18*, 416–439.

Ingraham, A. (2005). A test for collusion between a bidder and an auctioneer in sealed-bid auctions. *Contributions to Economic Analysis and Policy, 4*(1), 10.

Iossa, E., & Martimort, D. (2011). *Post-tender corruption and risk allocation: Implications for public-private partnerships* (CEIS Research Paper).

Ishii, R. (2009). Favor exchange in collusion: Empirical study of repeated procurement auctions in Japan. *International Journal of Industrial Organization, 27*(2), 137–144.

Ishii, R. (2013). Bid roundness under collusion in Japanese Procurement Auctions. *Review of Industrial Organization, 44*, 241–254.

Japan Fair Trade Commission. (2010). Annual report for fiscal year.

Kawai, K., & Nakabayashi, J. (2014). *Detecting large-scale collusion in procurement auctions* (working paper).

Klemperer, P. (2002). What really matters in auction design? *Journal of Economic Perspectives, 16*(1), 169–189.

Klemperer, P. (2004). *Auctions: Theory and practice*. Princeton, NJ: Princeton University Press.

Klitgaard, R. (1991). *Controlling corruption*. Berkeley, CA: University of California Press.

Kosenok, G., & Lambert-Mogiliansky, A. (2009). Public markets tailored for the cartel – Favoritism in procurement auctions. *Review of Industrial Organizations, 35*, 95–121.

Kovacic, W., Marshall, R., Marx, L., & Raiff, M. (2006). Bidding rings and the design of anti-collusion measures for auctions and procurements, Chapter 15. In N. Dimitri, G. Piga, & G. Spagnolo (dir.), *Handbook of procurement* (pp. 381–411).

Krishna, V. (2009). *Auction theory* (2nd ed.). Cambridge: Academic Press, Elsevier.

LaCasse, C. (1995). Bid rigging and the threat of government prosecution. *The RAND Journal of Economics, 26*(3), 398–417.

Laffont, J.-J., & Martimort, D. (2000). Mechanism design with collusion and correlation. *Econometrica, 68*(2), 309–342.

Laffont, J.-J., & Tirole, J. (1991). Auction design and favoritism. *Internation Journal of Industrial Organization, 9*(1), 9–42.

Laffont, J.-J., & Tirole, J. (1993). *A theory of incentives in procurement and regulation*. Cambridge: MIT Press.

Lambert-Mogiliansky, A. (2011). Corruption and collusion in procurement – Strategic complements. In *International handbook on the economics of corruption*. Cheltenham: Edward Elgar Publishing.

Lambert-Mogiliansky, A., & Sonin, K. (2006). Collusive market-sharing and corruption in procurement. *Journal of Economics & Management Strategy, 15*(4), 883–908.

Langus, G., Motta, M., & Aguzzoni, L. (2013). The effect of EU antitrust investigations and fines on a firm's valuation. *The Journal of Industrial Economics, 61*(2), 290–338.

Lee, I. (1999). Non-cooperative tacit collusion, complementary bidding and incumbency premium. *Review of Industrial Organization, 15*, 115–134.

Lee, J.-S. (2008). Favoritism in asymmetric procurement auctions. *International Journal of Industrial Organization, 26*(6), 1407–1424.

Lee, I., & Hahn, K. (2002). Bid-rigging in auctions for Korean public-works contracts and potential damage. *Review of Industrial Organization, 21*(1), 73–88.

Lengwiler, Y., & Wolfstetter, E. (2006). Corruption in procurement auctions. In *Handbook of procurement – Theory and practice for managers*. Cambridge: Cambridge University Press.

Lyk-Jensen, P. (1996). *Some suggestions on how to cheat the auctioneer: Collusion in auctions when signals are affiliated* (working paper). Greqam.

Marion. (2007). Are bid preferences benign? The effect of small business subsidy in highway procurement auctions. *Journal of Public Economics, 91*(7–8), 34.

Marshall, R., & Marx, L. (2007). Bidder collusion. *Journal of Economic Theory, 133*(1), 374–402.

McAfee, R., & McMillan, J. (1992). Bidding rings. *The American Economic Review, 82*(3), 579–599.

McMillan, J. (1991). Dango: The price fixing conspiracies. *Economics and Politics, 3*, 201–218.

Menezes, F., & Monteiro, P. (2006). Corruption and auctions. *Journal of Mathematical Economics, 42*(1), 97–108.

Milgrom, P. (2004). *Putting auction theory to work (Churchill lectures in economics)*. Cambridge: Cambridge University Press.

Miller, N. (2009). Strategic leniency and cartel enforcement. *The American Economic Review, 99*(3), 750–768.

Moore, J. (2012). Stabilité externe et anticipation des offres concurrentielles par les ententes dans les marchés publics: une analyse empirique. *Revue d'économie industrielle, 4*.

Moszoro, M., & Krzyzanowska, M. (2011). *Implementing public-private partnerships in municipalities*. Spain: IESE Business School-University of Navarra.

Motta, M. (2004). *Competition policy: Theory and practice*. Cambridge: Cambridge University Press.

Myerson, R. B. (1981). Optimal auction design. *Mathematics of Operations Research, 6*(1), 58–73.

OECD. (2003). *Les ententes injustifiables: progrès récents et défis futurs*. OECD.

OECD. (2007). *Ten anonymous studies on bribery in public procurement*. OECD.

OECD. (2008). *Lignes directrices pour la lutte contre les soumissions concertées dans les marchés publics*. OECD.

OECD. (2010). *Collusion and corruption in public procurement*. Policy Roundtables.

Olken, B. (2007). Monitoring corruption: Evidence from a field experiment in Indonesia. *Journal of Political Economy, 115*(2), 200–249.

Ohashi, T., & Erickson, H. P. (2009). Revisiting the mystery of fibronectin multimers: The fibronectin matrix is composed of fibronectin dimers cross-linked by non-covalent bonds. *Matrix Biology, 28*(3), 170–175.

Paarsch, H. (1992). Deciding between the common and private value paradigms in empirical model of auctions. *Journal of Econometrics, 51*, 191–215.

Padhi, S., & Mohapatra, P. (2011). Detection of collusion in government procurement auctions. *Journal of Purchasing & Supply Management, 17*(4), 207–221.

Peltzman, S. (1971). Pricing in public and private enterprises: Electric utilities in the United States. *Journal of Law and Economics, 14*(1), 109–147.

Pesendorfer, M. (2000). A study of collusion in first-price auctions. *The Review of Economic Studies, 67*(3), 381.

Porter, R., & Zona, J. (1993). Detection of bid rigging in procurement auctions. *Journal of Political Economy, 101*(3), 518–538.

Porter, R., & Zona, J. (1999). Ohio School milk markets: An analysis of bidding. *The RAND Journal of Economics, 30*(2), 263–288.

Potters, J., Rockenbach, B., Sadrieh, A., & van Damme, E. (2004). Collusion under yardstick competition: An experimental study. *International Journal of Industrial Organization, 22*, 1017–1038.

Pouyet, J. (2002). Collusion under asymmetric information: The role of the correlation. *Journal of Public Economic Theory, 4*(4), 543–572.

Robinson, M. (1985). Collusion and the choice of auction. *The RAND Journal of Economics, 16*(1), 141–145.

Riley, J., & Samuelson, W. (1981). Optimal auctions. *American Economic Review, 71*(3), 381–392.

Saussier, S., & Yvrande-Billon, A. (2007). *Economie des Coûts de Transaction. Repères*.

Smith, R. A. (1961, April and May). The incredible electrical conspiracy. *Fortune, 63*, 132–180, 161–224.

Soreide, T. (2002). *Corruption in public procurement: Causes, consequences and cures* (Chr. Michelsen Institute Report).

Soreide, T. (2008). Beaten by bribery: Why not blow the whistle? *Journal of Institutional and Theoretical Economics, 164*(3), 407–428.

Spiller, P. (2010). Regulation: A transaction cost perspective. *California Management Review, 52*(2), 147–158.

Spiller, P. (2011). *Transaction cost regulation* (working paper).

Stephan, A. (2009). An empirical assessment of the European leniency notice. *Journal of Competition Law & Economics, 5*(3), 537–561.

Stigler, G. (1971). The theory of economic regulation. *Bell Journal of Economics and Management Science, 2*, 3–21.

Tangerås, T. (2002). Collusion-proof yardstick competition. *Journal of Public Economics, 83*(2), 231–254.

Tanno, T., & Hirai, T. (2012). *Collusion, breakdown, and competition in procurement auctions* (working paper).

Tirole, J. (1986). Procurement and renegotiation. *Journal of Political Economy, 94*(2), 235–259.

Tran, A. (2008). *Corruption in auctions: Evidence from internal records of a BribePaying firm* (working paper).

Veljanovski, C. (2011). Deterrence, recidivism and European cartel fines. *Journal of Competition Law and Economics, 7,* 871–915.

Von Ungern-Sternberg, T. (1988). Cartel stability in sealed bid second price auctions. *The Journal of Industrial Economics, 36*(3), 351–358.

Vickrey, W. (1961). On the prevention of gerrymandering. *Political Science Quarterly, 76*(1), 105.

Wilson, R. (1987). Auction theory. In J. Eatwell, M. Milgate, & P. Newman (Eds.), *The New Palgrave: A dictionary of economic theory.* London: Macmillan.

Printed by Printforce, the Netherlands